HERM KLIX

THE LIFE OF THE PARTY

THE LIFE
OF THE PARTY

A New Collection of Stories and Anecdotes

BENNETT CERF

Drawings by Carl Rose

HANOVER HOUSE

DOUBLEDAY & COMPANY, INC.
Garden City, New York

Library of Congress Catalog Card Number: 56–10756

CONTENTS

5

FOREWORD

A stranger dashed frantically into "Doc" Sherman's Madison Avenue pharmacy this spring, hollering, "Quick, Doc! I've swallowed poison by mistake! I must have an antidote!"

"You've come to the right place," beamed Sherman. "It seems there once were two Irishmen named Pat and Mike . . ."

The good doctor, who had filled thousands of prescriptions, knew that laughter is the "best medicine for weary bones"—that the very sound of it is reassuring and healing. There is nothing like a hearty laugh to clear the atmosphere—or deflate windbags and phonies!

The Life of the Party is my eighth collection of anecdotes and stories, designed, for the most part, just to provoke the laughs I value so highly. Like the contents of its predecessors, every item included is absolutely new—unless, of course, you've heard it before. I culled many of them from my "Cerfboard" column in *This Week*, "Trade Winds" in the *Saturday Review*, and my daily box, "Try and Stop Me" for King Features. The title of this book was suggested by my friend and dentist, the aptly named Dr. Edward Pullman. He has pulled many a good one in his day.

Oliver Gogarty, Irish raconteur and wit, advises, "Tell a funny story on every possible occasion, and tell it as well as you know how, too. People will remember your jokes and forget your speeches. Monuments are built over solemn asses—but people remember in their hearts the men who have made them laugh."

I remember an old legend about a human who told the Sun he had discovered one spot on earth that was eternally dark. "Impossible," scoffed the Sun. He hastened to the spot described

7

and searched high and low, but could not find even the suspicion of a shadow.

The moral is clear. Carry your own sunshine with you, and there will be fewer dark places in your life. In other words, let a smile be your umbrella. You'll get wet from time to time—but you won't give a darn!

BENNETT CERF

Mount Kisco, New York
September 1956

THE LIFE OF THE PARTY

CHAPTER ONE

BABES IN THE HOLLYWOODS

Picture making in Hollywood has one thing in common with serving in the infantry in wartime. For every minute of decisive action and excitement, there are twenty of the infinite boredom of "standing by" waiting for something to happen. It's a caution to watch internationally famous stars twiddling their thumbs— at about two thousand dollars a twiddle—while directors, scriptors, and technicians battle on into the night about a fragment of dialogue or the lighting of a set.

Some stars take to crocheting or knitting during these interminable lulls. Others answer fan mail or agonize over crossword puzzles. A few even read books. Cary Grant, one of the best

actors, as well as most charming personally, in the business, took advantage of a historic studio stalemate to invent a mythical picture company that first enlisted the enthusiastic co-operation of Ingrid Bergman (just before she decamped to Italy), Alfred Hitchcock, and Joe Cotten, and then bloomed prodigiously all over Hollywood.

The object of this intriguing time killer was to people an imaginary studio with characters whose names were most appropriate for their assignments. From a list submitted to me by Cary and his accomplices, I have selected the following outstanding examples:

> *Dolly Shot: the heroine*
> *May Cup: her mother*
> *Lee Dingman: the hero*

Mike Shadow: the villain
Pan Ova: a ballet dancer
Manny Takes: the director
Mimi O'Graph: the script girl
Phil Mer: the cameraman
Herr Dresser: the make-up man
Alec Trician: lights
Bill Board: publicity

Etc., etc., until you're so tired you Fala Sleep.

The insidious feature of Grant's game, of course, is that you've no sooner learned about it than you start applying it to your own business. I, for instance, immediately began dreaming up the perfect cast for a publishing house—fellows like Hy Perbole, the blurb writer; Eddie Tor, the blue-pencil wielder; Reggie Ment, the censor; Mae Hem, the mystery writer; Paul Verize, the shipping clerk; Ty Pograph, the printer; and Mister Market, the writer whose manuscript came in too late.

The death of Will Hays reminded Hy Gardner of the first list of "don'ts" Mr. Hays promulgated when he was appointed custodian of film makers' morals. There were twelve major "thou shalt nots" on the list, prompting the show-business bible, *Variety*, to headline the story, "Hays Two Up on Moses!"

A fat movie producer seized a lovely young starlet in his arms and kissed her violently four times. "What did you think of my performance?" he asked arrogantly after releasing the girl. "Magnificent," she scoffed. "But if I were you, I'd print only takes number one and four."

I was sitting in the patio of a famous film magnate's retreat at Palm Springs, California, while a sudden windstorm was sending swirls of sand high into the air around us. Like every other resident of the Springs, however, my host was convinced that *his* property was completely protected from occasionally violent wind gusts. "Notice how quiet it is right here?" he inquired complacently. "Anywhere else in town, this wind would bowl you over like a duckpin."

He completed his observation in the nick of time. At that moment two of his treasured palm trees were uprooted, and toppled over into the swimming pool.

Norman Reilly Raine recalls a famous Hollywood magnate who decided he wanted to produce an epic on Custer's last stand, but then promptly turned thumbs down on seven scripts. The final veto broke Raine's spirit completely. "I'm ready to give up," he admitted. "I really slaved over this last script. It's the best I can do. Just what is there about it that displeases you?" "I'll tell you," confided the magnate. "I hate Indians."

Here's a story I never heard before about Sam Goldwyn, the inimitable motion-picture pioneer, and it comes from Miriam Howell, who was one of his chief lieutenants some years ago. "Miriam," proposed Sam one morning, "we've got to get some new blood around here. I want to sign up some young writer, talented but completely unknown, who'll bring us fresh ideas and a fresh viewpoint." "Splendid," enthused Miriam, "and I know just the man for you." "What's his name?" asked Goldwyn. "He's a young playwright named John Patrick," said Miss Howell. "Never heard of him," said Mr. Goldwyn. "Who else can you think of?"

Arthur Mayer, author of the amusing Hollywood memoir, *Merely Colossal*, nominates Adolph Zukor, long-time headman at Paramount Pictures, as the politest gent in the world of the cinema. "I have a telegram to prove it," continues Mayer. "It reads, 'You're fired. Best regards.'"

An epic of Napoleonic times was being shot on location near the Twentieth Century-Fox lot when an airplane halted all activities by circling about for a full hour overhead. Finally an ingenious cameraman hollered to the director, "We could go ahead if you'd put in an explanatory line of dialogue. Let's have the hero shake his fist at the sky, and say, 'There goes that pig of a Raoul up there—a full hundred and fifty years before his time!' "

A favorite story of movie exhibitors concerns the beautiful princess in ancient Egypt who found a baby in a wicker basket drifting down the Nile and took it to her father, the Pharaoh. "Isn't this a beautiful baby?" she exclaimed. "Oh, Daddy, I want to adopt him." The Pharaoh snorted, "He doesn't look so beautiful to me. In fact, I'll state definitely I think he's as ugly as any I've ever seen." The princess murmured defensively, "He looked awfully good in the rushes."

Paramount had just finished shooting a scene from one of those biblical pictures in which ten thousand extras, dressed as Egyptians, Romans, and what not, wandered around the place, and everybody made a break for lunch at the same time. The director, pleased with his morning's work, was in an expansive mood when he entered the bar and grill across the avenue from the studio. Noting a tableful of extra girls still in costume near the door, he waved happily to them and told the bartender, "See what the gals in the Old Testament'll have!"

In Hollywood, veteran Mack Sennett, discoverer of Gloria Swanson, Madeline Hurlock, and a score of other callipygian bathing beauties, explained the real reason for all the woes of the movie magnates. "Things began going to pot," recalled Sennett bitterly, "the tragic day when Jean Harlow first stumbled upon a man in the studio who had a book under his arm. She promptly spent a whole week's salary enrolling in a school and getting herself educated. Before we knew what had hit us, every actor and actress in Hollywood started following suit. The fashion for reading spread through the colony like measles in a kindergarten. First thing you knew, they even started reading the scripts of their pictures. From that moment on, there was hell to pay."

Sennett first laid eyes on Marie Dressler when he was a kid in Northampton, Massachusetts. Miss Dressler appeared in a play called *Lady Slavey*. Enraptured, he decided on the spot to seek a career on the stage. His mother's lawyer agreed to give him a note of introduction. The lawyer's name was not yet famous. His note read: "Dear Miss Dressler: This boy wants to go on the stage. Yours truly, Calvin Coolidge."

Mabel Normand was the star Mack Sennett loved best, but he almost lost her services because one of his right-hand men, Chester Conklin, failed in the part of Sir Walter Raleigh. It was raining cats and dogs one morning, and the pavement in front of Keystone was inches deep in mud and water. Conklin spied Mabel on the other side of the street, wondering how to get across, and made a magnificent gesture. He whipped off his

brand-new coat and spread it in the mud. Miss Normand smiled gratefully, stepped daintily—and disappeared into a manhole.

Hollywood weddings differ from the regular formula in only one small detail, reports a returning tourist. Out that way the brides keep the bouquet and throw the groom away.

Mere mention of the name of Howard Hughes, the millionaire toolmaker and movie tycoon, makes Hollywood folk rush to tell you a hundred stories about his unconventional behavior. Hughes is notoriously careless about his attire; seeing him for the first time, visitors often refuse point-blank to believe that the unshaven, sloppily dressed young man with the soiled, scuffed white sneakers can possibly be one of the richest and most powerful figures on the West Coast.

At one time Hughes went on a long-distance telephone kick, tying up the only booth in a Los Angeles drugstore for hours at a time. The indignant druggist, unaware of Hughes's identity, finally ordered him from the premises. Hughes promptly had the phone company install a second booth. "Satisfied now?" he asked. The druggist was not only satisfied, but speechless. He had tried vainly for two years to get that second booth!

Another time, recalls Stewart White, Hughes was working on a deal involving twenty million dollars. He told his assistant, who was conducting the New York end of the negotiations, "Phone me the minute they say 'yes' or 'no.'" Then he added, "Come to think of it, you'd better call after six and get the night rate."

The Waldorf Astoria staff remembers the time Howard Hughes told a room clerk, "Hold onto my suite for me. I'll be back in a few days." Back he was, too, exactly seventy-two hours later. In the meantime he had flown completely around the world.

Neil Morgan tells of the time Hughes flew his giant Constellation air liner to a San Diego powwow, but returned to Hollywood by car with an aide. Weeks later an operations officer from the San Diego airport managed to get Hughes on the phone, demanding angrily, "Whatcha want us to do with that blank blank Constellation of yours?" There was a long pause, then Hughes murmured sheepishly, "So that's where it is! I knew I left it somewhere!"

General Electric threatens to add one more new element to the recent upheaval in the motion-picture field. In a process immediately dubbed "Smell-o-rama" by Schenectady wits, it promises to add odor to the general effect. Selected groups have been treated to secret screenings of a rose garden, in the course of which the lovely scent of rose perfume filled the theater. True, this is just an extension of an old idea introduced by Irving Berlin in one of his Music Box Revues where, while John Steele was warbling "In an Orange Grove in California," ushers sprayed the house with attar of orange blossoms. And in Washington this summer, the page on which an ad for a popular brand of dill pickles appeared had been sprayed with some substance that made every reader feel he was smack in the middle of Reuben's delicatessen.

The General Electric experiment was so successful that one man came out of the theater predicting it would up nationwide receipts by twenty per cent at least. "Think of all the delicious aromas with which we can assail the nostrils of our customers," he enthused—but suddenly he paled. "Good heavens," he whispered. "Don't look now—but isn't that fellow behind us a director of the Hoggenspieler Packing Plant? What can *he* have in mind?"

Hollywood is full of stories about the late Barney Dean, studio dialogue "doctor" and constant companion of Bob Hope, Bing Crosby, Jack Benny, and other great stars.

Barney never used a typewriter. He couldn't even remember people's names. Royalty meant no more to him than the lowest grip on a movie set. One day Bob Hope told him, "If you hurry, Barney, you can meet the King and Queen of Greece. They're

17

just leaving the music department." "What do I need with them now?" scoffed Barney. "Where were they last night when I needed them for a full house?" Later Barney was crossing Hollywood Boulevard at Vine against a traffic light. The policeman at the corner blew his whistle and hollered, "Hey there, you!" Barney, all innocence, asked, "How fast was I going, Officer?"

After Jack Benny had rung in the name of Barney Dean on three consecutive radio programs, his then supporting star, Phil Harris, exploded, "Who *is* this Barney Dean you're always talking about?" Benny retorted, "Just drop a cigar butt and you'll find out." Barney told Benny later, "I could have sued you, but I was afraid you'd prove it on me."

Bing Crosby took Dean with him once when he visited the sumptuous estate of a member of the Rockefeller clan. Barney kept silent while their car threaded through the miles of private roads leading to the manor house, but refused to get out when the butler opened the car door for them. "What's the matter?" asked Crosby. "Overwhelmed by the grandeur?" "It isn't that," explained Barney. "I forgot to bring my library card." After dinner Barney was visibly impressed by the huge indoor swimming pool and tennis court. When a fellow guest inquired, "Have you any idea where Mrs. Stotesbury might be?" Barney replied solemnly, "I think she's upstairs playing polo."

A Hollywood director, famous for his onslaughts on the English language, returned from New York, vastly impressed with the Metropolitan Opera Company's new look. "You've got to give credit," he enthused, "to those fellows, Bing and Bing!" Later he added, "My favorite is still *Madame Butterfield*."

Another director is married to a girl who is hipped on psychoanalysis. The day after their first son was born, the director appeared at the studio commissary, passed out the customary cigars, and announced cheerfully, "Well, I've deposited five thousand dollars in the bank to take care of the kid's complete analysis. Now, when he learns to talk, if he ever raises his voice to me once, I'll have no compunction whatever in beating the be-jabbers out of him."

It's hard to keep track of family trees out Hollywood way, with divorces and remarriages so prevalent among the movie elite. They say two lads at an executive's estate got into a big fight, with one star's son taunting another, "My father can lick the daylights out of your father." "Don't be silly," answered the other calmly. "Your father *is* my father!"

On every movie lot in Hollywood there's a little red school-house where starlets under eighteen who do not already boast high-school diplomas are required by California law to study at least three hours a day.

Of course these screenland scholars often are earning ten times as much as their teachers. And the three R's that interest them most are Rehearsin', Romancin', and Reducin'. Nor is it easy for a pedagogue to maintain the usual discipline with a roomful of kids answering to names like Judy Garland, Mickey Rooney, Shirley Temple, Betty Grable, and Elizabeth Taylor

19

(all studio students in their day). He's apt to begin by calling the roll and end by collecting autographs!

"To hold the attention of these movie moppets," a teacher at one major studio assured me, "you have only to remember that the problems must be presented properly. Ask them, for instance, to multiply two thousand dollars by fifty-two—with time and a half for overtime. Teach Johnnie to read the tiniest print in a contract. Show a little lady how to write her name in electric lights, instead of on paper.

"These youngsters really want to learn how to face *Life*—not to mention Hopper, Parsons, Skolsky, and the *Hollywood Reporter.*"

A Park Avenue psychiatrist was somewhat surprised to find one of Hollywood's most successful, publicized, and effervescent glamor girls waiting anxiously to see him. "Oh, Doctor," she explained piteously, "I need your help so badly! I can't sing; I can't dance; I can't act. It's so frustrating!" The psychiatrist adopted his most soothing manner. "You can quit show business entirely," he reminded her. "Oh no," she contradicted promptly. "I'm a big star!"

Two vacationing businessmen on the beach at Bermuda were having a fine time debating the many charms of movie star Jane Russell. "Don't know what everybody sees in her," deprecated one. "Take away her eyes, her hair, her lips, and her figure, and what have you got?" The other gave a heartfelt sigh and said, "My wife."

A famous film beauty was sun-bathing at her secluded pool, attired in absolutely nothing, when a brash photographer invaded the premises, snapped her picture, and made for the exit on the double. The star was after him in no time flat. "I'll teach you to play a dirty trick like that," she screamed. "You shot the wrong profile!"

A Beverly Hills nouveau riche, boasting about his new estate, topped it off by declaring, "And you ought to see the tennis court! I bet it's the biggest one in California." The reporter who brought in the story added, "This character is at heart just an old-fashioned kid. He drank six of them while I was interviewing him."

Harry Sauber tells about a writer, in search of material, who interviewed a bit player at a major Hollywood studio. How did he become an aspiring movie actor? Well, explained the player, he had been a handler in a Forty-second Street flea circus, and had been bitten by Felix, the star flea of the troupe. While recuperating, he came to the Coast for a visit and drifted into films. "I've heard plenty of people say it," enthused the writer, "but you are positively the first person who actually became an actor because he was bitten by an acting bug."

An alert visitor can pick up several useful hints in the golden sunshine of California, where the flying movie agents play. For instance, one opens every conversation with a client by saying bitterly, "I shouldn't even be talking to you, you so-and-so. I heard exactly what you said about me two days ago." This forestalls many a beef by a dissatisfied client. Chances are excellent he really did vilify his agent somewhere along the line and, if he didn't, he thinks he did. He now definitely has lost the offensive and is off balance for the rest of the meeting.

Leland Hayward, now one of the country's leading producers (*South Pacific, Mr. Roberts,* etc.), made his debut out Hollywood way as an agent—and a mighty shrewd one too. Last year he was bent on acquiring a certain property for a screen play, but objected vigorously to the price tag of seventy-five thousand dollars agent Irving Lazar had put on it. "Irving," implored Hayward, "who taught you to be such a pirate?" Lazar answered quite truthfully, "You did!"

Harry Kurnitz recalls the day a writer invaded the two-by-four office of a struggling Hollywood agent with a small package in his arms. "What's in that package?" demanded the suspicious agent. "An inflatable lifeboat that will hold eight men," said the writer. "One more wisecrack," decreed the agent, "and I no longer represent you. Now what's in that package?" So the writer opened the package, pushed the button on the compressed-air cylinder, and fled. The boat backed the agent so tightly into a corner it took the fire department to hack him out.

At a literary cocktail party a well-known agent made a spectacular exit. He fell down a flight of stairs. As he picked himself up, miraculously unhurt, he called up to the crowd above, "You noticed, I hope, that I hit only every tenth step."

Memorable moments in Hollywood high life:

1. A press agent called a columnist to report the death of a producer client. "I'm sorry," said the columnist firmly, "but I used his name last week."

2. A winsome chick reproved a bold Wilshire wolf with "You know I'm going to be married tomorrow! Call me in about three weeks."

3. Greta Garbo is rumored to have dreamed one night that she sprinkled six boxes of grass seed in her hair. She awakened moaning, "I vant to be a lawn."

4. Groucho Marx proposed this toast to a socialite hostess: "I drink to your charm, your beauty, and your brains—which will give you a rough idea of how hard up I am for a drink."

5. Zsa Zsa Gabor went on a caviar-and-filet-mignon diet and took off $135 in three days.

6. A visitor asked a starlet, "Did you buy that sable wrap out of your earnings?" The starlet gave a chuckle—or was it a Peale of laughter?—and replied, "I owe it all to my Power of Positive Winking."

7. A movie queen's personal maid knocked on the door of her portable dressing room and announced, "There's a bishop out

here who says he married you in 1943." "That's funny," mused the star. "I'm practically certain I never married a bishop." Later she added, "I can't help getting married all the time. I'm a sucker for a rite." She's a remarkable housekeeper, however. Every time she wangles a divorce, she keeps the house.

Marilyn, We Roll Along

Marilyn Monroe Miller is easily the favorite actress of every writer on the Fox lot: when she's around, who bothers listening to the dialogue?

"We sent her up on location to northern Canada," recalls publicist Harry Brand, "and the Royal Mounted Police forgot all about getting their man. They just concentrated on Marilyn—and she was wearing three sweaters and two pairs of pants, too! That girl doesn't believe in frozen assets. On her, the end justifies the jeans."

Between rehearsals, the story has it that Marilyn went trout fishing. She hooked a whopper, but he finally broke loose and swam like all get-out to rejoin the other trout. "Wow, fellows," he gasped. "You should have seen the one I got away from."

A fashion editor was asked to describe the dress Marilyn had worn to an Academy Award dinner. "Well," answered the editor cautiously, "in most places it looked a lot like Marilyn."

At the Fox lot one summer, life was enlivened by weekly baseball pools. Each of sixteen actors or actresses drew out of a hat a pill that represented one of the major-league ball teams, and paid a dollar therefor. At the end of the week, the total sixteen-dollar pot went to the actor whose team had scored the most runs in games played during that period. Marilyn Monroe had been taking aureomycin pills to cure a cold, and as a scene was being rehearsed for *The Seven Year Itch*, she thoughtlessly took one from her purse and gulped it down. Suddenly she realized she had made a slight mistake. "Help," she wailed. "I just swallowed the Baltimore Orioles!"

Mae West, who is reputed to know a thing or two about sex appeal herself, was asked recently by a Las Vegas reporter for *her* critical estimate of Marilyn Monroe. "She's a good kid," conceded Miss West, "and they've handled her publicity well. But I just don't think she has the equipment."

What Miss West needs is a new oculist.

Herb Stein has written an entire Hollywood success story in just three sentences: 1. I haven't got a phone yet, but you can get me through the drugstore at our corner. 2. Give me a ring, old thing. I'm in the book. 3. "The subscriber has requested that we do not give out her new number."

That hardy perennial of movie classics, *Gone with the Wind,* has been reissued for the steenth time. Alan Green suggests it's about time they rename it *Gone with the Second Wind*.

Cecil B. DeMille was asked by Leo Guild why he made so many biblical pictures. DeMille chuckled. "Why let two thousand years of publicity go to waste?"

One of the men who deliver sandwiches and soft drinks to the personnel in the offices of M-G-M has the harmless foible of referring to famous personages by their first names. He's forever dropping pearls like "I bumped into Dore last night," or "Marlon's new part fits him like a glove," or "If I were Grace, I'd make the Prince appear in her next picture."

Recently he was given a pair of seats to a special showing of *Julius Caesar*. Next morning he didn't let his audience down. "Well, folks," he announced cheerfully, "I caught Julius last night."

Visiting Hollywood a few years before his death, French playwright Henri Bernstein was heard to observe, "Genius, geniuses everywhere I turn! If only there was some talent!"

A star came to New York between pictures with a wad of five thousand dollars burning a hole in his pocket. Problem: should he buy a small piece of a pal's new musical revue, or get the little woman the mink coat for which she had been yearning? He compromised by buying into the show but promising his wife *two* coats if it was a hit.

After the tryout, the star sent his wife this wire: "I've got bad news for you. Your coats closed in New Haven last night."

CHAPTER TWO

ANIMAL LIFE

Reigning Cats and Dogs

I am a firm believer in the old theory that there is a time and a place for everything—and that goes double for funny stories.

For instance, I told a story to an assemblage of several thousand schoolteachers in Detroit recently that won me about three times as solid a response as I figured it warranted. There was a reason!

The story concerned a prosperous New York merchant who went South on vacation to do a little hunting. He rented a hound-dog for five dollars at the lodge he patronized, and sallied forth. It soon became apparent that this dog was a champion. In one hour the merchant was back with a full bag, his reputation as a huntsman greatly enhanced.

The next year he demanded the same dog. "You mean 'Teacher,'" the lodge owner assured him. "He's so good we've raised the price to ten dollars." The year following, the dog's name had been changed to "Principal," and the price was up to twenty dollars.

The huntsman grumbled but couldn't do a thing about it. He just had to have that dog! So again he arrived at the lodge and put in his claim. But the owner registered despondency and sighed, "You can't have that dog any longer, mister. It's our fault. We've ruined him for hunting. This spring we renamed him 'State Superintendent of Schools,' and from that moment on all he's done is sit on his fanny and bark!"

Now, here's why those teachers laughed so hard. The gentleman who had introduced me, and was the only man sitting on the platform behind me, was the State Superintendent of Schools in Michigan!

Governor and Mrs. Averell Harriman have an oceanside estate in Hobe Sound, Florida, and one sure sign they are in residence is the sight of their prize dachshund frisking about on the beach. The name of this dachshund is Gary Cooper.

Last winter a jokester sent a post card to the dog addressed "Gary Cooper, c/o the Harrimans." An alert real-estate promoter spotted the card at the post office and figured he had a hot prospect to work on. He rushed over to the Harriman place, declaiming, "It's imperative that I see Mr. Cooper immediately."

"He must be around here somewhere," said an obliging maid. "Here, Gary! Here, Gary!"

A man boasted day and night about the wonderful dog he owned. Walking on the beach with this beloved pooch, he met a friend and promptly launched forth with, "You've got to see the new trick I just taught Fido." He picked up a stick and hurled it into the water. With one bound, Fido was after it, but not for him so commonplace a feat as swimming in the briny! Fido ran lightly on *top* of the waves, retrieved the stick, and, returning on the water's surface, deposited it at his master's feet.

"I'll show you that was no accident," boasted the dog's owner. A second time he threw the stick, and a second time Fido fetched it via the surface of the sea.

"Well?" exulted the owner. "What do you think of a dog that can do a trick like that?" "Not too much," deprecated the friend. "He can't even swim!"

George Gobel complained that he couldn't teach his prize boxer, Irving, not to chase after automobiles. A noted dog expert assured Gobel, "Every boxer chases cars." "I know," said George, "but Irving catches them."

"A small town," opines A. W. Perrine, "is a place where a fellow has to walk around a dog enjoying a nap on the sidewalk."

One dog woke up when five-year-old Kathy skipped by, barked happily, and followed her home. Kathy did not know that her new friend was a female. She loved the dog so that her parents couldn't find it in their hearts to call the A.S.P.C.A. She had her moment of triumph some weeks later when she came home from school and found her dog being pursued by every male dog in the neighborhood. "How do you like that, Mom?" she inquired proudly. "Our dog is just a natural-born leader."

In Los Angeles, Matt Weinstock tells about a lady who loves cats who was dining with her husband in her apartment one night when she fancied she heard a cat meowing a floor or two away. "I'll bet that pussy is lonely," she remarked to her husband, and playfully meowed back.

To her surprise the cat answered her! She repeated her meow, this time putting extra feeling into her performance, and there then ensued the darnedest cat conversation ever heard in that neighborhood. It continued for a full half hour, while the husband marveled.

The next day her triumph was deflated when a neighbor dropped down to borrow some sugar. "The funniest thing happened last night," said the neighbor. "I meowed at a cat and he meowed back—and we must have kept it up for forty minutes!"

A Cleveland resident, reports Paul Steiner, lost confidence in a cat who snoozed unconcernedly in the sun while dozens of mice scurried happily by, so he bought a mousetrap. Its first victim was the cat.

At the country estate of a distinguished Doubleday editor, a small boy's head appeared over the fence, and a meek voice inquired, "Please, Mr. Beecroft, could I have my arrow back?" "Certainly, my boy," responded the editor with that spontaneous love for the young that has made him famous. "Where is it?" "I think," said the small boy, "that it's stuck in one of your cats."

Animal Spirits

"I had a bit of a hassle," admitted an intrepid horseman, "with my fiery steed in Central Park this morning. He wanted to go in one direction, and I wanted to go in the other." "How did you settle it?" he was asked. "Oh," he answered airily, "the horse tossed me for it."

An Eastern lady, vacationing at a Nevada dude ranch, essayed a ride on a spirited pony and was promptly sent flying head over heels into a pile of—well, dust in a corner of the corral. "This pony bucks," she cried angrily as she struggled to her feet. A cowboy who had watched the performance with keen enjoyment drawled, "Shucks, lady, that wasn't no buck. That pony only coughed!"

Up in Maine a man bought himself a horse and, after he had paid for it, asked, "Now that the deal is closed, tell me honestly: is the horse any good?" The shrewd Yankee who had sold the animal answered, "Depends on what you mean to do with him." "I'm a sea captain," said the buyer, "and I plan to take him aboard ship tonight." "You're lucky," said the Yankee. "On land he's no good at all."

Danny Kaye comes up with a story about a friend named Nussbaum who took it into his head to go to the Malay Peninsula to hunt tigers. When he came back a friend demanded, "What is a nice, well-brought-up fellow like you doing risking his life with tigers, yet?" "You don't understand," said Nussbaum loftily. "This was a safari to end all safaris! There is no thrill like stalking through the jungle, knowing that a great man-eating tiger may leap at you any minute." "Nu," said the friend, "how many tigers did you kill?" "None," admitted Nussbaum. "The safari was a failure then?" persisted the friend. "Of course not," maintained Nussbaum. "It was a glorious success. When you're hunting tigers, none is *plenty*."

A man strolled into a neighborhood tavern with a huge, mangy yellow dog in tow and sat minding his own business until another guest, leading a ferocious-looking bulldog, challenged him.

"Whatcha doing with a mutt like that?" he demanded. "You should get a pedigreed dog like mine." The first man answered quietly, "Five hundred dollars says my yellow 'mutt' can lick the daylights out of that bull of yours."

The bet was made, and sure enough, the yellow dog made mincemeat of the bull in about two minutes flat. The bartender swept up the carnage and asked respectfully, "Where did that yellow dog come from anyhow?"

Its owner explained, "A friend sent him to me from Africa. All I had to do was cut off his mane and tail!"

That reminds me of the time Tallulah Bankhead forswore canine companionship for a time and acquired a playful lion cub as a pet. "Winston Churchill" she called him. Her friends fled when he came around for a romp. Once he almost bit off Noel Coward's hand. When Coward cried bloody murder, Tallulah silenced him with, "Don't be a spoilsport. Winston is just teething."

Arthur Wise, Los Angeles financier, writes about the bank clerk who entered a pet shop and announced he was in the market for a parrot. "I have a dandy here," boasted the proprietor. "He can say Uncle Herbert, Aunt Minnie, Hooray for the Dodgers, and Wait Till Next Year." "Never mind all that," interrupted the bank clerk. *"Is he tender?"*

The favorite animal story of the late H. T. Webster, creator of Caspar Milquetoast and "Life's Darkest Moment," concerned the kangaroo who suddenly leaped twelve feet over the barrier at the Bronx Park Zoo and took off in the direction of Yonkers at eighty miles an hour. A keeper dashed up to the baffled lady who had been standing in front of the kangaroo's cage and demanded, "What on earth did you do to that kangaroo to make him run that way?" "Nothing, really," the lady declared. "I just tickled him a little." "You'd better tickle me in the same place," suggested the keeper grimly. "I've got to catch him!"

There was a state fair in the Middle West recently where interest ran high in the award for the champion bull. Two entries were already famous in those parts and feeling—and wagering— ran high on which would win out. When the time came, the judges couldn't decide themselves. The chairman stepped into the center of the arena and announced, "These bulls are so evenly matched, we simply can't make up our minds which one is best. We're going to leave it to the governor's son here to name the champion."

The governor's son was exactly six years old. He gravely inspected the two magnificent bulls and finally piped, "I pick this one."

The crowd cheered, the blue ribbon was pinned on his selection, and then the chairman asked, "Why did you choose the one you did?" The governor's son answered, "Because I think he'll give the most milk."

CHAPTER THREE

ARTISTS AND MODELS

On a sub-zero day in midwinter a lovely young model complained that the studio was too cold for posing in the nude. "You're right," agreed the artist who had hired her. "I don't feel like painting today anyhow. Sit down and have a cup of coffee and a sandwich with me." Some minutes later he heard a determined pounding on the door. "Quick," he commanded the model. "Get your clothes off! It's my wife!"

33

A Cincinnati camera club, tired of photographing the Ohio River and the local ball players, threw caution to the winds and hired a model for some nude photographic studies. But when the moment for action arrived, it developed that the model had been wearing such tight garters, their imprint on her legs could not be erased.

The members decided she must wait in an anteroom for an hour while they went out for dinner. When they came back, the marks on her legs were gone all right—but alas, she had been sitting the entire hour on a cane-bottomed chair!

One model agency believes in giving its girls unusual names. Three that seemed to carry things a bit far were: Miss September Maughan, Miss Eyeful Tower and Miss Berthe Daye Sutes.

Models of distinction:

1. The cover girl who suddenly turned up at Palm Beach on the arm of an eligible playboy. "Hallelujah!" marveled a friend. "Where did you dig up this one?" "I'm not sure," admitted the playboy. "I opened my wallet and there she was!"

2. The model from Honolulu who taught all the other girls the hula. "It's easy," she maintained. "First you put a crop of grass on one hip. Then you put a crop of grass on the other. Then you rotate the crops."

3. The model who was so ugly that when she walked into a studio three mice jumped up on chairs.

4. The model who refused to pose for one magazine illustrator. Her reason: "He's tall, dark—and hands."

5. The model Peter Lind Hayes discovered in New Rochelle. "She has absolutely everything a man desires," insists Peter, "including muscles and a mustache."

The late H. T. Webster had completed a dozen cartoons in a single day and decided he needed a bit of relaxation. He chose twenty friends at random and sent them a one-word telegram: "Congratulations!"

34

Only two phoned to ask what he was talking about. The other eighteen sent notes of thanks. Each had recently completed some minor achievement he deemed entirely worthy of Webster's congratulatory wire!

Salvador Dali, the famous but eccentric painter, refused to come to America with his wife Gala until Caresse Crosby, Boston socialite and collector, agreed to shepherd them. They sailed aboard the *Champlain*, Dali bundled up in sweaters and mittens in a third-class cabin near the engine room. "I stay next to the engine," he explained, "so that I'll get there quicker." To each of his precious pictures he had affixed a string; the other ends of the strings were tied to his clothing or his fingers. He was packed and ready to leave the ship four days before they steamed past the Statue of Liberty.

When the reporters streamed aboard, Caresse told them about Salvador Dali. None of them had ever heard of the gentleman, but they trooped obediently after her to his cabin. One look at his magnificent mustachio and another at his canvases, and Caresse, alas, was completely forgotten. "A portrait of my wife," announced Dali in French. "What's that on her shoulders?" asked a pop-eyed reporter. "Lamb chops," said Dali. That did it! The next morning, Dali and his lamb chops hit the headlines, and Caresse, for possibly the only time in her life, was relegated to a footnote on page nine.

In his disarming autobiography, *Lying in State*, Stanton Griffis tells about a day he and a Wall Street friend wandered into a Paris gallery to see an exhibition of modern pictures. The friend thought one or two of them would improve the décor of his private office.

"How do you go about buying these things without getting the daylights socked out of you?" he asked. "Put in low bids on all of them," advised the knowing Mr. Griffis. "When the show is over, you'll probably find that a couple have fallen virtually into your lap."

The frock-coated manager indicated that this procedure was highly unusual, but graciously consented to enter the bids. A few mornings later, Mr. Griffis received a frantic phone call from his friend. "My God," wailed the friend. "I've bought forty-six pictures!"

CHAPTER FOUR

'TENSHUN!

"Life's certainly taken a turn for the better at Camp Lee since a beautiful blonde was assigned to our barracks," boasted a GI in a Richmond bar. "What is she—a WAC?" asked an incredulous bystander. "Not at all," said the GI. "She's just one of 'the boys.' Does the regular routine, eats and sleeps like one of us, even takes showers where we do." "For the love of mud," gasped the bystander. "How does she get away with it?" The GI winked and said, "Who's gonna snitch?"

A squad of draftees in Oklahoma was engaged in enlarging and painting barracks, being driven like Furies by a tough and uncompromising sergeant. Just behind them, another squad of soldiers was busy tearing down the barracks as soon as they were painted. A roving correspondent watched the operation with some wonderment for a few minutes, then asked the painting sergeant how come. The sergeant replied, "I got my orders and they got theirs, but I'll tell you one thing, boy: I'm having a heck of a time staying ahead of them!"

When asked to furnish his school and college affiliations, a New England job applicant paused briefly, then wrote, "Korea, Clash of 1952."

On sick call one morning, a draftee heard two hardened veterans discussing the doctor in charge. "He doesn't kid around," asserted one. "Fellow came in saying he had ptomaine poisoning, so the doc cut off his big toe." "Yeah," agreed the second, "and remember the guy with erysipelas? The doctor just sliced away his left ear." By this time the draftee had turned a sickly green. "Let me out of here," he begged. "I've got asthma!"

John Straley tells about a lonesome draftee who had frittered away all but a twenty-five-cent piece of the money he had saved on a wild and vaguely disappointing weekend. The last quarter was to be his bus fare back to camp. Slumped at the bar, however, the quarter slipped out of his hand, and, before he could retrieve it, the proprietor's pet monkey had leaped from his perch, grabbed the coin, and swallowed it.

The grouchy proprietor, furthermore, flatly refused to make restitution. "Hang on to yer money better, bud," he growled. "I ain't responsible for dat monkey's actions." The outraged draftee hauled off and socked the grinning monkey right in the solar plexus. "Grab my last quarter, will you?" he began, but then let out a yell of glee. "I'm independently rich," he cried, scooping up coins from the bar, where the monk had coughed up nine dollars and seventy-five cents!

The sergeant glared at an undersized, sharp-eyed rookie and demanded, "You, there, what's the first thing you do when you clean a rifle?" "Look at the serial number," was the immediate reply. "The serial number!" roared the sergeant. "*Why?*" "To make certain," explained the rookie, "that I'm cleaning my own rifle."

General Al Gruenther reports that an army unit near NATO headquarters is out to get a famous Parisian glamor girl. Seems she's been contributing to the delinquency of a major.

Young Johnny Malone always had wanted to be a sailor, and he enlisted the day after he was eighteen. His first letter home, however, denoted a certain measure of disillusionment. It read: "Dear Mom: I joined the Navy because I loved the way the ships were kept so spick-and-span—but I never knew until this week who keeps them so spick-and-span. Love, Johnny."

A Missouri boy, a plebe at Annapolis, wrote a letter home, explaining, "The first thing I had to learn down here was how to use my sextant." "Well," declared his mother, aghast, "the things they teach in college nowadays!"

The news from Norfolk is that enlisted men are showing a new respect for their officers, regardless of their sex. A sailor was observed retrieving a handkerchief that had been dropped by a trim WAVE lieutenant, and handing it to her with a heartfelt "I think you dropped this, toots, sir."

Bob Sylvester reports that the Navy is working on an atomic submarine which will stay under water for four solid years— coming up just long enough to allow the crew to re-enlist.

HORATIO ALGER

CHAPTER FIVE

BUSINESS AS USUAL

A deserving young man went to work one Monday morning in the lowest position in a huge manufacturing plant. His starting salary was only ten dollars a week, but determinedly he began his climb up the ladder.

Inside of a month he was head of the shipping department at a hundred a week. Two months later he was in the front office, earning a thousand a week. And exactly one year after his humble start, the big boss called him in and said, "My boy, you've done well. You are hereby named president of the company, at a hundred thousand a year!"

"Thank you," said the young man.

"Thank you, he tells me," grumbled the big boss. "Haven't you anything else to say for yourself?"

"Yes," said the young man. "Please tell Mama I won't be home for dinner."

In Los Angeles, there dwelt a head accountant who labored for a big furniture house for forty years. Every morning he unlocked his desk at eight-thirty on the nose, peered into the center drawer for a moment, then locked everything up again. What was in that center drawer? Assistants, visiting salesmen, even the owner himself, never came close to solving the mystery. One day the accountant died suddenly, and after a decent interval everybody rushed to pry open the center drawer. It was found to contain just one little slip of paper. Printed in capital letters thereon were the words, THE SIDE TOWARD THE WINDOW IS THE DEBIT SIDE!

The new typist, fresh from college, was so pretty that nobody had the heart to reprimand her for obvious shortcomings. The boss saw her frantically searching through the files one morning, and after pausing to enjoy the rear view said consolingly, "There, there, Mary. If you've lost something again, it isn't serious enough to burst into tears about it." "It certainly is," said Mary, choking back a sob. "This time it's my lunch."

A short time before his death, Thomas A. Edison was asked the secret of his success. "Two things that had nothing to do with my knack for inventing things had a lot to do with it," he replied candidly. "One was good luck. The other was that nobody ever was able to convince me that it was unfair to my fellow workers to put forth my best efforts in my work. I'm glad there was no such thing as the eight-hour day when I was a young man. I won't say it isn't a boon to others—but if my own life had been restricted to eight-hour days, I don't think I would have accomplished a great deal. This country wouldn't be where it is today if the young men of fifty years ago had been afraid they might earn more than they were paid for!"

How many of you have heard of the Horatio Alger Award? Named after the author of rags-to-riches sagas that delighted— and inspired—the younger generation at the turn of the century, it is awarded annually to a group of self-made industrial leaders by the American Schools and Colleges Association. Among the outstanding citizens who snagged Alger awards in recent years were the late Tom Watson, of International Business Machines, whose first job as bookkeeping apprentice netted him exactly two dollars a week; Paul Hoffman, of Studebaker and Ford Foundation fame, who began his business career as a porter in a used-car lot in Chicago; Walter Fuller, who rose through self-education from lowly mill hand to head of the Curtis Publishing Company, and Adolph Zukor, who added forty dollars of borrowed capital to what he had managed to save from a two-dollar-a-week salary in a fur store, and opened a penny arcade. He became the guiding genius of Paramount Pictures.

Speaking of Mr. Watson of IBM, he was famous for his insistence on having signs commanding "THINK" plastered all over his palatial premises. Nobody ever discovered the identity of the miscreant who penciled "OR THWIM" on the bottom of all of them after the staff had gone home one night.

"And now," beamed the business-school teacher, "tell the class what you do when your employer rings for someone to take dictation." "I pick up my notebook," recited perky little Miss Hastings, "sharpen my pencils, and answer the buzzard promptly." Obviously, Miss Hastings was destined for success in the business world. Her first boss regarded her chassis with undisguised approval, but a few hours later was moved to point to the portable on her desk and remark, "There is one thing you must remember, my dear. If my wife bursts in suddenly any time without knocking, please apply yourself to that contraption. It's a typewriter."

Miss Hastings progressed rapidly. The boss learned to give her reports and say, "Make a dozen copies of this—and circulate the one with the fewest mistakes."

It was only a question of time till a subsequent boss (aged seventy) asked Miss Hastings to be his bride. The morning after the nuptials, the seventy-year-old groom was bristling with his usual vigor, but the young bride was listless and bedraggled. "When he told me," she wailed, "he'd been saving for twenty years—*I* thought he meant *money!*"

The *Town Journal* reports that a slick saleslady, after talking a customer into buying a mink coat at a Fifth Avenue specialty shop, asked gently, "How would your husband prefer being billed, modom? In a series of piddling amounts or in one staggering sum?"

A New York dress-shop owner is thinking seriously of framing a letter of complaint that reached him, by courtesy of the ingenious U. S. Post Office Department, the other morning. It reads: "The Big Store: Dear Mr. B. Store: Please cancel my order for maternity dress, Model 61, which you were supposed to deliver me three weeks ago. My delivery turned out faster than yours. Respectfully, etc., etc."

Zsa Zsa Hornblow, the doughty old maid who had inherited the Hornblow Nut and Bolt Factory from her father, Uriah Hornblow, and ran it with an iron hand, caught sight of a young fellow leaning idly against the wall, whistling and twiddling his thumbs. The outraged Zsa Zsa shrilled, "You there! What's your weekly salary?" "Thirty bucks," vouchsafed the idler. "Hmphh!"

snorted Zsa Zsa. "Here's thirty dollars. Now scram! Vamoose! You're fired." The young man pocketed the thirty and left, exuding good will. Zsa Zsa watched till he was off the premises, then demanded of foreman Al Vidor, "How long was that waster on the payroll of the Hornblow Nut and Bolt Works?" "He never worked for us, ma'am," said Al patiently. "He was just taking orders for Cokes and sandwiches for the drugstore."

A small-town druggist was down but not out. Closed by the sheriff, he posted this notice on the window: "Our doors are locked. The following services, formerly available here, may be had as follows: Ice water at fountain in park. General information from cop at the corner. Change of a dollar at bank. Matches and scratch pads at hotel. Rest rooms at home. Magazine for browsing at doctor's office. Bus information at the terminal. And loafing at any other location of your own choosing."

In Des Moines, Gardner Cowles, publisher of *Look*, goaded his sales force to new deeds of derring-do with the tale of an untried clerk in a clothing store who sold nineteen suits on his first day on the job. "A great start," enthused his boss, "but if you're really the world-beater you appear to be, you'll fob off this overloud, outmoded number with the broad purple stripes we've been stuck with for three years. Get sixty dollars for it, and I'll give you a raise immediately." Three days later the clerk reported that the monstrosity had been sold. "You're wonderful," conceded the boss. "Did you have a tough time persuading the customer to take it?" "The customer was docile as a lamb," admitted the clerk, "but I had one hell of an argument with his seeing-eye dog!"

A pawnbroker loaded his show window with unredeemed saxophones, banjos, tubas—and shotguns. "Very interesting display," commented a friend, "but does it sell merchandise?" "Does it!" enthused the pawnbroker. "One day a fellow buys a sax or a tuba. Two days later his neighbors buy the shotguns."

Walter Lowen tells about a salesgirl in a chain candy store who always had customers lined up waiting for her while other salesgirls stood twiddling their thumbs. The owner of the chain noted her popularity and asked for her secret. "It's easy enough," she replied. "The other girls scoop up more than a pound of candy and then start taking away. I always scoop up less than a pound and then add to it."

The president of a billion-dollar corporation faced his board of directors with an unusually grim look on his face. "I'm going to put it squarely to you, J.D.," he said to the first vice-president. "Have you been taking out my secretary after hours?" "Gosh, chief," blushed J.D. "I didn't think you'd mind." In turn, two lesser vice-presidents, the comptroller, and the chief statistician sheepishly admitted that they, too, had not been immune to the charms of the prexy's secretary. The newest and youngest member of the board, however, was made of sterner stuff. "I'm happy to say," he announced, "that I've had no extracurricular activities whatever with the young lady in question." "You're just the man we're looking for," boomed the president, relief in his voice. "Get right outside and fire her!"

A Stamford, Connecticut, businessman named Thomas Edward Saxe, Jr., has designated one corner of his inner sanctum as official headquarters for the most soothing and undemanding institution in the country today: the Sittin', Starin' 'n' Rockin' Club.

Its close to two thousand members (including a couple of movie stars, TV and sports personalities and ordinary folk like bank presidents and you and me) have neither meetings nor policies to fret about. The only thing they must do to stay in good standing—or sitting—is to propel themselves gently to and fro in a rocking chair a few minutes every day.

Saxe discovered one morning, while vacationing in Sarasota, Florida, that an old rockin' chair had "gotten" him. It relaxed his nerves, soothed his brow, brightened his skies. He resolved

then and there to form his club and pass on the good word. The news spread so quickly that he soon was swamped with applications.

"I had to call a halt," he says ruefully. "I was so busy mailing out new membership cards, I had practically no time left for rocking myself."

There's not a thing in the world, of course, to stop you from forming a club all your own. Your sole need is a handy rocking chair.

Just wait calmly every twenty-four hours with your personally selected clubfellows for the end of a perfect sway.

Mr. Huebsch told his secretary at 9:30 A.M. that he needed some documents in a hurry. When she hadn't produced them by eleven, he went after her in a rage. She didn't help matters by looking very aggrieved indeed and telling him, "Hold your horses, Mr. Huebsch! I haven't even found the filing cabinet yet!"

A group of well-heeled young executives were exchanging confidences on how they had overcome early difficulties. "Things were pretty tough for me," admitted Rogers when his turn came, "but I just gritted my teeth, rolled up my sleeves, spat on my hands—and borrowed another hundred thousand dollars from my father."

Anxious to get on in the world, a nice young couple were entertaining the boss and his wife at dinner—doing pretty well, too, until their ten-year-old hopeful burst into view. He cased the boss's wife with obvious interest, then asked his dad, "Does she really wrestle on TV?"

Marshall Field, founder of the great Chicago store, loved to tell this story at the expense of his friend, P. D. Armour, the meat packer. Armour once hired a new office clerk but didn't mention the time to report for work. The new employee showed up the first day at 8:00 A.M., to find P. D. Armour and his staff in shirt sleeves, plunged into the morning accounts. The next day the young man showed up at seven. Armour, hard at work, only glowered. The third day the new clerk managed to get in at six-thirty. Armour glared up from his paper-littered desk. "Young man," he bellowed, "just what is it you do with your forenoons?"

In a nationally known department store in Dallas, where, if you search hard enough, you can pick up a handkerchief for as little as $8.75, they staged a fashion exposition that had the customers hanging from the rafters. So many well-heeled Dallas ladies—and their husbands—turned up, in fact, there was no room left for the models to change their costumes on the exhibition floor. A special elevator whisked them up two flights, where an assembly line, similar to the Ford setup at its Highland Park plant, lay in wait for them.

One attendant yanked away their hats. Another unzipped them and peeled off their dresses. Another pulled off their shoes. At the end of the line, each model stood in her barest essentials waiting for her next costume to be trotted out.

47

Things were going swimmingly, the crowd cheering, the models changing into ever more dazzling—and expensive—ensembles, when a slight hitch marred the proceedings.

The haughtiest and wealthiest customer of the establishment stepped blithely into the wrong elevator. . . .

Do I have to go on with this story?

In the bridal department of a Fort Wayne emporium, writes Cliff Milnor, a customer stopped the usually quick-witted consultant cold. What she wanted was "a maternity wedding gown"! "Sorry," gasped the consultant, "but I doubt that you'll find a garment like that in the entire state of Indiana." "Time you people snapped up around here," said the customer scornfully. "They've got 'em in Kentucky!"

A famous Brooklyn department store decided to honor its two millionth customer. She was embraced by the store president, interviewed on TV, and loaded down with a dozen fancily wrapped packages of choice merchandise.

She then proceeded to her original destination—the complaint desk.

"I've got to get a present," confided a customer to a department-store clerk, "for a very rich old aunt who can hardly walk. Any suggestions?" The clerk considered a moment, then came up with, "How about some floor wax?"

After pulling out half the stock in an unsuccessful attempt to please a pernickety lady customer, the shoe salesman mopped his brow and inquired, "Mind if I rest a moment, lady? Your feet are killing me!"

An heiress was riding in an elevator in a Midwest department store when something went wrong with the mechanism. The elevator plunged to the basement, and the heiress landed on her posterior. She sued for the hundred thousand dollars she felt this affront to her dignity was worth.

"I take it," the defense attorney remarked caustically, "that when you realized a crash was inevitable, the sins of your entire life passed before your eyes?"

"Certainly not," snapped the heiress. "We only fell eleven floors."

A small boy invaded the lingerie section of a big department store and shyly presented his problem to a lady clerk. "I want to buy my mom a present of a slip," he said, "but I'm darned if I know what size she wears." The clerk said, "It would help to know if your mom is tall or short, fat or skinny." "She's just perfect," beamed the small boy, so the clerk wrapped up a size 34 for him.

Two days later, Mom came to the store herself and changed it to a size 52.

To be serious for a moment, Marihelen Macduff describes a young shopper in a fashionable Dallas emporium whose behavior in the brides' salon was puzzling the personnel. She would pick up one piece of material after another, and pace up and down with it held against her side—but never once did she look into the mirror.

"It's not the looks of my bridal gown that bother me at all," she finally explained. "I want to know what it will *sound* like. My husband-to-be lost his eyesight in Korea. I want him to *hear* me at his side."

Garfinkel was selling lightweight summer suits at such a low figure that one customer, at least, smelled a rat. "They shrink maybe when it rains?" he inquired. "Nonsense," answered Garfinkel heatedly. "Three yards in every hundred maybe at the most." The customer was convinced but, after the first rainstorm, angrily returned with a garment shrunken almost beyond recognition. Garfinkel, however, had a ready explanation. "Can I help it," he demanded, "if you were unlucky enough to get those three yards?"

A continental refugee in London had one big ambition in life: to be able to afford an English suit, made to order by a really first-class English tailor. He scrimped and saved, and finally had enough to order not only the suit, but all the trimmings to match—homburg, shirt, tie, oxfords, stick. The day came for the final fitting, and he was able to study the full ensemble in a full-length mirror. Suddenly he burst into tears. The tailor, dismayed, begged, "Tell me what's wrong, sir. Are you displeased with the fit? Do any of the accessories bother you?" "No, no," the refugee assured him between sobs. "The clothes are perfect. *But why did we have to lose India?*"

Himmel and Bimmel, who shared a floor of a loft building in the garment district, were fierce competitors in the cloak-and-suit industry, but managed to preserve a personal friendship nonetheless. Every day they would lunch together and catalogue their respective trials and tribulations.

"Son-in-laws," moaned Himmel one noon, "you expect to be dumb, but my son-in-law Morris is dumber even than you could imagine. Let me show you, Bimmel, what I got to contend with." Thereupon, he summoned Morris, handed him a five-dollar bill, and said, "Morris, I want you should go down to the corner and buy me a new automobile."

Morris took the bill silently, departed, and Himmel shot a look of triumph at his friend. Bimmel, however, refused to be impressed. "My son, Nathan," he announced, "is ten times dumber than your Morris." He called Nathan in, pressed a shiny half dollar in his palm, and said, "Nathan, run down by the barbershop in the basement and let me know quick if I am there." Nathan scurried off, leaving the two older men moaning and wagging their heads.

In the elevator, Morris and Nathan met and exchanged greetings. "My father-in-law thinks I'm stupid," grumbled Morris.

"But he gives me five dollars to buy him a hotomobile and never once says what make or color it should be." "My papa's worse even," consoled Nathan. "A half dollar he squanders so I should see if he's in the barbershop, when for just a dime he could have telephoned and found out for himself!"

The fixtures and equipment of a big barbershop in a metropolitan hotel are a lot flossier than those of a tonsorial parlor in a small town, but the atmosphere and conversation are remarkably similar and unchanging.

The same cutups perform both in the chairs and behind them; the same badinage, political soothsaying and sporting data are exchanged; the same amorous if doddering patrons furtively squeeze the hands of the same coy manicurists.

The familiar barber pole with the red stripes is a throwback to the time of King Henry VIII of England, when barbers were also allowed to practice minor surgery and dentistry. The red stripe presumably symbolized blood, and was designed as a guidepost for a majority of the citizenry who couldn't read. Later, American barbers added a dash of blue for patriotic reasons.

In one shop a customer demanded a brand-new face lotion. "I have a date with a luscious babe tonight," he explained, "and I want to have the most provocative tang possible." "Here's one guaranteed to knock her cold," enthused the barber. "It has an ether base."

Al, the tony barber at the New Weston, was surprised to get a tip from editor Haas *before* the latter climbed into his chair. "You're the first customer who ever tipped me *before* I gave him any service," commented Al. "That's not a tip," Haas announced brusquely. "That's *hush* money."

The world traveler entered the hotel barbershop, and as luck would have it, chose the chair of the barber who, for some reason, always seemed to average the biggest tips. "I suppose you shave a lot of famous characters in this shop?" essayed the traveler. "Not at all," the barber assured him gravely. "You're the first one this month, sir."

"Can you *prove* this is a good hair tonic?" an oft-fooled baldhead asked his druggist. "I'll tell you how I can prove it," asserted the druggist. "One lady customer took the cork out of the bottle with her teeth and twenty-four hours later she had a mustache!"

Herb Shriner, waiting his turn to have his hair cut, picked up a magazine for expectant fathers and came across this bit of advice: "It will help to place the diaper in the shape of a baseball diamond, with you at bat. Fold second base over home plate. Place baby on the pitcher's mound. Then pin first base and third base to home plate and you're all set." "All set, my eye," commented Shriner. "I tried that very trick on my first-born, but we had to call the game on account of wet grounds."

An overpersistent insurance solicitor followed the late W. C. Fields into a barbershop one afternoon. Fields, spluttering shaving cream, finally exploded, "I've told you 'no' ten times now. Just to shut you up, I'll put the proposition up to my lawyer the next time I see him."

"Will you take the proper step," persisted the solicitor, "if he says it's okay?"

"I certainly will," asserted Fields. "I'll get another lawyer."

The bigger they are, the harder they fall—for life insurance policies. That, at least, is the unqualified announcement by the Provident Mutual of Philadelphia and, when the demon statisticians and actuaries of a company like that get finished with their computations, there's no more margin for error than in time or tide.

The lowest insurance is held by individuals who are exactly five feet high, avers B. F. Blair, president of Provident Mutual.

52

Their policies average $2,979. The five-foot-six-inch clan averages $3,976. Strapping six-footers average $5,070. And the folks who tower over us at six feet four hold average policies of $6,180. The Provident Mutual people emphasize that they're not pointing out any moral with all this, nor have they any idea of whys and wherefores; they're just giving the facts, ma'am.

By actual count there are now over one hundred and sixty thousand full-time life insurance agents in the United States, and by a curious coincidence it seems that most of them were classmates of mine in college. That's what they tell me over the phone, anyhow. The minute I hear, "Hi, Beans"—a nickname nobody has used since the day I graduated—I know what I'm in for.

Ralph Engelsman, one of the most successful insurance men in the country, once took on a recruit straight out of the Social Register. "If you see enough prospects," this rich but honest neophyte was told, "the law of averages will work for you. Enough commissions eventually will come along to make every sales talk worth fifteen dollars and twenty-two cents."

One of the neophyte's first prospects was his richest uncle. "Sorry," he was told, "but I have enough policies." "That's all right," said the fledgling agent. "I just made fifteen dollars and twenty-two cents!"

When the uncle heard the explanation, he said cheerfully, "Any time you need another fifteen dollars and twenty-two cents, come around and let me turn you down again."

One of the greatest feats of salesmanship in the annals of the insurance business was performed by an irresistible force in Vermont who overcame an immovable body named President Calvin Coolidge. Cal signed for a thousand-dollar policy.

Apparently the inducement that appealed to him most was the free medical check-up, for when he appeared at the doctor's, he had his aged father in tow.

"If it won't cost anything," he said, "I'd like you to look Pa over at the same time."

A big Madison Avenue ad agency is buzzing with the rebuff suffered by a lady operative who was ordered to telephone several hundred big shots and ask what brand of cigarettes they fancied most. She got along fine until she lured Dr. Alfred Kinsey, author of *Sexual Behavior in the Human Female*, to the phone in Indiana.

"We'd like to ask you," said she, "what cigarette you smoke."

Dr. Kinsey, the tireless investigator, snapped, "I never discuss my personal affairs for publication," and hung up.

Two ulcers stopped to exchange greetings on Madison Avenue. Sighed one, "I feel terrible. I must be getting an advertising man!"

Undoubtedly this ulcer had heard about the account executive who worried so much his hair turned charcoal gray.

Average mortals never realize how many things they crave until a cagey advertising expert points out the facts to them.

A thriving little industrial plant in Panama employed twenty local women. One day they just stopped coming, and such inducements as higher pay and shorter hours didn't budge them an inch. They had earned all they needed for months at least, they explained: why work any more? The boss, after much worry, finally hit upon a solution. He sent each of them a thousand-page Chicago mail-order catalogue. They were back at their places—every last one of them—the following Monday.

Peter Lind Hayes tells the tragic story of a lady who bought a large-economy flask of "Poof" and blew her arm off.

A very wise public-relations counsel cautions letter writers to delete the pronoun "I" as much as possible. "A weekend thank-you note which opens 'I had a wonderful time,'" he points out, "is not half so captivating as one beginning, 'You are a wonderful hostess.' Both say 'thank you,' but, ah, my friends, the second is the one that will get you asked back!"

The junior account executive of an ad agency married a glamor puss, bought a suburban villa twice too big for his income, and threw a monster housewarming party. His directions to friends were most explicit: "Get off the Merritt Parkway at Exit 42, turn left, and look for the first Frank Lloyd Wrightish creation. You can't miss it. It's the one with the big mortgage."

Two-hundred-and-fifteen-pound Bill Zeckendorf is a shrewd, daring, and tremendously successful realtor who not only has visited all the states in the union but owns large segments of them personally.

His propensity for acquiring desirable real estate has made him a marked man. He has only to drive slowly down a street in any town in the country for values on either side to go sky-rocketing immediately. A messenger saw him step into an elevator recently with Bishop Fulton Sheen. As the door of the elevator closed, the messenger murmured sadly, "There goes St. Patrick's Cathedral!"

Fellow bought a house near a riverbank, despite the fact that the cellar seemed rather damp. "Snug as a bug in a rug," the realtor assured him. "This cellar is dryer than the Sahara Desert."

A month later the buyer charged into the realtor's office, prepared to wring his neck. "You and your Sahara," he cried. "I put two mousetraps in that cellar and when I went down to look at them this morning they had caught a flounder and a haddock!"

Are you looking for a distinctive name for that new place of yours in the country? A proud Tennessean has dubbed *his* dream house "Chateau Nooga." A Charles Addams monstrosity on the Jersey shore is called "Gruesome Gables." And a Baltimore minister, hoping his congregation will get the hint, lives in "The Wrecktory."

Eric Hodgins, author of *Mr. Blandings Builds His Dream House,* is understandably mystified about the vagaries of American suburbanites' architectural enthusiasms. "Why," inquires Hodgins gently, "do they select sites in the hottest parts of Texas to build Cape Cod houses, which are designed to keep you warm? Or put ranch houses, designed to keep you cool, in the coldest parts of Maine? Or build split-level houses, designed for perching on hills, in Iowa, where they have to build the hills to put them on?" The writer of the best answers to these questions will receive an extra copy of next week's real-estate section of his Sunday paper free of charge.

The sales manager of a fast-growing outfit sticks pins in a big relief map behind his desk to show where every one of his salesmen is located at a given moment. Ragsdale, of the Iowa sector, was not, in the opinion of the manager, living up to his early promise, and was summoned to the home office for a pep talk and reindoctrination. "I'm not saying you're in imminent danger yet of being fired," was the stern end of the sales manager's warning, "but if you'll look carefully at my map, Ragsdale, you'll note I've loosened your pin."

A tax collector was examining the books of a defiant—but slightly worried—supermarket proprietor when the clerk, climbing aloft to fetch a can of preserved peaches, upset a whole pyramid of same. Cans came tumbling down on the tax collector's noggin, sending him sprawling to the ground.

"Be careful, Irving, you fool," cried the proprietor. "Supposing that had been a customer!"

McTavish had been in America only a few days when he made his first sortie into a supermarket. An attendant opened the door for him, another provided him with a big pushcart. Before him was an array of fruits, vegetables, breakfast foods, and canned delicacies of every description. The enraptured visitor piled his cart high and headed for the exit.

There, effectively blocking his path, stood the cashier. "The devil take it!" cried McTavish, abandoning his cart. "I knew there'd be a catch in it."

The salesman for the forty-four-volume encyclopedia climaxed his pitch with a hearty "Yes, ma'am! You just put a tiny deposit down, and don't pay another penny for six months!" The prospect looked surprised and demanded, "Who told you about us?"

The most unusual salesman he ever met, avers Herb Shriner, is a fellow who made a modest fortune purveying lightning rods. Suddenly he lost interest in his work, however. He got caught in a storm with a bunch of samples in his arms.

A smart jewelry salesman took one look at the beautiful blonde and the sugar daddy acting as her convoy, and trotted out his most expensive item—a diamond-ruby-and-sapphire-encrusted clip depicting the American flag.

The blonde fondled it with an adding-machine look in her eyes and cooed, "It's positively scrumptious—but doesn't it come in any other colors?"

After weighty consultation with innumerable salesmen, John Straley has discovered why, month by month, their figures aren't quite what their bosses expected them to be:

January: People spent all their cash for the holidays.

February: All the best customers have gone South.

March: Everybody's preoccupied with income taxes.

April: Unseasonable cold—and people spent too much on Easter clothes.

May: Too much rain: farmers distressed.

June: Not enough rain: farmers distressed.

July: Heat has people down.

August: Everybody away on vacation.

September: Everybody back—broke.

October: Unseasonable heat—and customers are waiting to see how fall clearance sales turn out.

November: Everybody too upset over elections.

December: Customers too busy with holiday shopping to see any salesmen.

AFTER-DINNER SPEAKER   PRE-DINNER GUZZLER   ALL-DAY WORKER   ALL-NIGHT DRIVER

One exasperated boss, fed up with the alibis of lackadaisical salesmen, tacked the following notice on his bulletin board:

"It has been brought to the attention of the management that many salesmen not only are dying while on duty, but refusing to fall over when the act is completed.

"*This practice must stop at once.*

"Hereafter, when a salesman has not moved in several hours, department heads are ordered to investigate. Because of the close resemblance of death and the ordinary gait of our sales personnel, the investigation will be made quietly, so as to prevent waking the salesman if he is sleeping.

"If some doubt persists, extending a check to cover entertainment expenses is a fine test. If the salesman does not reach for it, it may be assumed he is dead. In that case, fifteen copies of a formal report should be typed at once, three of which are to be dispatched to Washington, and two to the deceased. The others will be promptly lost in the office files."

How do salesmen strike back at this kind of needling? One of them took it upon himself to compile this list of requisites for full membership in the selling fraternity:

"Must be a man of vision, ambition, and iron endurance, an after-dinner speaker, before-dinner guzzler, work all day, flatter all evening, drive all night, and appear fresh as a daisy the next morning.

"Must be able to entertain customers, wives, sweethearts, and receptionists, be a man's man, a lady's man, a lover like Gable, a diplomat like Churchill, a good sport, a Plutocrat, a Democrat, a Republican, a New Dealer, a Fast Dealer, a mathematician, and a mechanic.

"Must belong to all clubs and fraternal orders, and pay all expenses on 5 per cent commission plus 2 per cent excise tax, 1½ per cent old-age pension, and 2 per cent lost-sales tax.

"Is it any wonder 'good' salesmen are hard to find?"

A big manufacturer of dog food summoned his entire sales force to Los Angeles for a convention. The sales manager generated vast enthusiasm with his glowing account of prize-winning ad campaigns, sensational promotion gimmicks and revolutionary packaging. Only the company president remained unimpressed.

"If all you men are doing such a wonderful job," he demanded, "why are our sales off fifteen per cent—and dropping steadily?"

"There's one thing we haven't been able to lick yet," admitted the sales manager, considerably subdued. "The dogs simply won't eat our product!"

CHAPTER SIX

THE CREAM OF THE GUESTS

Extra men—presentable ones, at least—are so scarce in most circles these days that they can make their own rules. They demand a list of other guests, the names of their dinner partners, details of the menu and form of entertainment—and, in general, are the selfish, spoiled gents that have kept them single in the first place.

One insisted on a small additional service that struck my wife Phyllis and me as so reasonable, we now accord it to every weekend guest we invite: his own newspaper, fresh and unsullied, on his Sunday-morning breakfast tray.

"When there's only one paper in the house," grumbled the pampered fellow who made us see the light, "the host's fourteen-year-old son invariably has chewed it to bits hours before I wake up. Funny that the same host who thinks nothing of serv-

ing you the best victuals and imported beverages will boggle at a few cents extra to buy his guests their own newspapers!"

Clare Jaynes, Chicago authoress and socialite, thinks it's important that the guest room be furnished with appropriate literature. Her own guests, for instance, are confronted with the following titles:

> THAT MAN IS HERE AGAIN
> NOT AS A STRANGER
> INTRUDER IN THE DUST
> LOOK HOMEWARD, ANGEL
> THE LOST WEEKEND
> DEATH IN THE AFTERNOON
> SO LITTLE TIME

and, after considerable urging on my part,

> BENNETT'S WELCOME

63

A nearsighted society girl in New York, too vain to wear glasses, was at a dinner party when the butler handed her a note from the hostess. She gave it to Lord Doodlesworth on her left, beseeching, "Won't you read this for me, Your Lordship? I have something in my eye." His Lordship read, "Be nice to old Doodlesworth. He's a terrible bore, but we're hoping to be asked to his estate in England next summer."

Sam Levenson has an Aunt Beckie who is convinced this is the worst of all possible worlds.

The last time he came home from a weekend at her house he decided to shoot the works and sent her a magnum of champagne and a pound of caviar. A few evenings later he phoned her. "How are you, Aunt Beckie?" he asked. "Dying, of course," she moaned. "You never acknowledged my gift," he accused her. "Didn't you like it?" "I'll tell you," said Aunt Beckie thoughtfully. "The ginger ale wasn't so bad. But that huckleberry jelly . . . ! You must have left it standing next to some fish in the icebox all night!"

Leo Kaufman of Houston, Texas, in a reminiscent mood, tells of some of the rules one Ezra Kendall posted in an old Pittsburgh hotel years ago:

"To prevent patrons taking fruit from the table, there will be no fruit.

"In case of fire, jump out of the window and turn to the left.

"Do not clean your shoes with a towel—unless it has been stolen from another hotel.

"Notify us if you see a mouse in your room and we will send up the cat.

"Guests without baggage will leave their wives with the room clerk."

A plump gentleman ate a fine meal at the Waldorf with obvious relish, topped it off with some rare Napoleon brandy, then summoned the headwaiter. "Do you recall," he asked pleasantly, "how just a year ago I ate just such a repast in your excellent hotel and then, just because I couldn't pay for it, you had me thrown into the gutter like a veritable bum?" "I'm very sorry," began the contrite headwaiter. "It's quite all right," conceded the plump gentleman, lighting a cheroot, "but I'm afraid I'll have to trouble you again."

Ed Buckley, manager of New York's Hotel Roosevelt, was approached recently by the wife of a prominent publisher who asked him to donate the grand ballroom for a charity dance. Buckley explained to her that this was the peak season for rental of such space, and that it would be impossible to give it to her free. "But this is such a worthy cause," she protested. "All these wonderful but penniless authors and their broods . . ." Buckley again expressed regrets, then, remembering that she was the mistress of a sumptuous estate in the suburbs, suggested that she hold the dance in her own house. "What!" was the lady's indignant rejoinder, "and have all those bums cluttering up my living room?"

A stalwart mountaineer entered the lobby of a swank Huntington hotel, after a certain amount of difficulty with the revolving door, and signed the register with a big "X." The room clerk noticed that the new guest had left muddy tracks clear across the marble floor. "When you patronize a hostelry of this caliber," he remarked coldly, "you might at least wipe half the mud of West Virginia off your shoes." The mountaineer regarded the room clerk with honest amazement and asked softly, "*What* shoes, bub?"

The glamorous blonde, ambling through the lobby of Houston's finest hotel, was inclined to be hoity-toity, until she encountered the town's number-one oil driller. Then she became charm itself and inquired coyly, "How much did you say your name was?"

A group of very pious—and very frugal—gentlemen recently attended a conclave in a Chicago hotel. When they decamped, a waiter sadly told his wife, "Dem gentlemen arrived wid ten dollars in one hand and ten commandments in de udder—and neither wuz broken when dey left!"

The vast old Grand Union Hotel in Saratoga is but a memory now, but native son Frank Sullivan recalls the days when society packed the premises, Victor Herbert conducted the orchestra, and Monty Woolley's dad was the manager. That was years ago, of course—before young Woolley's chin bore even a remote hint of the sassafras that was later to become his trademark in Hollywood.

Sullivan secured a room for Marc Connelly once at the height of the season, but, instead of being grateful, Connelly reported it was so far down the corridor that, "even on a clear day, I can't see the lobby." As for his bed, Connelly declared it more uncomfortable than a slab of concrete, with spikes protruding therefrom. "That's a historic bed, you unfeeling lout," protested Sullivan. "George Washington definitely slept in it." "Hmphh," mused Marc Connelly. "Now I know why he never complained when he got to Valley Forge."

Gal from a local editorial office—the athletic type—went up to a highly publicized ski lodge for a weekend of risking life and limb on the glistening slopes. The morning after her arrival she complained to the manager that twice during the night she had to get dressed and go to the lobby for a carafe of ice water. "My dear young lady," said the manager, "why didn't you simply press the buzzer beside your bed?" "The buzzer?" exclaimed the girl. "The bellboy told me that was the fire alarm!"

To celebrate their fiftieth wedding anniversary, a dignified lawyer took his wife to Europe. Neither had been abroad before, but a more worldly and sophisticated junior partner volunteered to make their Paris visit a breeze. "I know the manager of the

finest hotel on the Champs Élysées," he assured them. "I'll write him that you're coming." He did too. "This gentleman has done a lot for me," is what he dictated, "so I want to be sure that you give him the best of everything: corner suite, room service, tips on where to go, etc., etc., etc."

The manager himself greeted the lawyer in Paris, and though he seemed a bit surprised to meet the wife, shrugged his shoulders and conducted the couple to their suite. Everything was lovely—including three young ladies, very scantily clad, who sat demurely in a row in the sitting room. "Who are they?" gasped the lawyer, blushing violently. "Ah, monsieur," the manager assured him, "it is as your friend requested. Those are the three et ceteras."

A waitress in a beanery was serving a customer when a bald-headed gent entered and planted himself at a table in the rear.

67

"That's old Professor Snead," vouchsafed the waitress. "He's got a twin brother and they're alike as peas in a pod, only this one's stone deaf. Watch me have some fun with him." She minced over to him, smiled prettily, and said in a loud voice, "Well, you bald-headed old baboon, what kind of food are you going to pour into that fat stomach of yours today?" The bald-headed gent answered softly, "I'll have ham and eggs, toast, and coffee. And by the way, my brother is the deaf one."

An editor of many years' standing couldn't help scanning the menu of his eating club for typographical errors, and one day he was convinced he had found one. "Oh, Adolph," he observed, "I note that you are featuring homburger steak today. You mean hamburger steak, don't you?" "Not at all," maintained Adolph. "This morning our new English cook dropped his hat in the meat grinder."

James McNeill Whistler, the celebrated artist, rather prided himself on his knowledge of French. In a fashionable Paris restaurant one evening he insisted upon ordering the dinner and got very angry when a friend tried to help the waiter understand everything that was being said. "I am quite capable of speaking French without your assistance," he grumbled. "That may well be," soothed his friend, "but I just heard you distinctly place an order for a flight of steps."

The late Bob Benchley's son, Nat, tells of a time his father was showing some friends around Paris and insisted they dine at a restaurant where he had eaten some memorable pressed duck. But he couldn't remember where the restaurant was located. Over the friends' protests, he continued his quest for hours and finally stumbled on the place.

It was only when the orders of pressed duck were being placed before his guests that Benchley remembered what had made it so memorable. It was the worst pressed duck he had ever eaten.

A shrewd restaurateur in Milwaukee has plastered a huge sign on his window proclaiming, "T-bone, 25 Cents!" When you get close enough to read the small print, however, you note this reservation: "With Meat, Four Bucks!"

Munro Leaf, author of the immortal *Ferdinand the Bull*, was driving his car across the country, and made it a practice to stop for chow at railroad inns where big trucks were parked in front. "Those truck drivers," he told his wife, "know these roads in their sleep—and they've learned by experience where the best eats are to be found." Once, however, the lead proved false. Despite the presence of four monster trucks in the parking space, the food served inside was virtually inedible. A waitress noticed Leaf's discomfiture. "I know what's bothering you," she whispered. "The boss bought those old trucks at a salvage sale. He figures they bring in more customers than an electric sign. There aren't even any motors in them!"

On Fourteenth Street in New York there is an old German restaurant named Luchow's, which grows more popular, it seems, as time goes on. Broadway and Hollywood celebrities flock there in particular on Sunday nights. One promising starlet was making her first appearance in the Big Town and her publicity-conscious agent said, "The place in which you'll attract the most attention tonight is Luchow's." "That suits me fine," enthused the starlet. "I haven't been to an honest-to-goodness Chinese eatery in heaven knows when!"

E. M. Statler, who founded the chain of hotels that bore his name, understood the psychology of waiters perfectly. Rufus Jarman, in his engrossing book about the Statler Hotels, *A Bed for the Night*, asserts that, not only Mr. Statler, but every experienced waiter in his employ, knew the approximate size of the tip almost before a guest sat down at the table.

Indications: (1) Guests who study the menu at great length are usually not good tippers. (2) Men who wear inexpensive gaudy neckties or loud striped shirts are poor prospects. (3) The type of drink ordered is particularly revealing. "Beer for everybody" ranks lowest, closely followed by "rye and ginger ale." "Scotch and water" is most promising. (4) Also suspect are pipe smokers (oh, come now!).

Waiters figure that pipe smokers are likely to be the nonconformist type, and if there's one thing a waiter hates, it's a nonconformist.

A motorist stopped at a big roadside tavern for a bite of supper. His waitress had eight tables to take care of, but only one customer seemed to find fault with the service. He became so noisily abusive, in fact, that the motorist chivalrously volunteered, "If that lout is bothering you, I'll be happy to toss him out on his ear." "Lay off, mister," the waitress whispered. "That's my husband and we've worked this act down to a science. He makes the other customers feel so sorry for me that they all give me extra-large tips."

Up to the porte-cochere of an ultraswank summer hotel drove a gleaming Rolls-Royce, replete with liveried chauffeur and footman. In the back seat lolled a lady swathed in mink and diamonds, and next to her sat a very little girl, also dressed to the teeth. The doorman bowed low to the lady and lifted the little girl out of the seat. "Beautiful child," he observed. "Can she walk yet?" The lady cast her eyes skyward and said fervently, "Heaven willing, she'll never have to!"

Old Mr. Gotrox was even grumpier than usual as he stomped up and down the veranda of his summer hotel. The reason for his irritation finally was revealed when he admitted, "For two solid hours last night I had to listen to that blithering bore Allister telling me about his confounded rheumatism." "That's not like you, Gotrox," one old crony was emboldened to say. "Why didn't you trump his story with the account of your diabetes?" "Shucks," scoffed Gotrox. "I led with that."

Charles Lederer, in New York to clip coupons, sheepishly admitted the authenticity of one of the funniest anecdotes in Ben Hecht's *A Child of the Century*. Dining at the elegant Colony Restaurant in New York, with a glamorous musical-comedy queen he was wooing, Charlie, recalls Hecht, sat listening owlishly to a lecture from her on how he must mend his careless ways. Getting up at noon and climbing into any ill-assorted articles of clothing that happened to be at hand, she insisted, was not the proper way to live. As the beautiful lady concluded her discourse, Lederer, who had sat seemingly spellbound, arose—and handed her his trousers. He had removed them surreptitiously during her lecture. "Here," he proposed, "you wear these," and walked coldly out of the restaurant in his shorts.

Of Palm Springs, the California desert resort, Cleveland Amory reports, "Not everybody you see at the lavish hotels is a millionaire," but adds, "Of course, they were when they arrived there." He implies that to exist in this wonderful California desert country you must be as rich as the seventy-seven-year-old member of the Rockefeller clan, who married a lady many years his junior. "What did he give his 'child' bride as a wedding gift?" asked somebody. "Blocks," was the answer. "Yes, blocks. Forty-ninth and Fiftieth—on Fifth."

Harry Hershfield tells of the first day a night-club comedian spent in the invigorating air of an Adirondack resort. One of the comedian's lungs tapped the other and exulted, "Get a load of this air. It's the stuff I've been telling you about!"

The Shangri-La-by-the-Sea was run on the American plan, and Mr. Mandelbaum was determined to get his money's worth. He had to give up, however, after four helpings of beef. "I can still chew," he sighed to his wife, "but I can't swallow any more."

Mr. Gans rubbed the sand out of his eyes in time to observe his son dragging the top half of a bikini bathing suit along the beach. "Now, sonny," he wheedled, "I want you to show Daddy *exactly* where you found it."

If old Jake Keim, who promoted the first boardwalk in Atlantic City, could see the throngs of today, the hotels, and the annual "Miss America" jubilee, he probably would gasp, "What did I start down here anyhow?"

Mr. Keim wasn't aware that his boardwalk was revolutionary. His little rooming house, prospering in the aftermath of the Civil War, had been protected from the waves by a sand dune. When it was removed, the tide changed his hostelry into a swimming pool. Keim talked the city into building the boardwalk.

It was a mile long and collapsible—sometimes unintentionally. Each fall the planks were disconnected and put away for safekeeping. In every Atlantic City budget from 1870 to 1879 there was one item of seventeen dollars, expense for "rent of barn for storing boardwalk."

Those tides were responsible for another Atlantic City institution too. In 1883, a lad named Bradley opened a candy kitchen on Mr. Keim's boardwalk, and was selling a very superior brand of taffy there. Then a giant wave whooshed over the place, and Mr. B. found himself with a mess of water-soaked confectionery.

A less enterprising soul would have quit and gone home. Bradley, however, evolved a new principle on the spot. "Salt water is *good* for taffy," he proclaimed, with a note of desperation in his voice.

To his amazement, the public believed him. "Salt-water taffy" has been a staple of the community ever since.

For years a mecca for visitors to "the nation's playground" was Captain John Young's Million Dollar Pier. It featured a nine-room Elizabethan cottage intended for the owner's personal dwelling. Since it was at the very end of the pier, seventeen hundred feet from shore, it was ruled out of the jurisdiction of the state of New Jersey. So the captain gave it the address of "No. 1, Atlantic Ocean."

Captain Young fished by merely sticking a rod or net out the window. Soon he was advertising a daily net haul which visitors could witness at two bits a head. The catch included various fish, horseshoe crabs, empty beer bottles, and an occasional unwary swimmer.

They say one shark became so mesmerized by the "ohs" and "ahs" greeting his daily capture and release that he turned up in the net for seventeen consecutive performances.

CHAPTER SEVEN

THE DANCE OF LIFE

A young mother-to-be visited her gynecologist for a routine check-up, and was told that she would be blessed with twins. The doctor decided the husband should know immediately, too, so had the nurse drag him out of the front seat of his car below. "What's the big idea?" he protested. "I'm liable to get a ticket for being double-parked outside." "Well, son," said the doctor gently, "your wife's in the same situation inside."

"Doc" Sherman tells about the youthful couple who entered his Madison Avenue drugstore in search of a potent new baby tonic. "Here's one," promised Doc, "that will make your youngster husky, handsome, and happy." "That's just what we want," said the young lady, "but who takes it, my husband or I?"

Tax-conscious Bob Hope sees nothing surprising in the fact that babies start bawling the moment they are born. "In the first place," points out Hope, "they're hungry. And in the second place, by the time they're five minutes old, they owe the Department of Internal Revenue $1,900!"

A thoughtful pediatrician reminded a comparatively new father, "Never spank your child on an empty stomach. Be sure to eat something first." Then he noticed that the baby's hair had turned white. "This kid worrying about something?" he asked. "It's not the kid at all," the father answered him. "It's my nearsighted wife. She keeps powdering the wrong end."

Opening gambit of a sad, sad recital: "No sooner had we sold Junior's buggy than . . ."

When the wife of a high-powered copy writer in Westport gave birth to a baby daughter, he proudly announced by wire to his friends, "We have skirted the issue."
A year later, the mother made the mistake of leaving the baby in her husband's care while she closeted herself in the library to pay the month's bills. Pa buried himself behind his newspaper and forgot about the baby until he heard a series of thumps, followed by a horrendous wail. Clearly baby had fallen down the stairs.
"Martha," called the father excitedly. "Come quick! Our little girl just took her first forty-eight steps!"

If your kids are anything like mine, they dearly love receiving presents—but hate even more having to write thank-you letters therefor. My Jonny got around to thanking his Uncle Herbert for a Christmas gift along about March 25. What he wrote was, "I'm sorry I didn't thank you for my present, and it would serve me right if you forgot about my birthday next Thursday. . . ."

That note ranks with the intercepted correspondence of a boy and girl who sat next to each other in a third-grade class.

Wrote the boy: "Dear Judee: I luv you. Do you luv me? Jimmy." Answered the girl: "Dear Jimmy: I do *not* love you. Love, Judy."

A little girl, born and bred in Anderson, Indiana, had never seen the ocean and looked forward to her initial vacation in Florida. Arrived in the Southland, her daddy enfolded her in his arms and treated her to a first taste of the surf. She was squealing with joy when she rejoined her mother on the beach. "I just love the ocean, Mommy," she enthused, "except when it flushes."

A Boston six-year-old, obviously impeccably reared, came home from a party in fine spirits, to be asked by his mother, "Were you the youngest one there?"

"Not at all," he answered loftily. "There was another gentleman present who was wheeled in in a baby carriage."

"Gee, Pop," implored a youngster. "Why can't I go out in the green fields and play and run around like all other boys?" The father's terse reply was, "Shut up and deal!"

A reader in North Carolina reports that her three-year-old son was having trouble unfastening the back button of his underwear. He interrupted a hot canasta session to ask her, "Hey, Mom, how about opening my bathroom door?"

Taxicab driver in Washington had a unique experience one day last week. A lady signaled him to stop, then lifted four wee kiddies into the back seat. "Be with you in a mo," she promised, then disappeared into a house. She was back in about ten minutes, calmly hustled the kids out of the cab, and asked, "What do I owe you?" "I don't get it," confessed the mystified driver. "Just an inspiration," she explained. "I had to make an important long-distance call and it was imperative that I get the children safely out of the house."

Eight-year-old Claudia was packed off to Waterbury for a visit with her old-maid aunt. Her last minute instructions were, "Remember, Aunt Hester is a bit on the prissy side. If you have to go to the bathroom, be sure to say, 'I'd like to powder my nose.'" Claudia made such a hit with Aunt Hester that when the time came for her to leave she was told, "I certainly loved having you here, my dear. On your next visit you must bring your little sister Sue with you." "I better not," said Claudia hastily. "Sue still powders her nose in bed."

Little Mary Brown went walking with her dad in the park and came home to report that she had seen a great big lion gamboling on the greensward. Her mother promptly chastised her for lying and made her go upstairs to ask God to forgive her. Mary came down again after a while, and her mother asked, "Well, Mary, did you ask God's pardon for lying?" "I did," reported Mary, "and do you know what He said? He said, 'Don't even mention it, Miss Brown. I often mistake those great big yellow dogs for lions Myself.'"

In his autobiography, the late Vice-President Alben Barkley told of the lad who asked his father, "What's an ancestor?" "Well," said Pop, "for example, I'm an ancestor." "Yeah?" was the reply. "Then how come people brag about them?"

The famed Kentucky legislator also reminded us that "a child enters your home and makes such a racket for eighteen or twenty years that you scarcely can stand it, then departs, leaving the house so dismally silent you think you'll go mad."

The proprietor of a children's specialty shop in a New England shopping center was so busy dreaming up slogans like "Kwality Klothes for Kute Kiddies" that he neglected to pay his help a living wage. The long-suffering employees finally were goaded into picketing the establishment, but they showed a fine appreciation of the sensibilities of their clientele.

The picket signs read, "We'the out on thtwike."

Somebody asked editor Herb Mayes's younger daughter, "Does your old man have a den?" "He doesn't need one," was the answer. "He just growls all over the house."

Young Chris was diligently practicing away on the piano when there came a determined banging on the door. It was the cop from the corner, looking very formidable indeed. "Gotta investigate a call from the lady who lives next door, Chris," he said severely. "She swore two fellers named Chopin and Debussy was being murdered in here."

Observed Don McNeil to an appreciative audience at his TV Breakfast Club show: "It used to take an uncommonly strong man to tear a telephone book in half. Now that feat is easily—and frequently—accomplished by the average father of a teen-age daughter."

Ralph Moody, author of the award-winning book for boys and girls, *Little Britches*, receives a lot of fan mail from youthful admirers, but one letter he particularly cherishes came from a forthright lad in a Wyoming rural school.

"There is five of us in our class," it disclosed. "Our teacher just read us your book and I like it. You rite such bad English I can understand it. Love."

Reverend Otis Moore of New York reports on the predicament of eight-year-old Clara, who unfortunately was receiving a richly deserved spanking from her exasperated mother. In the middle of the proceedings, a little boy from across the way marched in and gave evidence of remaining till the bitter end. Clara stopped howling long enough to twist around and say very clearly, "Scram, John. Can't you see that Mother and I are busy right now?"

John was manly enough to admit later that he also was subjected to the humiliation of an occasional paddling in the woodshed. "Pop always proposes a toast before he whops me," added John. "He says, 'Bottoms up!'"

"When I was but a lad," recalls Duke Ellington, "I put books inside my pants for padding when a good spanking was evidently in the cards for me. Ever since, I've known the value of a literary background."

A chronic bachelor with a pronounced dislike for children became so smitten with a curvaceous blond widow that he up and married her, despite the fact that she was encumbered with an eight-year-old son.

A few weeks after the honeymoon, the kid was asked how he was getting along with his new daddy.

"Great," enthused the lad. "He's really fun. Thinks up new games for us to play all the time. Every day this week, for instance, he's been taking me out in Long Island Sound about two miles—and then I swim back."

"A two-mile swim every day sounds like pretty rough going for a kid your age," was the comment. "Doesn't it tire you out?"

"Nah," said the kid. "The swimming part is a cinch. I must admit, though, it isn't always easy getting out of that darn sack!"

"The trouble with our school system nowadays," explains educator William Brish, of Maryland, "is that the teachers are afraid of the principals, the principals are afraid of the boards of education and the boards are afraid of the parents. But the children of today—they're afraid of nobody!"

Of course children are not all quite so obstreperous as the little monster who crawled all over Tallulah Bankhead one afternoon. "Our little Philip is certainly a problem," admitted the mother. "We don't know what to make of him."

Miss Bankhead seized a moment when Mama's head was turned the other way to give Philip a hearty cuff on the ear and suggest, "How about a nice rug?"

Small fry, avers Basil Davenport, are having a hard time keeping their TV Wild West programs and adventures by rocket ship separate in their minds. One boy decked out in a space helmet hailed his dad with, "Put 'er thar, you ornery old horned toad, or I'll plug you with my six-shooter."

"You've got the wrong cue," corrected Dad. "You're talking Western, not space."

"I," said his son with considerable composure, "am from West Mars."

Mrs. Abernathy's eleven-year-old daughter, Nell, came home from camp with a gold medal for packing her trunk more neatly than any other girl. "How did you do it," marveled Mrs. Abernathy, "when at home we can never clean up the mess you leave behind?"

"It was cinchy," explained Nell complacently. "I just never unpacked it all summer!"

A new teacher suddenly appeared to take charge of a fourth-grade class in a fashionable Chicago suburb.

At the conclusion of her first session, the teacher was handed a note by a shy little girl who had been sitting in the front row. "I think you are going to be a wonderful teacher," it read, "and I have fallen in love with you already. P.S. The girl sitting next to me thinks you're a fat slob."

There's a little boy at a Beverly Hills school who poses quite a problem for the teacher every day. Because his father is a movie producer with an income estimated at something like eight thousand dollars a week, the son's sense of values is not the same as the other students'. One composition he turned in, for instance, has become a genuine collector's item in the school. It began, "This is the story about a very poor family. The father was very poor, the mother was very poor, the children were very poor, and the three butlers were the poorest of all."

Asked to recount the story of Noah in his Bible class another day, the lad began, "Well, it seems that God told Noah it was going to do some tall raining, so he'd better build himself a yacht. . . ."

Dr. Frank Littleton was on duty in a state medical bureau in the Blue Ridge Mountains district when a mother entered with a husky, tough-looking son of about three, and promptly proceeded to nurse him, to the consternation of the entire staff.

"My dear lady," sputtered Dr. Littleton, "that boy is too big to be nursed. You should have weaned him long ago."

"I know," admitted the mother sadly. "But every time I try, he throws rocks at me."

I never quite believe the stories I hear about boners pulled on eighth-grade examination papers, but even if this one isn't quite true, it bears repetition:

"One beautiful evening in the twelfth century, Queen Eleanor of Aquitaine entered Coventry, and after removing all her

clothes, rode through the streets astride a snow-white stallion.
On her way, she bumped into Sir Walter Raleigh, who was embarrassed by her appearance and threw his cloak around her,
crying, '*Honi soit qui mal y pense*,' which means, 'You need it
more than I do.' The Queen graciously responded, '*Dieu et mon
droit*.' ('By golly, you're right.')

"The entire incident is known as the Magna Charta."

And these three quotes allegedly come straight from exam
papers in a progressive school near New York:

1. My teacher told me the name of the ruler of Ethiopia is
Hail Silly Assy, but frankly I don't believe it. 2. Gothic architec-
ture is easy to spot by virtue of its use of flying buttocks. 3. The
safest kind of girl to take out is one who wears glasses. If you
breathe heavily on them, she no longer can see what you're doing.

Eileen Bernard, an editor of American Cyanamid's house
magazine, has come up with a definition of a grade-school

teacher that will do until a better one comes along. "A teacher," she says, "is Courage with Kleenex in her pocket, Sympathy struggling with a snow suit, and Patience with Papers to grade. A teacher really does not mind sniffles, squirmings, stomach-aches, spills, sloth, and sauciness. Neither does she disintegrate before tears, trifles, fights, futility, excuses, parents who spout, little boys who shout, and little girls who pout. Most of all, a teacher is one who likes somebody else's children—and still has strength left to go to the PTA meeting. Thank Heaven for the Teachers."

(Editor's postscript: How about seeing to it that she gets a living wage?)

The transition from prep-school adolescent to sophisticated college freshman, of course, gives the average boy or girl a new sense of responsibility, depth of character, and awareness of world problems.

Typical examples:

1. The Princeton freshman who, when asked, "Are you famil-iar with the works of Sigmund Freud?" answered brightly, "No, but I think I know his brother, French."

2. The precocious Vassar babe who boasted, "I had a date last weekend with a general." Her roommate, impressed, in-quired, "Major general?" "No," was the reluctant reply. "Not yet."

3. The wise lad at Northwestern who was asked for the feminine of "bachelor," and answered, "Lady in waiting."

4. The prodigy from Stanford who came home for his first Christmas vacation as a college man. His mother unpacked his trunk, and discovered a sports jacket with a hock-shop ticket at-tached thereto. The prodigy explained, "I checked it at a dance one warm evening, Ma, and I guess I forgot to remove the tag." A minute later his mother found a similar ticket on a pair of pants. "Oswald," she demanded sharply, "just what kind of a dance was this, anyhow?"

84

A successful banker, back on his college campus for a class reunion, visited his old economics prof, and picked up the current semester's final exam. "Holy smoke," he exclaimed, "these are precisely the questions you asked our class fifteen years ago. If you always ask the same questions, don't you know the students will get wise, and pass them on from class to class?"

"Sure," answered the prof blandly, "but in economics, you see, we're constantly changing the answers."

At Kansas State College, Professor H. W. Davis mourned, "The worst thing about being a professor is that after a while you begin to look like one." Another Davis on the faculty, first name Earl, cited as his idea of perfect graphic description, Carl Sandburg's line, "Lincoln crossed his right leg over his left knee, and planted both feet solidly on the ground."

A married lady on the Kansas State teaching roster had a rather unnerving experience just before I visited there. Not being able to locate a sitter, she brought her baby with her to an afternoon tea, and carried under her arm a toidy seat in pink plastic. Her hostess reached for the seat and boomed, "Welcome! Let me hang up your darling new hat!"

Residents of Chapel Hill are partial to a tale of D. C. Jacobsen's about an extremely frugal member of the University of North Carolina faculty. This worthy gent, it appears, had just drawn thirty-five dollars from his bank, bent upon acquiring some reference tomes at Paul Smith's Intimate Bookshop. No sooner had he turned away from the paying teller's window, however, than his path was blocked by the formidable figure of native son Kay Kyser, the popular band leader, who retired while he was about three millions ahead.

"I'm bound for lunch," announced Kay. "How's for coming with me?"

"Love to," agreed the professor. Then, glancing down at the

seven crisp five-dollar bills in his hand, he added hastily, "I'll join you as soon as I've made this deposit."

Latest story from one of those jerk-water colleges with outrageously overpublicized basketball teams is that the coach asked his assistant, "What's biting our all-star center? He's been moping and sulking for two whole days." "It's his father," explained the assistant, "who keeps writing him for money all the time."

"Wimpfheimer," said the philosophy pro sternly, "I'm sure you can tell us who wrote *Critique of Pure Reason*." Wimpfheimer, who had had a hard night carousing at the Williamstown Book Shop, admitted sadly, "Professor, I. Kant." "Amazing," said the professor. "This is the first correct answer you've given me in your five years as a freshman!"

Blasé undergrads today may not take college rivalries as seriously as their granddads were wont to do, but the very sound of "Yale vs. Harvard" still brings the light of battle into the eyes of any true son of Eli or Cambridge.

There was the day, for instance, when an ex-football gladiator from Yale, 214 pounds of All-American, got himself married to a rich and beautiful girl, the catch of the season. Society turned out en masse for the nuptials.

When the bride and groom knelt before the bishop, the congregation gasped.

Painted by a Harvard rascal on the sole of the groom's No. 16 left shoe, in brilliant crimson, was "To Hell," and on the right, "with Yale!"

Some new definitions whipped up for California freshmen by the ever-helpful Jim Marshall:

Alaska: A prelude to "No"
Aspersion: A burro in Teheran
Automaton: A person who eats in the Automat

Amazon: First part of a sentence (Example: Amazon of a gun!)
Buccaneer: Current price of corn
Flattery: An apartment house
Gubernatorial: A peanut in swimming
Incongruous: Where the laws are made
Lemon Juice: An introduction: Lemon juice you to Miss Lyon
Pasteurize: Something you see moving
Pseudo: Counterfeit money
Syntax: What the author of stuff like this has to pay the government.
Weasel: It blows at noon

Not long ago, a college on the Atlantic seaboard found itself in urgent need of two million dollars for a special project. Fortunately, a fabulously wealthy young heiress was lined up to supply the necessary funds. But alas, the college comic magazine chose that moment to publish what the editors believed was a hilarious parody of her social career. The heiress tore up her check, and the editors were kicked out of college.

This incident underlines the fact that there is no more hazardous job than editing an undergraduate humorous publication. Ever since the distant era when I narrowly averted disaster editing the Columbia *Jester*, entire boards have been given the heave-ho at regular intervals for getting too fresh with the faculty, treading on the sensitive toes of trustees, or, most often, printing jokes that might best have been saved for fraternity smokers.

In the latter instance, the offending issues promptly sell at a premium, and old grads who haven't been heard from in years pop up suddenly to renew subscriptions.

Undergraduate humor has a comforting sameness about it through the years. Barring one dismal stretch when ultra-sophistication was the order of the day, and every collegian was trying to imitate the style of *The New Yorker*, the editors have adhered to a dependable, earthy formula wherein boys will be boisterous and girls live up to the most eye-opening of Dr. Kinsey's belated discoveries.

If the following selections from this season's college comics sound vaguely familiar, it is only because the same stories, or reasonable facsimiles thereof, were appearing when the editors sported handle-bar mustaches and you still could snag a free lunch with a ten-cent schooner of beer:

"I can't stand necking," she protested softly, "so what do you say we sit down?"

She talked in her sleep so he sent her home to mutter.

"I'm knee-deep in love with that dame. You see, she has a wading list."

Statistics prove that blondes make the best students.

"You're looking great. What happened to that pain in the neck?" "Oh, she's at the bridge club."

"Doctor, what's your favorite sport?" "Sleighing." "I mean apart from business."

"That's a pretty dress you have on." "Yes. I only wear it to teas." "Whom?"

"Did you go to the Junior Prom this year, dear daughter?" "No, Mom. I ripped my shoulder strap playing tennis."

Coed to druggist: "You heard me. I want a green lipstick. I'm entertaining a railroad man this evening."

"I wouldn't say for sure that my girl was hungry tonight, but it was the first time I ever saw sparks fly from a knife and fork."

"Have you heard about my friend Kerch?" "Kerch who?" "Gesundheit!"

Freshman to English prof at end of term: "Thanks. You was a very good teacher."

"Doctor, did you say eating radishes would make my skin break out?" "No. I never make rash promises."

Randy: "I'll stick to you like glue, my love." Elly: "The feeling's mucilage."

Stuff like that!

A balding and paunchy gent, back from a vaguely disappointing thirty-fifth reunion of his old college class, decided he needed a complete check-up, and went to his doctor. "I just haven't got my old pep any more," he confessed sadly. The doctor examined him fore and aft and assured him, "There's nothing wrong with you that carrots, and plenty of them, can't cure. Take as many as you like." A month later, the doctor noted a distinct improvement. "Just go on eating carrots," he prescribed. The patient jumped from his chair, crying, "Carrots! Good Lord, Doc, I thought you said claret. I've been drinking a bottle a day!"

"I set out in life," reminisced the old grad sadly, "to find that pot of gold at the end of the rainbow. Now I'm fifty-eight, and all I've found is the pot!"

An old moneybags latched onto a provocative blonde of twenty at Palm Beach—or could it be that she latched onto him?—married her, and brought her home to his Fifth Avenue mansion, where the butler eyed her with all the warmth and fervor of a dead codfish. "Isn't she a humdinger?" whispered the old goat triumphantly. "Could be, sir," ventured the butler, "but I do hate to see a man begin a full day's work so very late in the afternoon."

A cranky old party invested in one of those new hearing gadgets that are so small they are practically invisible, and was assured he could return it for full credit if it didn't prove twice as effective as the cumbersome device he had been wearing for years. He came back two days later to express his delight with the new aid. "I'll bet your family likes it too," hazarded the clerk. "Oh, they don't know I've got it," cackled the old party. "Am I having a ball! Just in the past two days, I've changed my will twice!"

Classified ad in a New England newspaper: "For sale: handsome second-hand tombstone. Outstanding bargain for a family named Perkins."

Tucked away in serene, windswept graveyards all over the country are old tombstones in varying states of preservation that bear epitaphs far out of the usual and expected patterns. Interest in them is such that there are over fifty full-sized volumes on the subject catalogued by the New York Public Library. One of the newest and liveliest of the compilations is *Stories on Stone*, by Charles L. Wallis (Oxford University Press).

Politics, points out Mr. Wallis, is such a serious business to some citizens that they seek to re-echo their convictions even from beyond the grave. There was a dedicated Republican named Grigsby, for instance, in Attica, Kansas, who insisted that this epitaph be inscribed on his stone: "I hereby enter my dying protest against what is called the Democratic Party. I have watched it closely since the days of Jackson and know that all the misfortunes of our nation have come to it through the so-called party. Therefore, beware of this party of treason." Mr. Grigsby, incidentally, expired in 1890.

The gravestone of B. H. Norris, of Montgomery City, Missouri, on the other hand, exhorts, "Kind friends I've left behind, Cast your votes for Jennings Bryan."

A monument to the family of Robert Hallenbeck in Elgin, Minnesota, records, "None of us ever voted for Roosevelt or Truman!"

The grim humor of the pioneers found expression in such still-existent gravestones as "Here lies John Coil, a son of toil, who died on Arizona soil. He was a man of considerable vim, but this here air was too hot for him"; "Here lies George Johnson: Hanged by Mistake"; and (in Rapid City, South Dakota):

Here be the bodies of Allen, Curry, and Hall
Like other horse thieves they had their fall.
So be a little cautious how you gobble horses up,
For every horse you pick up adds sorrow to your cup.
We're bound to stop this business, and hang you to a man,
For we've hemp and hands enough in town to swing the whole
  damn clan.

There's a tomb in New Orleans' Metairie Cemetery that bears not a Bible verse, but the unusual inscription, "See Louisiana Reports, 1905. Page 39." It seems the lady who had ordered the tomb was lost at sea, but the Louisiana Supreme Court ordered the executors of her will to build the tomb anyway.

The thrifty executors, protesting to the end, had the last word. They obeyed the court order but they also had the tomb marked to show precisely why it was erected.

The ladies' dress business had been in the doldrums so long that Mr. Lapidus reversed his field and became an undertaker.

"Things are humming," he told a customer, and to prove his point, showed him four open caskets, all filled. Suddenly two of the corpses sat up, and the customer recoiled in horror. "Take it easy," soothed Lapidus. "Those are just my partners trying to make the place look busy."

Epitaph suggested by an Oklahoma student:

> *Weep a bit*
> *for E. Z. Lott:*
> *He was lit;*
> *His lights were not.*

Wes Laurence has a new "Little Willie" poem to add to your collection:

> *Playing his wooden oboe, Will*
> *Swallowed the horn at the top of a trill.*
> *Said Mother, watching Willie go:*
> *"What mighty aches from oak horns grow."*

I am indebted to the *Detroit Athletic Club News* for the story of a widow lady near the Vermont border who hadn't been known to smile or show a vestige of sentiment for twenty years. When she suddenly informed her regular summer boarders from

Detroit that she'd like to visit her husband's grave, they accordingly were overcome. Nevertheless, they drove her to the cemetery.

She dutifully began looking for the proper headstone, pausing occasionally to make a disparaging remark about the deceased, but finally she threw her flowers onto the ground.

"The heck with him," she decided. "I never knew where the so-and-so was while he was alive, and it ain't a bit different now!"

CHAPTER EIGHT

"THE FARMERS AND THE COWBOYS . . ."

The Farmers . . .

A farmer, paying his first visit to the state insane asylum, discovered one inmate propped up against a tree, blissfully watching the grass grow. The inmate idly inquired, "What's your racket, bub?" "I'm a farmer," was the answer. "Do tell," said the inmate. "I once did some farming too. Darn tough work. Ever try being crazy?" "I certainly did not," said the farmer heatedly. "Well, you ought to," concluded the inmate, relaxing even more completely. "It's got farming skinned seven ways."

Janet Peters tells about the time she persuaded the old carpenter from a Maine summer resort to pay his first visit to New York. He observed the traffic and general hubbub of the big town without comment, but when he reached Fifth Avenue and Thirty-fourth Street, he walked purposefully to the edge of the curb. Raising his thumb at arm's length, shoulder level, he squinted intently up at the great Empire State Building and commented, "Got it pretty plumb, didn't they?"

When the city slicker's foreign racing car got stuck in the mud and ran out of gas in the bargain, Ebenezer hitched his mule to it and after two hours' heaving and shoving under the broiling August sun, extricated the car and hauled it four miles to the nearest garage. When Eb returned, his wife said, "I hope you charged him good for all that work." "Two dollars," said Eb complacently. "Two dollars!" screamed his wife. "I swear, Pa, sometimes I wish you'd do the pullin' and let that mule handle the executive end of your business!"

Having spent his own youth on a farm, a big-city banker was determined that his spoiled young son should get at least a whiff of the same sound training, so he persuaded his old neighbor, Seth Parsons, to take the lad on as extra hand for July and August. About July 15 he called up Seth to ask, "How's the boy making out?" "I ain't the one to bandy words with you," declared the forthright farmer. "If that boy of yours had one more hand, he'd need a third pocket to put it in."

Vrest Orton tells of two ancient Vermonters who were reminiscing around "Pop" Johnson's old cracker barrel. "I never been licked but once in my life," boasted one, "and that's when as a boy of ten I made the mistake of tellin' the truth." His compan-

95

ion whittled quietly for a moment, then remarked, "Well, Sam, it suttinly cured ye."

A farm hand in Kansas ambled up to the owner of the place and drawled, "Thought ye might like ter know the bull's got loose and been chasin' yer wife around the pasture fer the past half hour or so." The owner jumped to his feet in panic and shouted, "You blasted fool! Why have you waited so long to tell me?" "What's the matter, boss?" asked the farm hand in some surprise. "Your wife short-winded?"

My old Uncle Herbert from Vermont was visiting New York recently, and was frankly appalled by the heavy traffic choking every thoroughfare. "You gotta nice town here," opined Uncle Herb, "but it looks to me like you fellers let yourselves get quite a bit behind in your haulin'!"

Main route Number 66 went through the very heart of Goose-creek Hollow, and the natives fumed when tourists tore through at about ninety miles an hour. Sheriff Deveen was finally prevailed upon to put up a couple of warning signs.

A week later he demanded of the chief agitator, "Well, Howie, them signs you hollered for had any effect yet?" "Sure did," replied old Howie glumly. "All the cars what used to go through at twenty miles an hour has slowed down to ten!"

Two typical Bucks County farmers met at a tavern around haying time, and the first one asked the proverbial question, "How's crops?" "Waal," allowed the second, "the gas station and the cheeseburger concession is just about holdin' their own, but durned if they ain't holdin' over *Springtime for Henry* for a second week in my barn."

Everybody in Herb Shriner's home town, he admits, always knows what everybody else is doing, but they read the local paper anyhow, to see if anybody's been caught at it. There are three sources of news: INS, the UP, and the A. & P.

February is about the coldest month. "Sometimes," recalls Herb, "the temperature goes to twenty below—and that's where you feel it most. In April, sprucing up begins. We're sort of in-between folks, though: too poor to paint and too proud to whitewash."

Comes summer and there's some trouble over insects getting into the corn. "But shucks," concludes Herb, "we just fishes 'em out and drinks it anyhow."

Walter Lonnergan tells about a backwoods stalwart who made his first trip to the big city, and was conducted to the vestibule of a new skyscraper. One door seemed to fascinate him. An old, weather-beaten lady stepped in, a red light flashed, and off she went. Seconds later the elevator descended, the door opened, and out stepped a magnificently beautiful girl.

"Gee whillickers," marveled the backwoodsman. "I should have brought my wife with me!"

Harry Hansen, distinguished critic, and editor of the *World Almanac*, recently undertook to show the sights of New York to a Nebraska farm girl who had never in her life been east of the

97

wide Missouri River before. A trip to the top of the Empire State Building would prove an eye opener, figured Harry, so up they went. "Observe!" ordered the distinguished cicerone. "Down there is J. P. Morgan's house and the Chrysler Building. Northward looms Radio City and, beyond it, Central Park. There are Macy's emporium and the Great White Way. And yonder the *Queen Elizabeth* is picking her way down the Hudson, headed for the open sea!"

The Nebraska lass observed all, then contributed her first remark to the festivities. "I guess," is what she said, "all towns look pretty much alike, don't they?"

"Yes, I'm the man who advertised for a top-notch lion tamer," nodded the owner of a small-time carnival. "Are you applying for the job?"

The husky farm hand before him nodded briefly, patted the gun in his holster, picked up a chair and a whip, and said, "Let me at him!"

"Not so fast," warned the owner. "There was one application in ahead of yours. We'll have to give her first whack."

"Her?" echoed the farm hand incredulously.

"Yes, it's a girl," admitted the owner. "I was surprised too. Here she comes."

With that a beautiful blonde hove upon the scene. She had a full-length fur coat wrapped around her, but not one bit of the usual lion-taming equipment—no gun, no whip, no chair.

"You're not going into the cage like that!" gasped the owner. "My lion is the meanest, most savage beast ever brought back alive."

"I don't scare easy," yawned the girl. "I've handled bulls; I can handle a lion." With that she unlocked the door and strode unconcernedly to the center of the lion's cage. There she flung open her fur coat. Underneath it, she was wearing nothing at all!

The lion's eyes bulged, it gave a deep M-G-M roar—and leaped at her. But there was no bloodshed. The lion swabbed his great red tongue across her cheek, gently kissed her hands and

98

feet, licked her face again—and climbed back on his stool in the corner!

The carnival owner shook his head unbelievingly, and demanded of the farm hand, "Do you think you can do better than *that?*"

"Hell, yes," boasted the farm hand. "You get that damn lion out of there and I'll show you!"

The Hillbillies . . .

Jeb Russell contributes this bit of Ozarkana:

Couple of Eastern tourists were driving along a back road in Arkansas, when their right of way was disputed by a rootin', tootin' band of mountaineers, some on horseback, others on muleback, their whiskers streaming in the wind as they urged on their mounts with bloodcurdling war whoops. The tourists noticed a native woman eying the pack without too much interest, and inquired, "Sheriff's posse, ma'am?" "Nope," she answered. "Possum hunting?" "Nup, not that neither." "Well, then, what on earth are those fellows chasing?" "It's like this, strangers," explained the woman. "Buzz Wetherby's son Lance is twenty-one years old today, and the boys is tryin' to run him down to put pants on him."

Census takers in remote sections of the Arkansas hills have special problems to cope with. One, for instance, encountered a rugged girl—not more than twenty—with four children. "May I have their ages?" he inquired. The girl knitted her brows. "Let's see if I can recall," she mused. "One's a lap child, one's a floor creeper, one's a porch child, and the oldest is a yard young one."

Jack Lait, Jr., has discovered that hillbilly records have one virtue their severest critics cannot deny. When they're worn out, you can't tell the difference.

Latest hillbilly story concerns the poor fellow who had to spend a night in Little Rock and saw an electric light for the first time in his life. Returned to his mountain shack, he sank into his favorite chair and told his wife, "Don't know how them city folk catch any sleep. There was a big light burning in my room right through the night." "Why didn't you blow it out?" asked the wife. "Gol dang it—I couldn't," grumbled the hillbilly. "It was in a bottle!"

A moonshiner in West Virginny felt called upon to emphasize the potency of his brew. "All I kin tell you fellers," he said, "was that yesterday I spilled a coupla drops in front of a cow that had a bell round its neck. While I was in the house eatin' lunch, a coupla mosquiters buzzed up and sampled my likker. Whin I come out, them damn mosquiters had et up the cow and was ringin' the bell for the calf!"

In Crane, Missouri, Margaret Lucas tells about a city fellow who was rash enough to buy a mule, but soon realized he didn't have the faintest notion of how to make it obey his commands. So he hired a professional mule trainer.

That worthy approached the mule with a murderous gleam in his eye and a heavy wooden board in his hand. He took a round-house swing and socked the mule's back just as hard as he could. The mule didn't even blink. The trainer whacked him again.

"Gosh a'mighty," protested the owner, "are you fixing to murder my mule?"

"It's easy to see you know nothing about these critters," said the trainer grimly. "First thing you gotta do is win their attention."

Clem Hatfield's general store in the Blue Ridge country was located halfway down a steep hill. One day the regular assemblage of old gaffers on the porch saw a cloud of dust coming down the hill, and identified it as old Zim, a moonshiner from the backwoods. "Yep," nodded the postmaster. "Bet he's after that letter I told him was waitin' fer him three or four weeks back."

To the amazement of the audience, old Zim suddenly stopped shuffling and broke into a trot. By the time he passed the store he was positively galloping down the hill. The postmaster shifted his chewing terbacky and commented disgustedly, "Lookut the old fool! Too durn lazy to hold back!"

A hillbilly bride went off gaily to the other side of the mountain with her masterful new bridegroom, but when she discovered how much he liked his moonshine she trudged all the way home again to her pappy. That worthy was sitting in front of his cabin, scratching himself and lapping up the contents of a hefty whisky jug.

"Don't stand thar blabbering, gal," he told his daughter sternly. "Drinkin' ain't the wust thing thar be. How much does your man consume a day?" The daughter thought a moment, then guessed, "I bet it comes to a full quart a day, Pappy." "Lan's sake," chuckled Pappy. "You ain't got a thing to worry about. I *spill* more than that every day!"

Oil and gas men in the South are using a new type of aluminum pipe with a simplified coupler that has reduced costs and speeded up operations amazingly. Demonstrating the pipe at key meetings is Keen Johnson, former governor of the state of Kentucky.

At one meeting, Johnson recalled to Jim Clark a day when he was still governor. A mountaineer had been convicted of a feud killing—on circumstantial evidence—and sentenced to die. Petitions and pleas from interested parties had failed to impress the governor, but a note, scrawled in pencil on a piece of old scratch paper, from the prisoner himself, won him a commutation to life imprisonment.

"Dear Guvnor," it read. "I is skeduled to be execooted on friday and heer it is wensday. Yores trooly, Joe D."

... and the Cowboys

Lucius Beebe, official historian of Nevada's fabulous Virginia City, and all surrounding territory, tells of two cowpokes who recently revived the code of the Old West and opened fire on the broad highway in the best Jesse James tradition. The cowpokes were not very good shots, and bystanders sought shelter hastily beneath such incongruous shelters as hot-dog stands, 1956 two-toned sedans, and a delivery wagon full of laundry. Several bullets lodged in the laundry bundles, and one local wit declared that, for the first time in laundering history, the proprietor had a legitimate excuse for the condition in which he returned his customers' shirts.

Life in Nevada, says Beebe, is like this: One ancient met another who was toting under his arm two loaves of bread and six bottles of whisky. "Land's sake, Lem," he marveled, "what in heck you gonna do with all that bread?"

In a frontier town in West Texas, a cowboy rushed out of a saloon, essayed a running broad jump, and landed kerplunk on his sit-spot in the middle of a puddle in the roadway.

"Hurt yourself?" asked a bystander languidly.

"Reckon I'll live," allowed the cowboy, dusting himself off, "but I'd sure like to get my hands on the varmint who moved my horse!"

Trouble clearly was indicated in a Wild West saloon when a rootin', tootin' cowboy got into a hassle with a foreman from a rival outfit. Suddenly guns were blazing and everybody ducked for cover—everybody, that is, but one mild-mannered galoot who calmly maintained his position at the bar, sipping his drink. When the commotion died down, the proprietor of the saloon said, "I certainly admire your nerve, young feller. You're the coolest proposition we seen around these parts in a month of Sundays." " 'Twarn't nothing," deprecated the mild-mannered one. "I knowed I was safe. I owe everybody in the place money!"

Ray Harris of Albuquerque, commenting on the wild rush to discover uranium in New Mexico and thereabouts, says one city chap he knew, never before away from asphalt pavements in his life, mooched out into the desert with a newly purchased Geiger counter. "Did he find any uranium?" Harris was asked. "Not one ounce," reported Harris, "but he found four other prospectors named Geiger."

The Desperate Daltons

It's over sixty years since the infamous Dalton gang met its Waterloo in the town plaza of Coffeyville, Kansas, but to hear the proud citizens of that bustling community tell it, the bloodshed and excitement might have happened yesterday.

Coffeyville, seventy-five miles due north of Tulsa, and about one hundred miles from Wichita, also boasts of late-resident Walter Johnson, immortal pitching ace of the Washington Senators, and of America's greatest wit, Will Rogers, born in the nearby village of Oologah in 1879. It furthermore points with pride to the high school where a raw-boned fledgling named Wendell Willkie taught briefly in 1913.

But on the day when I visited Coffeyville, conversation inevitably veered back to the liquidation of the Dalton outfit.

In light of actual records, the fearsome reputation of the Daltons is difficult to understand. Their career of crime covered less than two years, and consisted principally of a series of clumsy, singularly unimaginative train robberies, featured by wanton killings and piddling booty. Bob Dalton was the leader, with his brothers Emmett and Grat for chief accomplices. A variable retinue of desperadoes completed the roster.

The Indian territory where they operated was thinly settled by farmers and cattlemen, and casually policed, else they would have been halted much sooner.

The Daltons were related on their mother's side to the four most dreaded—and publicized—outlaws of the day, Jesse James and Cole, Bob, and Jim Younger. Lurid paperbacks and the yellow press had built these criminals up to be glamorous and romantic fellows (how different is it these days?), and it is reasonable to suppose that Bob Dalton was seeking only to carry on the noble family tradition.

The raid on Coffeyville must have struck him as the epitome of daredeviltry, for this was his home town, where everybody knew him. His own father lay buried here, and so did his brother Frank, shot down, ironically enough, fighting bandits as a U.S. deputy marshal.

On the morning of October 5, 1892, Bob, Emmett, and Grat Dalton, plus two accomplices, galloped into Coffeyville and held up two banks on opposite sides of the plaza: the First National and Condon & Co. The Daltons' flimsy disguises—prop mustaches and goatees—fooled nobody, eyewitness Henry Isham least of all.

Isham dashed into his hardware store and passed out shotguns and revolvers in jig time to everybody in sight.

There followed a furious, five-minute exchange of shots, in which four bandits were killed outright (along with four inno-

cent townsfolk), and Emmett Dalton was seriously wounded.
And the loot? Though the bandits had seized over twenty thousand dollars in cash from the two banks, they dropped it when
the shooting started.

Despite the confusion, when Condon & Co. balanced their
books that night, there was a shortage of only twenty dollars!
More remarkable still, the First National had an unaccountable
surplus of $1.98!

Survivor Emmett Dalton probably would have been strung up
on the spot, had it not been for the quick wit of Dr. W. H. Wells,
who bandaged his wounds. "Do you think the varmint will die?"
the doctor was asked.

"Hell yes," he replied. "Did you ever hear yet of a patient of
mine recovering?"

As a matter of fact, Emmett lived a full forty-five years longer,
fourteen years in jail and the rest in California, where he made
more money talking and writing about his brief career of crime
than the Dalton gang netted on all its raids put together!

To a publisher and author, at least, the moral is clear.

CHAPTER NINE

THE GOOD OLD DAYS

Two Roman gladiators startled Nero and his court with their valiant exploits. Forty to fifty competitors at a time perished under their swords. Crowds cheered their every move. In no time flat, you might say, they were the Joe DiMaggio and the Willie Mays of gladiators.

Finally officials decided to give the two boys a real test. They were scheduled to take on eighty soldiers on horseback. They had massacred the lot of them in fifteen minutes and were calmly sipping Cokes when Nero himself burst into their dressing room. "Next Sunday," he gloated, "we're putting you up against a hundred hungry lions! They've been eating up all the prophets anyhow. And just so you can't plan any strategy in advance, we won't let you even see each other again until you march into the arena."

The big day dawned bright and clear. The arena was sold out. Speculators were getting fifty gold pieces a ticket. And as the two gladiators were reunited, one began, "You should have been with me Wednesday night! I'm sitting in my studio when who should come barging in but the Empress. She was alone—and had on a slinky dress and wore some intoxicating perfume." "Holy smoke!" exclaimed the other. "Go on, go on!" "I'll have to finish the story later," yawned the narrator. "Here come those silly lions!"

A couple of noble Romans decided the time had come to burn down the city, but one said, "Maybe we're too late. I hear Nero himself harbors a similar notion." "Let's hurry and beat him to it," urged the other. "I'm all for eliminating the fiddle man."

Champion optimist of the world, nominated by David Green, is the general in Caesar's army who, when forced to flee before vandal hordes, sent this report to headquarters: "According to preconceived plan, we have proceeded to a point of vantage which lay eighty miles behind us."

A lad at Harvard claims to have discovered a bit of unrecorded dialogue between Julius Caesar and his false friend, Brutus. The latter asked Caesar, "How many bagels with lox did you consume this morning, Julius, old boy?" The answer, as you may have suspected, was, "Et tu, Brutus."

Diogenes, the story goes, decided to return to earth a short time back to resume his search for a really honest man. Holding his lantern aloft, he journeyed from California to New York, and

on to England and France, but his efforts went for nought. And the worst was yet to come. He finally crossed the border of Hungary and tarried in Budapest. There he not only failed to find an honest man—but somebody stole his lantern!

One of the perils of reading a lot of books when you're an adult is that some of your most cherished childhood illusions are likely to be shattered. Gory tales of pirates and buccaneers, for instance, who buried millions of pieces of eight, made off with beautiful princesses, and forced other captives to walk the plank ——they're all malarkey, insists Patrick Pringle in a volume called *Jolly Roger* (Norton).

He's done an infinite amount of research in piratical lore, says Pringle, and has never come upon a single instance where anybody "walked the plank." Pirates were too anxious to collect ransoms or put their prisoners to work to polish them off for mere bravado.

And Captain Kidd, most celebrated pirate of them all? Strictly a phony, sneers Pringle: a small-time operator who ended on the gallows, penniless.

In fact, most pirates, after dividing spoils with their crews and paying hush money to rascally officials, didn't have enough loot left to fill a single chest. What a blow to anybody who grew up thinking *Treasure Island* was the real McCoy!

Prepare yourself for another shock. Could it be that all the stories we learned in school about the intrepid patriots who masterminded the Boston Tea Party are mostly bunk? That's what John Hyde Preston stoutly maintains in his *A Short History of the American Revolution* (recently reissued by Pocket Books).

As Preston tells it, the East India Company, faced with an enormous loss on millions of pounds of tea, won the Crown's permission to send, duty-free, three shiploads, valued at seventy-five thousand dollars, to Boston, where they proposed to sell the cargo at a far lower price than tea had ever been offered to the colonists before.

Why was the price of tea so high in Boston? A group of leading citizens, says Preston, had built up a whopping business in tea smuggled from Holland. Now, suddenly, their monopoly was threatened. The tea merchants, led by none other than the wily Samuel Adams, had to convince the other merchants that if British tea was allowed in, other goods would follow and push the local merchants right off the map.

How would they like that? Not at all, roared the merchants, and a party of the most respectable of them promptly painted and dressed themselves like Indians and dumped the British tea into the harbor.

Personally, I don't like that version at all. Preston can have all his facts; I'll go along with the legend of the Boston Tea Party I always believed. How about you?

Another memory of the American Revolution dear to us all is the famous painting of George Washington crossing the Delaware on Christmas Night, 1776, just before his victory at Trenton.

Now there comes along an old meanie named Elsie Hix who, in *Strange As It Seems* (published by Hanover House), points out that the picture was painted in Germany by an artist named Leutze who never got closer to our shores than Hamburg. Furthermore, the river he depicted was the Rhine, and every one of the soldiers a hundred-per-cent German model. And the American flag waving over Washington wasn't even in existence at the time. It was not adopted until six months later!

Yes, we pick up all sorts of stories about the great and the near great in our schoolbooks and, later, in our newspapers, radio and TV shows, and gossip columns.

It's well to bear one thing very much in mind, however: they ain't necessarily so!

Cal Whipple's *Yankee Whalers in the South Seas* is chock-full of salty anecdotes, and should sell particularly well in Philadelphia, the city of blubberly love. I particularly liked the story of the cautious whaling captain from Nantucket who became embroiled with a British skipper, and found himself challenged to a duel. The American, having the choice of weapons, decided on pistols, and proposed a dueling spot which he knew and his opponent did not. It turned out to be the crest of a hill. After the antagonists marked off their twenty paces, they couldn't even see each other, much less shoot!

When the whaling ship *Essex* was sunk in 1820, writes Whipple, only eight members of the crew lived to tell the tale, and all of them carried for the rest of their lives the memory of having become cannibals in order to survive. Captain Pollard, one of the eight, was challenged years later by a writer who claimed relationship to a member of the *Essex* crew who had not returned. "I wonder if you remember him?" inquired the writer. "Remember him?" cackled Captain Pollard. "Hell, son, I et him!"

Peter de Vries tells a story about the time Stephen Douglas was a young man debating in the political campaigns in Illinois. There was always a lanky, raw-boned lad sitting up front, watching his every move, listening to him intently. Douglas finally asked him point-blank, "Why do you come to hear me debate so regularly?" "Because," answered the boy, "some day I hope to be up there on the platform myself."

"That's fine," Douglas enthused. "What's your name?" "Abe," said the boy. "Abe what?" persisted Douglas. And the boy answered, "Abe Feldspar."

Abe Lincoln once attended the theater in Springfield, and arrived just as the curtain rose. His eyes riveted on the stage, he thoughtlessly placed his tall silk hat on the seat next to him, open end up.

Entered a lady of very bountiful proportions, headed straight for the empty seat. She sat. There was a crunch. She jumped up.

The hat was now a black silk pancake. Mr. Lincoln picked it up ruefully. "Madam," he declared, "I could have told you my hat wouldn't fit you before you tried it on."

Even Abraham Lincoln didn't always succeed in what he was trying to accomplish, but he seldom failed to admit his occasional failures. Robert Yoder recalls that he had one story that helped a lot at such times. It concerned a farmer who was confronted with a tree stump too big to pull, too wet to burn. "I'll tell you how I got rid of it," the farmer explained, "if you won't divulge my secret. I plowed around it."

Ted Dealy, Dallas journalist, likes to memorize the last words of famous men, and these, he says, are four of his favorites:

Goethe: Let there be light!

Nathan Hale: I regret that I have but one life to give for my country.

Stonewall Jackson: Carry me over the river, boys, and let me rest under the trees.

General Custer: Where did all those blank blank Indians come from?

From downtown San Francisco, today's businessman looks up to the rugged eminence of Telegraph Hill, now topped by a tower given by Lilly Hitchcock Coit. In pioneer days there was a semaphore there to let merchants know that a ship from the East was in sight, and due to drop anchor in an hour's time.

A ham actor in the eighteen-fifties once spread his arms dramatically on stage and rashly spoke the line, "What does this mean?" The entire audience, well versed in the semaphore signals, bellowed as one, "Side-wheel steamer coming in!"

In the very middle of an impenetrable Appalachian forest, an explorer came upon a mighty oak with these words carved upon it: "I was the first person to travel through these wilds. Daniel Boone." Directly underneath, however, was inscribed: "That's what you think! Eleanor Roosevelt."

In the early part of the nineteenth century, English Court circles were enlivened by the wit and wardrobe of a wealthy young gadabout named George Bryan Brummell—Beau Brummell for short. His bons mots were quoted from Bath to Vienna; his waistcoats and pantaloons were of such vivid hues that only a Lucius Beebe or Alfred A. Knopf would dare to appear in modern-day counterparts.

The trouble with Beau Brummell was that he didn't know when to leave well enough alone. Tiring of wasting his devastating wisecracks on pushovers, he began to cut the then Prince of Wales (afterward George IV) down to size. This was a formidable undertaking, since the Prince weighed 240 pounds. The payoff came one day when the Prince made what he considered a most impressive entrance to Court, only to hear Beau Brummell whisper to the Prime Minister, "Who's your fat friend?" The fat friend responded with the royal equivalent of "Throw that bum out of here," and soon Beau Brummell was an exile in France, where he gambled away his inheritance and came to a very bad end indeed.

To this day, of course, Beau Brummell's name is used to denote a fashion plate. By the same token, romantic males are labeled Don Juans and Casanovas. General A. E. Burnsides' side whiskers are still called sideburns, a Vandyke is a chin decoration similar to those depicted in paintings by the Flemish artist, and a Mae West life belt is—well, rather inflated.

The word sandwich comes to us from John Montagu, fourth Earl of Sandwich; a punched theater pass is an Annie Oakley, in honor of the gal who could shoot a hole in a jack of spades from a distance of a hundred yards; and a signature is a John Hancock, the first name affixed to the Declaration of Independence.

Gat comes from Gatling gun, perfected by R. J. Gatling. John Loudon McAdam introduced the type of road surfacing known as macadam. A malapropism is a ridiculous misuse of words, the title coming from the "old weather-beaten she-dragon" in Sheridan's famous play, *The Rivals*. The saxophone derives its name from the inventor, Antoine Joseph Saxe, and people who play the instrument after midnight in apartment houses are often treated to a drink known as a Mickey Finn, also named after its inventor.

Finally, let us not forget that Napoleon bequeathed us a pastry, Lord Derby a hat, Nellie Melba a toast, Amelia Bloomer a singularly unglamorous lady's garment, William Morris a chair, Mary Tudor a "Bloody Mary," Lord Zwei a back, and Joe Miller many of the jokes "originated" by columnists today.

Unauthenticated but intriguing is the tale of a journey made by Queen Victoria by train to London from a holiday at Balmoral Castle in the Scottish Highlands. The special train that bore her, Prime Minister Disraeli, and other important members of her entourage had been delayed by a heavy storm, and the engineer had his throttle wide open in an effort to make up lost time.

Suddenly he gasped with dismay. A figure loomed up on the track ahead, shrouded in black, waving its arms frantically. Every movement was outlined by the headlight of the onrushing locomotive.

The engineer jammed on his brakes and brought the train to a grinding halt. The Queen and Mr. Disraeli were hurtled from their chairs. The terrified train crew piled out into the night.

Just fifty yards ahead, a bridge had been washed out. Few seconds more, and Queen Victoria and everyone else aboard would have been lost—an irretrievable disaster that might well have changed the history not only of England but of the entire world.

Everybody breathed a silent prayer of thanks—and then looked for the mysterious figure that had flagged the train. It had vanished completely. The crew was about to reboard the train, when, in a flash, the figure reappeared on the track ahead, again waving its arms grotesquely. And then the engineer gave a shout—and pointed.

Imprisoned in the headlight of the engine was a tiny moth. The mysterious figure was nothing more than the reflection on the snow of its frenzied death dance as it zigzagged crazily closer and closer to the consuming beam!

In one of the rambling, low-ceilinged, early-nineteenth-century houses still found in northern Westchester County, New York, I have come upon a book that must have been a godsend to young ladies bothered by the niceties of behavior in what some folks still insist were the good old days. The book is called *Hill's Manual of Social and Business Forms,* and it was published about 1870 in Chicago by Moses Warren and Company.

Was a girl unfortunate enough to lose her heart to a fellow

addicted to use of that vile weed, tobacco? This, insisted arbiter Hill, was the way to brush him off:

"Dear Sir: I am in receipt of your courteous letter containing a declaration of love and, to make a candid confession, I reciprocate your affectionate regard. But you have one habit which makes it imperative that our further correspondence should cease.

"I have reference to the use of tobacco. 1. This addiction would impoverish my home. Only ten cents a day expended for a cigar, in a lifetime of forty years, with its accumulation of interest, amounts to over four thousand dollars! 2. It might wreck my happiness. The use of tobacco deadens the sense of taste, so that the user involuntarily craves strong drink in order to taste it. 3. It would surround me with filth. I am immediately faint at the thought of dragging my skirts through the spittle of a smoker; I turn with disgust at atmosphere tainted with the stench of tobacco smoke. In any room in which vulgarity and obscenity prevail, there is always tobacco smoke in the air.

116

"Nevertheless, I remain, your friend and well-wisher. Marietta Wilcox."

Of course, this was long before cigarettes became popular. Chances are that Marietta Wilcox's great-granddaughter gaily smokes two full packs a day.

Poor old Pa still had something to say about his daughter's matrimonial plans in the '70's. Mr. Hill suggested that an unwanted suitor be polished off as follows:

"I am compelled to inform you that, though my daughter has treated you with much friendliness, she will be unable to continue with you a love acquaintance, owing to a prior engagement with a gentleman of worth and respectability, which contract she has no occasion to regret."

Oswald, my coat and gloves!

Ladies who visited the better hotels in the old days found signs posted in bedrooms warning them to keep their menfolk from spitting on the carpets, lying in bed with their shoes on, or driving nails into the furniture. In New England, some guests who used cuss words in the public halls were either fined, or made to accompany the proprietor and his family to church services.

One hotel owner in New Hampshire with a sense of humor added, "Lady guests must not criticize the cooking. If you don't like it, go out to the kitchen and try to do better," and, "In case of fire, please do not call the Fire Department. Our local fire fighters usually do more damage than the fire."

Teddy Roosevelt's political trade-marks were a big stick and a wide-brimmed black sombrero. He came by the sombrero, asserts Hermann Hagedorn, in *The Roosevelt Family of Sagamore Hill*, purely by accident. Just before the nominating convention of 1900, one of T.R.'s children bopped him on the side of the head with a rock. The kid went out to work on his control, and T.R. went in to apply lotions. The lump just grew and grew, however, so Teddy seized the sombrero to conceal his condition from the public. When he saw the hit that it scored, he wore a sombrero for the rest of his life!

They say that the handwriting of the late Joe Cannon, onetime Speaker of the House of Representatives, was so illegible that a fellow congressman once told him, "This letter you sent me yesterday, Uncle Joe, really takes the cake. I showed it to about fifty acquaintances, and between us we managed to figure out everything but the last four words." "Let me see it," exclaimed Uncle Joe angrily, and seized his own scrawl. After a minute's scrutiny, he hollered, "You durn fool, those last four words are 'Top Secret and Confidential!'"

Here is what I believe to be a brand-new Cal Coolidge story and, since it comes straight from Herbert Hoover, there is no question about its authenticity.

Mr. Hoover, then Secretary of Commerce, was alone with

118

Coolidge in the President's study at the White House one evening when a phone began ringing. There were seven or eight phones on the desk, and Cal picked up all the wrong ones first. He was reasonably exasperated by the time he happened upon the right one, explaining in an aside, "This is a direct wire from the State Department. Hasn't rung in three years." (Editor's note: Those were the days!) "No wonder I didn't recognize the sound of the bell!" Into the phone he rasped, "What on earth are you calling me for at this hour of the night?"

The caller was Secretary of State Charles Evans Hughes and he explained, "We've just had word that Queen Marie of Rumania is planning a visit to the United States and I presumed you would want to know about it." Mr. Coolidge had only one comment to make before he hung up. "Hmphh," he mused. "I hope you'll see to it that she pays her own expenses!"

The late Calvin Coolidge, retired from the presidency, became even less talkative than when he was in the White House. Skeptics doubted Henry Newsome, therefore, when he swore he had persuaded Cal to make a speech—for nothing too—at a local banquet in Vermont. "I will admit," conceded Mr. Newsome, "that when Cal first opened his mouth dust flew out."

Mr. Coolidge even refused to speak at one whistle stop when he was campaigning for President. He looked over the crowd and stamped back into his private railroad car. "This crowd," he explained succinctly, "is too big for an anecdote and too small for an oration."

Dayton, Ohio, was the scene of one of the first press interviews ever given by the late Wendell Willkie. He held it in his hotel suite, after a banquet, and still wore his dinner clothes. Nervous at the outset, he quickly regained his confidence, and when the reporters and photographers departed, Mr. Willkie was well aware that he had made an excellent impression. Although he didn't know it, there was still one reporter on the scene: John Moore, now managing editor of the Dayton *Journal-Herald*, had gotten caught behind the door when the others trooped out. That's how he happened to be on deck when Mr. Willkie clapped his open hat on his head, waltzed gaily over to the mirror, and exclaimed happily to himself, "Well, Wendell, I'll be gosh-darned!"

That proverbially crusty politico, Harold Ickes, was stopped one day on his way to an important confab at the Pentagon Building by a silly old socialite who cooed, "If it isn't dear Mr. Ickes! And how do you find yourself these brisk wintry mornings?" Dear Mr. Ickes, striving to break loose from her iron grip, barked, "I just throw back the comforter, madam, and there I am!"

In *Say It Ain't So*, Mac Davis tells the story of a small-town kid in Missouri who loved to play ball. "It's no use," he was always told. "You can't see well enough. We don't want anybody on our team who has to wear glasses." "There must be something I can do," the kid insisted. "All right," he finally was told. "Since everybody seems to like you around here, you can go out there and umpire."

So the kid went out and umpired and got himself into a lot of hot water. But he managed to get by, and most of his decisions stuck. It was good training for him. The kid was Harry Truman.

Harry Truman likes to tell about the time a visitor called on his mother just a few weeks after he had been inaugurated as President. "My, but you must be proud of your boy Harry," gushed the visitor. "Of course I am," said Mrs. Truman, "but I've got another son just as fine—right out there in that field, plowing."

Mrs. Bess Truman, back in her modest Independence, Missouri, home after all those glittering years at the White House, took the change characteristically in stride. So did her distinguished husband. Mrs. T. did experience considerable difficulty in persuading the ex-President to resume operation of the power mower. "I spent the better part of our first summer back home trying to induce Harry to get out there and use it on the lawn," says Mrs. Truman. "Finally he heeded me—at exactly eleven o'clock on a Sunday morning, with all the Methodists and Baptists in town going by our house on the way to church. When I saw Mr. Truman cutting the grass on that lawn in his shirt sleeves, I was horrified. 'Harry! Come in here this minute!' I cried. There's not a doubt in my mind he planned the whole thing deliberately to save himself from ever touching that mower again. And he hasn't."

CHAPTER TEN

GUYS AND DOLLARS

In the hope that this will be the year in which you will accumulate all those American dollars that have eluded you heretofore, the next few paragraphs will be devoted to some facts about U.S. currency. They were supplied by Miss Dorothy Steinberg, of the Treasury Department.

Our currency notes include twelve denominations, all but one of which bear portraits of a former President or Secretary of the Treasury. Before reading further, can you tell what guys adorn our various dollars? There's some excuse if you do not readily recall the ones aboard the bills for $500, $1,000, $5,000, $10,000 or $100,000, since I imagine you don't get to handle more than two or three such bank notes a week, but you should be observant enough to recall the others.

The one-dollar bill glorifies George Washington, the two-dollar bill Thomas Jefferson, the five-spot Abraham Lincoln, the tenner Alexander Hamilton. On the twenty you'll find Andrew Jackson, on the fifty Ulysses S. Grant, on the hundred—the one exception to the general rule—Benjamin Franklin.

Then, ascending in our space ship to the wide green yonder, there's William McKinley on the $500 bill, Grover Cleveland on $1,000, James Madison on $5,000, Salmon Chase (Lincoln's Secretary of the Treasury from 1861 to 1864) on $10,000, and Woodrow Wilson on $100,000. Wilson doesn't get around much these days! Seriously, the $100,000 note is not in general circulation—even in Texas. It is a gold certificate and is issued only to Federal reserve banks.

Currency notes of the present size (2.61 x 6.14 inches) were issued in July, 1929. These notes, when new, will stack 233 to one inch. They cost about one cent per note to produce and the average life of $1.00 (unless Jack Benny gets hold of it) is approximately ten months.

The old series bills (3.15 x 7.4218) are now virtually extinct, for the most part in the hands of collectors.

All U.S. coins, except those minted in Philadelphia, where the government began the coinage of money in 1793, carry a letter to identify the city of their origin (and to keep the record absolutely straight, Philadelphia used a "P" on wartime alloy nickels coined there from October, 1942, to December, 1945).

Coins minted today in Denver bear a "D," and in San Francisco, an "S." Mints no longer in operation were located in Carson City (CC), Charlotte (C), Dahlonega, Georgia (D), and New Orleans (O). Any other initials on U.S. coins represent the designer's signature.

A young assistant in whom J. P. Morgan had great faith became involved with a chorus girl and his name suddenly was being bandied about in the headlines. "I'm disappointed in you," Morgan told him bluntly. "But, Mr. Morgan," protested the young man, "it's just that I'm not a hypocrite. I haven't done a thing that most other young men as fortunately situated as myself haven't done behind closed doors!" "You may be right," admitted Morgan, "but dammit, that's what doors are for!"

Just graduated with high honors from Harvard, young Smathers sought a job in one of Boston's swankiest banking establishments. Awaiting one of the vice-presidents, Smathers idly struck up a conversation with a freckle-faced office boy in short pants. "Tell me, Buster," he inquired loftily, "do you think there's an opening in this musty institution for a sharp young college graduate?" "There certainly will be," Buster assured him, "unless they raise me to twenty bucks a week by this coming Friday."

A millionaire banker (self-made) sent his kid brother to Harvard, where his real studies were devoted to the girls in the chorus at a night club in Boston. He fell madly in love with one of them and finally proposed marriage. "You're a darling," she replied pensively, "and you must be brave when I tell you I cannot marry you. I will always be a sister to you, however." And the next day, true to her word, she married the millionaire banker.

How many of you remember Samuel Insull? His spectacular career began when he was in his teens, in England. The Thomas A. Edison Company installed telephones in London, and employed him as their first switchboard operator. For a man of Insull's ability it was just a hop, skip—and a swim from there to the presidency of the Edison Company in Chicago.

Once established in Illinois, Sam Insull built up a fantastic empire, pyramiding his holdings, and fitting great utility companies into a jigsaw puzzle even he must have found it difficult, eventually, to decipher. Before the bubble burst in 1932, the market value of Insull-controlled securities totaled four billion dollars! (The gory details can be found in Emmet Dedman's *Fabulous Chicago.*)

After the crash, the once-mighty financier found himself not only bankrupt and jobless, but a fugitive from justice as well. He turned up, in disguise, in Istanbul, Turkey; and among the star reporters rushed over to cover his extradition was Jim Kilgallen, newshawk for INS and father of panelist Dorothy.

Until Kilgallen's arrival, Insull had managed to duck the photographers, but Jim cornered him, hiding in an Istanbul fruit shop, and persuaded him to talk. Coming back to America with him on the same boat, Jim sent home some exclusive interviews that made his rivals gnash their teeth with envy.

The day before the boat landed in New York, however, Jim Kilgallen suddenly realized that he had neglected to make out his expense account—the list of payments known in every newspaper office as a "swindle sheet." He sauntered into the writing room on the top deck, sat down at his portable and started his compilation.

He had reached almost the bottom of the page, and the total was reaching interesting proportions, when he became aware of someone staring over his shoulder. It was Insull.

He read Kilgallen's list to the end, shook his head, then commented wonderingly, "And they indicted me!"

Millions of other investors and speculators had suffered the same fate as Insull by the time the depression hit rock bottom in 1932. The memories are still too painful to probe—particularly to anybody who had common stocks in his portfolio at the time— but I do like to recall the crusty old Wall Street man who was dolefully reading about the latest drop in prices when his little boy tugged on his sleeve and reminded him, "You promised to buy me a toy railroad set."

The father assured him solemnly, "If you'll wait just a few days longer, I'll give you the whole New York Central."

Those were the times when advertisements grew so scarce that great national monthly and weekly magazines shrank from the pre-depression average of 250 pages to a mere shade of themselves.

One suburbanite in Ohio who stubbornly had maintained that

the gloom was unwarranted finally admitted to his wife that things had gone to pot. "What has convinced you at last?" she asked.

"A mild gust of wind," he told her sadly, "just blew our *Saturday Evening Post* off the front porch."

That's when the Wall Street boys really were jumping—and from pretty high up, too. Financial geniuses were turned back into washroom attendants overnight. Deals were no longer worth the tablecloths they were written on. They had to invent a new kind of ticker which automatically changed from tape to rope every time the market took another dive.

Happy days came back to Wall Street, however, and the bull market roared so lustily that even some of the customers made money.

The pages of recent issues of the *Bawl Street Journal*, an annual burlesque of the dignified and impeccable *Wall Street Journal*, reflect the deep contentment of the financial community. For wily editor John Straley and his coupon-clipping staff, the goose hangs high.

Their jokes are like their own securities: uninterrupted dividend payers for many years. No companies or institutions are too mighty to escape being targets for their parody ads.

Sinclair Oil regrets, "We cannot fuel all of the people all of the time." Beekman Hospital promises, "Our doctors will keep you in stitches." The Bureau of Internal Revenue's message is simple: "Thanks, fellas!"

R. W. Pressprich & Co. "would like to get their hands on an attractive young secretary." A. M. Kidder & Co. inquire, "Looking for an active, undervalued stock? So are we!"

The Fulton Fish Market proclaims, "Our market is always strong. Smelts to high heaven." Acme Exterminators boast, "Our clients have millions." J. P. Morgan & Co. assure "Small accounts ($100,000 and up)," that they are "cordially invited."

The only bank teller they've caught defaulting in the past two

years made the fatal error of putting back too much. He was sentenced for being generous to a vault.

One stockbroker has chalked up such profits that in Las Vegas he didn't even peep when he lost $115 in a stamp machine. He just strode manfully up to his hotel bar and demanded, "One for the road, brother: an asphalt and soda."

A banker in Phoenix, Arizona, read a number of surveys, all of which indicated that women control the greater part of the nation's wealth. "Apparently," he commented, "the hands that rock the cradle also cradle the rocks."

This is the story of an opportunity that was missed. In 1905, John P. Burkhard was the publisher of a new magazine for sportsmen called *Field and Stream*. Hearing that an ex-bicycle maker named Henry Ford had turned to the production of automobiles in Detroit, Burkhard hastened to assure him that full-page ads in *Field and Stream* would attract the moneyed customers he was seeking.

"How much?" asked the cautious Mr. Ford. The price was set at $60 a page for a twenty-month contract. Mr. Ford offered in payment $1,200 worth of stock in the Ford Motor Company or a new Ford coupé which retailed at the same figure. The publisher, just as cautious as Mr. Ford, unhesitatingly took the car and turned it over to his printer for credit.

Just how many millions that $1,200 of stock in Ford Motors would be worth today is something I'll let statistically minded readers figure for themselves.

Equally fabulous is the story of General Motors stock. The corporation came into existence in 1908. Let's say you also were in existence by that time and had the foresight to have bought ten original shares at the issue price of $100 per share and held on to them through thick and thin. Today, by virtue of various exchanges and successive stock split-ups, you would own 15,141 shares with a market value of something in the neighborhood of $700,000. Furthermore, you would have received dividends and rights totaling close to $400,000 more. In other words, a $1,000 investment would have netted you well over a million dollars. Buy America!

Bernard Baruch was asked once for an opinion on the stock market. He refused to single out any one stock, but did vouchsafe two rules he observed scrupulously himself: 1. Never pay any attention to what a president of a company ever tells you about his own stock. 2. When the market's gyrations on the up side hit the front page of the New York *Times*, sell! . . . Broker Washington Dodge remembers a Japanese trader who picked the very bottom of the market in 1932, and advised his customers to go in and buy (how right he was!) in a message unique among documents of its kind: "Here is a good omen: the elevator which seemed impatiently has now hit bottom and will quickly express without its hat and coat. All traders must not miss boat, now that castor oil season is over, and beautiful flowers and bugles will be blowing heartbreak for damfool amateur bearish."

The wife of a big Wall Street trader gave their gangling, thirteen-year-old son a significant glance and told her husband, "Irving, you've been evading your duty long enough. It's high time you explained to your son the facts of life." Dreading every minute of it, Irving herded the lad into the study, cleared his throat nervously, and began, "My boy, I'm going to tell you all about the bulls and the bears."

CHAPTER ELEVEN

HEAVENS ABOVE

One of the skeptic Voltaire's pronouncements was, "In a hundred years the Bible will be a forgotten book found only in museums." When the hundred years were up, the home in which Voltaire made his prediction was occupied by the Geneva Bible Society.

Dr. Alexander, whose sermons electrify thousands in Oklahoma every week, reports that the severe water shortage in those parts has made radical changes necessary in the baptismal rites of all sects. The Baptists of Oklahoma, insists Dr. Alexander, are now using the sprinkling system. Methodists and Presbyterians use a damp cloth. And the Episcopalians and Congregationalists are just passing out rain checks.

From Dr. Otis Moore comes the story about a pastor friend of his who shifted his base of operations from Springfield, Massachusetts, to Worcester. A member of his new flock stopped the pastor's daughter one Sunday morning and inquired, "Does your father preach the same sermons here that he did in Springfield?" "Yes, he does," admitted the daughter, "but he *hollers* in different places."

Dr. Leo Green tells about an architect who promised to build a badly needed new auditorium for the church if he could be allowed to keep the construction plans a secret until the inaugural ceremonies. A record crowd turned up for the opening. The preacher, scheduled as usual to speak only until noon, was, as usual, just getting warmed up when he should have signed off.

But that's when the new plan became operative. At twelve-three sharp, a trap door opened, the preacher dropped into the basement, and the happy congregation went home to Sunday dinner.

In Glendale, California, writes ace columnist Matt Weinstock, a husky lad entered John Valentine's bookstore and purchased two leather-bound Bibles. "One of them," he explained, "is for myself, the other for a guy at our shop I'm trying to convert. Gambling is rampant there and this fellow is the ringleader." As the clerk wrapped the volumes, she remarked, "I hope you succeed in converting him." "I do too," said the purchaser. "They've laid me five to three I can't."

A little girl in Idaho had a novel excuse for not having prepared her Sunday-school lesson. "There's only one Bible in our house," she explained, "and that one is the reversed version."

Recommended to intemperate witch-hunters is A. Gayle Waldrop's story of a religious sect called the Doukhobors. Many years ago they emigrated from Russia to escape the tyranny of the czars, and found the freedom to worship as they desired in Canada. Unfortunately, however, the Doukhobors have one cherished ritual which puts them in definite conflict with the accepted Canadian way of life. They believe that, on a certain day every spring, it is appropriate that they give homage to the Lord in a state of complete nakedness.

On the chosen day this spring, accordingly, a good Doukhobor appeared in the market place of a Canadian town and proceeded to divest himself of all his clothing. An outraged constable came to arrest him, but the Doukhobor fled and, being unencumbered by clothing, soon outdistanced the pursuing arm of the law.

The constable decided he could run faster without his coat. Then, in rapid succession, he discarded his shirt, shoes, and finally his trousers. When at last he was naked as a jay bird, he managed to collar the fleeing Doukhobor.

The trouble, alas, was that when the two nude figures reentered the market place, not a single soul could tell which was the Doukhobor and which was the constable.

The six-year-old son of a Protestant lady in Bronxville had for a steadfast playmate the little Catholic girl who lived at the end of the block. One afternoon the two children were soaked to the skin by a flash thundershower, and the boy's mother, without further ado, stripped them and propelled them into a hot tub to prevent sniffles. An hour after the little Catholic girl had been packed off to her home, the boy came to his mother and announced with vast satisfaction, "Well, at last I understand the difference between Protestants and Catholics!"

Hollywood pictures in which nuns have figured as heroines have proven popular with general audiences, but are viewed with some doubts by the nuns themselves. Sister Mary Jean Dorcy, a Dominican nun from the School of St. Peter Martyr in California, notes wryly in her book, *Shepherd's Tartan:* "Hollywood found that the ignorance most people have about convents makes for good box office, so they created nuns in celluloid. We are now expected, not only to keep our rules and promote the active good works of the Kingdom of God, but also to be as beautiful as movie stars, to be experts at boxing and baseball, to emote in the grand manner at a moment's notice, and to frolic around in jeeps!"

Does that remind you of any pictures you've seen in recent months?

A young priest was hearing confession one Saturday evening when there appeared before him an unfamiliar young girl. "I've been away in another city for the past two years," she explained, "studying acrobatics. May I show you what I learned?" "By all means," said the young priest. The girl thereupon proceeded to do a complicated series of back flips and pinwheels, ending by standing on her head. During the course of her exhibition, two older ladies of the parish entered. "Glory be!" gasped one of them. "Would yez look at what the good father is giving for penance today—and me in me old last year's bloomers!"

There was great rejoicing in church circles of a town in Arkansas when the leading reprobate and liar of the county announced that he had seen the light and desired to be baptized. They doused him in the icy waters of the creek while all the town watched and applauded. As he came up with his teeth chattering, a friend hollered, "Hey, Tom, that water cold?" "No, sir," the prodigal son cried bravely. "Better duck him again, Parson," advised the friend. "He ain't quit lyin' yet!"

A minister, trying to impress his young daughter with the necessity of silence while he was writing his Sunday sermon reminded her, "You know it's the good Lord who really tells me what to say." "If that's true," demanded the daughter, "why do you scratch so much of it out?"

Herb Shriner tells about the minister in his home town who warned his congregation that alcohol and gasoline don't mix. One skeptic insisted on finding out for himself, and reported later, "The reverend's wrong. They mix all right—but they sure taste terrible."

The pastor of a church in a small town was loved and respected by his congregation, but his salary was necessarily small, and when a prosperous congregation in a large city offered him double the fee to shift his allegiance, the localites could not possibly match the offer.

"I suppose," mourned a member of the flock to the preacher's son, "your father will accept the call to that big city."

"Dunno," admitted the boy. "Dad's on his knees in the study at this very moment praying for guidance."

"And your ma?"

"She's upstairs packing the trunks."

An orthodox Jewish lad broke the news to his mother one evening that he intended marrying little Maggie Kelly, who had lived next door all his life. Mama was shocked into silence for a moment, but soon rallied her forces. "That's fine, Morris, my boy," she declared. "Only if I were you, I wouldn't tell Papa just yet. You know he has a heart condition. And I wouldn't tell your sister Sarah. Remember how strongly she feels on religious questions. I wouldn't mention it to your brother Abe for a while either. Such a temper he's got! He might break your jaw. Me, it's all right you should tell. I'm going to commit suicide anyhow."

In the Bronx, Helen Goldblatt saw a throng lining the Grand Concourse to cheer Cardinal Spellman. Loudest of the cheerers was a little old Jewish lady holding her granddaughter aloft to catch a glimpse of the passing prelate. "It's very nice of you to get so excited over Cardinal Spellman," observed Miss Goldblatt. "Cardinal Spellman?" echoed the startled old lady. "I thought it was Mischa Elman!"

A young man graduated from an orthodox rabbinical college and came home proudly wearing his long black alpaca coat, skullcap, prayer shawl, and ringlets—all badges of his calling. His mother looked him over carefully when he entered the room, then exclaimed, "Well, Papa, look who's here: *Joe College!*"

In Chicago, Dr. Morris Fishbein, warning businessmen who never took time out to rest, reminded them of the harassed merchant who came to his rabbi and mourned, "I'm in terrible trouble. I can't support my wife and seven children, and every year there comes still another baby. What should I do?" The wise rabbi told him, "Don't do anything at all."

Lewis Browne, a famous and successful author when he died, began his career as a rabbi on the West Coast. When an envious competitor heard this, he inquired sarcastically of Browne at a dinner, "A rabbi once, eh? Were you defrocked?" "Not at all," answered Browne calmly. "I was unsuited."

Three progressive, high-powered rabbis were boasting to one another about the advanced views of their respective congregations.

"We're so modern," asserted the first, "we've installed ash trays in every pew so members can smoke while they meditate."

"Pah," minimized the second, "that's nothing. We now have a snack bar in the basement that serves ham sandwiches after services."

"You boys," advised the third, "aren't even in the same class with *my* congregation. We're so reformed we close for the Jewish holidays!"

A Protestant minister entered the Pearly Gates when his appointed time arrived, and was presented with a spanking new Chevrolet by St. Peter. He went tootling all over heaven in it very contentedly, though he was a bit put out to observe Father Flanagan, his old neighbor from the Catholic church, whizzing by in a new-model Buick convertible. When Rabbi Goldstein, however, drove up in a sleek Cadillac limousine, with a liveried chauffeur and footman, the Protestant was so annoyed he marched back to St. Peter to register his protest. "This is rank favoritism," he pointed out. "Why should I get just a Chevvie and Rabbi Goldstein that snazzy Cadillac?" "S-s-sh," whispered St. Peter. "You don't seem to understand. He's related to the boss!"

The minister of a small town was awakened in the dead of night by a suspicious noise. Out of the darkness came a voice: "One move, and you're a dead man. I'm hunting for your money." "Let me get up and turn on the light," begged the minister, "and I'll hunt with you."

In a little flat in London one Christmas Eve, writes Edmond

Segrave, not a single gift had been purchased for the bright lad of the house. It was not that his parents didn't love him—they just didn't have a penny to spare.

"He's always loved to read," recalled the unhappy father, clutching at straws. "I know a grumpy old publisher who always entertains his authors and staff in high style the day before Christmas. Maybe he'll be in good enough humor to give me a damaged book or something from his overstock." The father's hunch paid off. "Help yourself in the shipping room," said the publisher indulgently.

And so on Christmas morning there was no pile of toys to confuse the boy—just one small package. But his eyes shone with joy when he opened it, and the parents shared in the glow.

A few days later, the publisher received a note from the boy. "Thank you," it read, "for the magic carpet, the elixir of life, and the beautiful golden key."

"What's all this folderol?" grumbled the publisher. "I just gave the fool boy a book!"

137

A tragic moment in the life of a fading Broadway star comes when he finally must face the fact that the parade has passed him by.

No longer is he offered the choice of a half dozen fat parts at the start of the season. Stony-eyed autograph hounds gaze blankly into his face. Columnists have forgotten even how he spells his name. If he has neglected to save for this very rainy day while the cash was pouring in, the awakening is doubly painful.

One such disillusioned Thespian, recalls Eddie Cantor, had fallen so far from glory that he didn't know where his next month's rent was coming from and, with the Christmas season approaching, gratefully accepted the one job that was offered to him, playing Santa Claus in a big department store. He donned the traditional costume and whiskers and, with a brave attempt at joviality but a sinking heart, climbed to his seat in the toy department.

A long line of children was waiting to be dandled on his knee and to whisper lists of all the presents they craved. One little boy was so much gayer and more charming than the rest that the actor felt a sudden surge of warmth in his heart. "I'd like to have a look at your mommy," he told the boy. "Here she comes for me now," was the reply.

The actor looked up and caught his breath—he was gazing straight into the eyes of the glamorous woman who once had been his leading lady. More, she had once been his wife; but their marriage had failed years before, and he had read that she married a respected and prosperous businessman.

Fortunately she did not appear to penetrate his disguise. "You have a fine boy here," he said, summoning all his courage to keep his voice from breaking. "He wants a space suit, a rocket ship, and an autographed picture of Captain Video."

The lady winked gravely at Santa and said, "I know you'll get them for him, won't you?" "But, Mommy," interrupted the boy, "how will Santa Claus find me? Give him our address!"

The mother indulgently went to a nearby desk to fill out a

card, which she placed in an envelope and left in Santa's hands. He sighed with relief when she disappeared down the corridor. Then he opened the envelope.

The card read, "Merry Christmas to the greatest actor I ever knew." Clipped to it was a check for one thousand dollars.

CHAPTER TWELVE

THE HIGH AND THE FLIGHTY

Cleveland Amory's sparkling *The Last Resorts,* a book about the
decline and fall of onetime society strongholds, such as Newport, Bar Harbor, Saratoga and Palm Beach, is a hilarious saga

to such as you and me, but to surviving members of the snobbish and outrageously spoiled plutocracy who once held sway there it is nothing short of a dirge.

One old dragon who read it threatened to sue Amory for attributing a statement to her which she swears she never uttered. "Better keep your mouth shut," counseled a friend. "It's the only clever thing I've heard you say in thirty years."

Amory attributes the decay of the once-glittering resorts to an offshoot of Gresham's inexorable law: bad millionaires drive good millionaires out of circulation.

The phonies, the nouveaux riches, and the show-offs move in; the dignified old parties flee for their lives. "These newcomers," mourned one die-hard, "have marked the '400' down to $3.98." Taxes and the scarcity of servants have taken their toll, too, of the show places that once cluttered the landscape at spas and beaches.

"Today we're living on capital," mourned one blue blood, "and that's that. I can't even remember when I wore a white tie last!"

And, oh, how morals have changed in the once-hidebound domains of Old Society! In the days of Edith Wharton's *The Age of Innocence*, the "right people" looked askance at a divorcée. Today, one generally accepted man and wife boast eleven ex-spouses between them!

A Mrs. Messmore at East Hampton sighs for the days "when it was considered fast to play net at tennis."

Another dowager recalls a time when society debutantes would hesitate to show their insteps. "Today," she adds grimly, "they usually show their step-ins!"

Newport, Rhode Island, once was the summer home of Edgar Allan Poe, Bret Harte, Oliver Wendell Holmes, Henry Wadsworth Longfellow, Henry James, and Julia Ward Howe, but when the millionaires started building their now-obsolete hundred-room "cottages," the literary set folded their tents and stole

silently away. The society folk remained dimly aware that a few of them were still lurking around, however. Mrs. William Astor, queen bee of the colony, announced one day that she was planning a really "Bohemian" party. "How daring," exclaimed the late Lady Mendl. "What extras are you inviting?" Mrs. Astor pondered a moment, then answered, "J. P. Morgan and Edith Wharton."

The pampered rich don't feel quite so defenseless when they're surrounded by other unfortunates like themselves. One heiress from Toledo, for instance, took up residence for the season in Paris, but it failed to meet her expectations. An indefinable something was missing. Suddenly she discovered what it was.

"Paris is wonderful at last," she confided in a letter home. "You have no idea how many people from Toledo have suddenly begun passing through!"

The headwaiter at one of Chicago's nobbiest hotels still

trembles when he recalls the evening four unmistakable V.I.P.'s
—Dorothy Thompson, Vincent Sheean, and Mr. and Mrs.
Henry Luce—popped up at the height of the dinner rush.

There was no table free and the foursome milled about, somewhat miffed, in the lobby for some minutes. A friend of the
management spotted them, and pulled anxiously at the headwaiter's sleeve. "Do you know who those people *are?*" he
whispered hoarsely. "I do indeed," said the headwaiter. "I have
been told four times, sir."

The dry cleaner had promised to return Mr. Backer's trousers
in time for the Harriman ball, but at 6 P.M. of the evening in
question they were nowhere in evidence. Mrs. Backer got the
cleaner on the phone and threatened, "If those pants aren't here
in fifteen minutes, I'm going to sue you for promise of breeches!"

In *My Philadelphia Father*, socialite Cordelia Biddle tells how
Colonel Anthony Biddle once decided to become a concert

singer and hired the famous Philadelphia Academy of Music for his debut. The audience consisted almost entirely of Biddles and Biddle employees, but, even so, they soon remembered urgent engagements elsewhere. Biddle was so outraged he jumped on a train for Florida. When he returned home he was accompanied by a dozen live alligators. In the middle of a blizzard, he burst into the office of a strange doctor, bellowing, "Damn it, I've been bitten by an alligator." The doctor looked out at the snow and said soothingly, "Just sit down there till you get hold of yourself."

Colonel Biddle and his family were immortalized by King Edward VII of England. "In Philadelphia, when I was the Prince of Wales," His Majesty recalled one day, "I met a large and interesting family named Scrapple. They served me a rather delicious native food, too—something, I believe, called biddle."

A Boston society matron who didn't know what she was up against once tried to persuade the late W. C. Fields to speak at a garden-club-federation banquet. "Surely you believe in clubs for women," she exclaimed. "I most certainly do, madam," Fields assured her with immense dignity, "but only if every other form of persuasion fails."

The hopelessly spoiled son of a multimillionaire suddenly discovered that money couldn't buy everything. The girl he adored flatly refused to marry him. Disconsolate, he climbed into his imported eighteen-cylinder automobile, and ordered the chauffeur, "Drive off a bridge. I'm committing suicide."

A new maid turned up at the Vanderbricks to help at a big dance. "From seven to eight," Mrs. Vanderbrick instructed her, "you are to stand at the ballroom entrance and call the guests' names as they arrive."

"What jolly fun that will be," enthused the maid. "I know a couple of beauts!"

Two gardeners met at the village seed-and-implement depot. "I hear you're up at Golden Acres this year, working for that banker fellow Rockerbilt," said one by way of greeting. "Me working for Rockerbilt? You've got it all wrong," the other assured him. "Rockerbilt gets up at six-thirty every morning to get aboard an overcrowded, rickety train to commute to the hot city so he can keep up his estate and pay us all our weekly wages. *Rockerbilt is working for me!*"

John Gunther, whose *Inside Africa* is the sixth of an amazingly successful series, was weekending recently at a luxurious Long Island estate. The Japanese butler, Mitzumo, was an especial admirer of Mr. Gunther's talents. On Sunday morning a neighbor, coming to pay his respects, asked, "Is John Gunther available?" Mitzumo giggled and reported, "No, Mr. Inside out!"

Servant problems are pressing, the country over, but Las Vegas housewives (sure, there are some!) have something extra to contend with. One of them told a new cook to dice some beets for dinner. Two hours later the cook reported, "Ma'am, cutting up them beets was no trouble at all, but putting all those black dots on them is plumb driving me crazy."

A resident of the fashionable Nob Hill section of San Francisco hired an affable new Chinese houseboy, but found his name too difficult for everyday use. "I can't go around calling you 'Fu Yu Ling Tsein Mei' all the time," she exclaimed petulantly, "so I'll just label you Russell, if you don't mind." "O.K., lady," beamed the Chinese lad, "but please to tell me your name again." "I," said the lady loftily, "am Mrs. Eustace Tewksbury Foppingham." "You're too damlong too," decided the lad. "I just call you Charlie."

Mrs. Commins summoned her new chambermaid and told her angrily, "I was able to write your name this morning in the dust on the mantelpiece." "Yes," agreed the maid, "and you're not half as smart as you think. You spelled it wrong."

Gone for good in Hollywood is the ostentatious gambling for excessive stakes. They still tell of one maid who never had worked for picture folk before, and was initiated on an evening when one of the most fabulous of the oldtime stars was hosting a wild and woolly all-night poker game.

Her eyes popped when one player threw a red chip in the middle and announced, "I open for one hundred dollars." She dropped the tray with a crash when another tossed in a blue chip and said, "I raise you five hundred dollars." But the climax came when a third player produced a single yellow chip and declared, "Let's make it one thousand dollars and keep out the pikers."

When the last guest had gone, the maid tiptoed into the game room, stole all the chips, and took the next train back to Elmira.

The old plutocrat, his wheel chair pulled up to the window of his Fifth Avenue mansion, smacked his lips as a lovely young nursemaid wheeled her charge toward the park entrance. "Quick, Tague," he cried to his butler. "Bring my teeth! I want to whistle."

The directors of an exclusive Fifth Avenue Club were discussing an unfortunate occurrence involving two prominent members. It seems member Number One had returned home unexpectedly, and finding his wife in the arms of member Number Two, had tattooed the latter's anatomy with a load of buckshot. "What awful publicity for the club!" groaned the secretary. "Can you think of anything worse?" "I certainly can," admitted the president. "Had he come home just an hour earlier, he'd have shot *me!*"

"I thought I was drowning for sure," droned Smithers, the club bore. "I was going down for the third time, mind you, and suddenly my whole life passed before my eyes. In sharp, clearly delineated pictures, it all came back to me."

"Hmphh," snorted Old Man Perkins from the depth of his leather chair. "I don't suppose one of those sharp pictures was one of me lending you that ten spot back in the fall of 1932?"

An eagle-eyed underling at *Tide* magazine spotted this catastrophic typographical error in the rules book of a very doggy women's club: "Officers must limit all announcements to three minutes. If they exceed their time, the president should use her navel to silence them." Muses the *Tide* man: "We hope Madame President has the stomach for that sort of thing."

A press agent for the Copacabana night club insists that a lady accosted another in the powder room, inquiring, "Haven't we met in Cannes?" "Which one?" said the other. "This one—or the one at the Colony?"

After a troupe of Spanish dancers had completed their act at the Shamrock Hotel's night club in Houston, a Texas oilman from the wide-open wells tapped the star on the shoulder and told her, "I shore liked them castanets, ma'am. My wife and I was wondering if you could show us how you wind them up."

Those dresses Marlene Dietrich wore in her personal-appearance junket at Las Vegas weren't as revealing as the papers would have had you believe. Marlene had them lined with flesh-colored silk, with necklaces and bracelets cleverly concealing the materials' ends. She had three gowns, all the same model, but different colors. "I told them: 'Put nothing on top,'" laughed Miss Dietrich. "Always when I appeared on a stage, people looked down at my legs. I got tired of seeing only the tops of people's heads, so this time I tell my designers I want people to look up. So they designed this dress. People looked up all right!"

Each dress set Miss Dietrich back $3,000—but, since her weekly stipend was just ten times that amount, she took the bill in stride. She also admits she lost, gambling. "I was at those slot machines every spare moment," she told me, "and I lost constantly." "How much in all?" I asked. "A lot," said Marlene. "Fifteen dollars!"

This may help explain why Marlene Dietrich is not only America's sexiest grandmother—but also its richest.

A famous dive near the Loop in Chicago was raided by the police, and such guests and entertainers who hadn't effected their escape via the windows were hustled into the patrol wagon. Miss Veronica Vere de Vere pushed everybody aside in her obvious desire to be first into the wagon. "What's the rush?" asked a cop. "I know what I'm doing," replied Miss Vere de Vere. "The last four raids I had to stand!"

Two of the moving spirits at a convention banquet drank so many toasts that finally they scarcely could move at all. "Lucky for me," one congratulated himself. "When I'm in this condition, I let somebody take me home and then I fall sound asleep the minute I hit the old bed."

"My trouble," confessed the other, "is hitting the old bed."

Two stories about intoxicants that seldom miss:

1. An intrepid explorer set out singlehanded for the Amazonian jungle in Brazil. Authorities equipped him with all the necessary gear, topped off with a miniature bottle of gin, another of vermouth, and a tiny mixer.

"What's this for?" asked the explorer. "You know I don't drink."

"That's in case you're hopelessly lost, without another human around for miles," was the answer. "Mix yourself a martini. Somebody's absolutely certain to pop up and tell you, 'Don't make it *that* way: make it *this* way.'"

2. A gent stepped up to a bar and asked for a martini compounded of twenty-four parts gin, one part vermouth. The bar-

tender, startled but game, said, "Yes, sir. Like a slice of lemon peel twisted in it?"

The gent grumbled, "If I want a lemonade, I'll ask for it."

Don Haggerty watched firemen extinguish a blaze in a Forty-fourth Street boardinghouse, and carry to safety the intoxicated gent in whose room the fire had originated. "Confound it," roared the chief, "haven't you got sense enough not to smoke in bed when you're in this condition?" The drunk protested mournfully, "Honest, Chief, I didn't set fire to that bed. It was burning already when I got into it!"

In his invaluable new treatise, *Never Say Diet*, Corey Ford claims that the following elbow exercise is bound to produce results: "Stand in vertical position, with elbows braced on edge of mahogany bar and right foot resting firmly on rail eight or ten inches above floor. Grasp glass in right hand and bend slowly until rim of glass touches lips. Lower elbow, refill glass, and repeat routine until chin is level with bar. Once proficiency has been attained, this exercise can even be continued in a horizontal position."

Fellow a little the worse for wear—and gin—stumbled into a taxi and ordered, "Take me over to Broadway and Forty-ninth Street." The driver informed him, "You're at Broadway and Forty-ninth Street right now." "Splendid," was the response. "Jush splendid. But next time, don't drive so fast!"

Fenwick suddenly planted his nineteenth highball on the bar, reeled dizzily across the saloon, and collapsed unconscious in a heap at the door. "That's the best thing about good old Fenwick's drinking," chirped a crony in admiration. "He always knows when to stop."

Far off in Switzerland, the touring proprietor of a bar and grill and an experienced guide were climbing up the Matterhorn, when they were caught in a snow slide. Ultimately a Saint Bernard dog toiled through to them, a keg of brandy tied under his chin. "Hurrah," cried the guide. "Here comes man's best friend."

"Yep," agreed the barman, "and look at the size of the dog that's bringing it!"

In an obscure gin parlor on Third Avenue, two gentlemen who were several sheets to the wind discovered, not only that both were Yale graduates, but were members of the same class. After many tearful embraces, and just before they both passed out cold, they swore to meet at this same bar, come hell or high water, ten years later to the day.

The first of them actually kept the date. He entered the gin parlor sheepishly, not believing there was one chance in a million the other would remember. But by all that was holy, there was Yale man Number Two propped up at the bar on the very stool he had occupied ten years before!

"What do you know!" marveled Number One. "I never dreamed you'd even be able to find this joint after ten long years!"

Number Two turned a bleary eye on him and growled, "Who left?"

A Wall Street broker encountered an old classmate who had fallen on evil days. Automatically he reached into his wallet and handed the down-and-outer a five-dollar bill. "What's this?" sneered the ungrateful recipient. "Two years ago you met me and gave me fifty bucks. Last year you retrenched to twenty. And now you hand me a measly five spot."

The trader, embarrassed, explained, "Two years ago I got married. Last year we had our first child. All those extra expenses and mouths to feed . . ."

"So that's it," roared the down-and-outer. "Raising a family on my dough, eh?"

"Has anybody ever offered you dinner in exchange for a respectable lick of work?" asked a Peoria lady as she regarded the seedy-looking tramp at her back door with obvious disapproval.

"Only once, ma'am," said the tramp hopefully. "Aside from that I've been shown nothing but kindness."

A wandering hobo had discovered through the years that doctors were comparatively soft touches, and his spirits rose when he saw a medico's shingle outside the door he was approaching. A beautiful young lady answered his peal on the bell. The hobo, looking as woebegone as possible, wheezed, "Do you think the good doctor could find an old pair of pants for an old fellow who's down on his luck?" The girl chuckled and replied, "Quite possibly, but I doubt that they'd do you much good. You see, I happen to be the doctor."

CHAPTER THIRTEEN

IT'S A BIG COUNTRY!

The Capital

At the height of the social season in the nation's capital, Senator Theodore Green of Rhode Island, a bachelor still at eighty-six, seemed a bit confused by it all. Over cocktails at a foreign embassy, a writer asked him how many parties he was attending that evening.

"Six," confessed the senator, and pulled out his pocket diary. "Trying to figure out where you're going next?" joshed the writer. "Not at all," replied the senator. "I'm trying to figure out where I am now!"

Another senator was buttonholed by Detroit industrialist Harvey Campbell, who demanded, "Look! I have the face of Claudette Colbert, the torso of Marilyn Monroe, and the legs of Betty Grable. Who am I?" "What do I care who you are?" cried the senator. "Kiss me!"

A passel of kids from one of those mammoth new city-housing projects was taken for a tour of Washington as an Easter-vacation treat. At Mount Vernon the guide announced, "This is where the father of our country made his home."

One youngster wasn't content with any such loose generalities. "On which floor," he demanded, "was his apartment?"

Secretary of Agriculture Ezra Benson found a small boy wandering disconsolately about the lobby one day, awaiting his father, who had business to transact with a minor executive in the Department. Benson told the lad, "If you've nothing to do for a while, why not go up that flight of stairs and have a look at the forty-foot mural on the next floor? I think you'll find it interesting."

The youngster bounded up the stairs three at a time, but a few moments later Secretary Benson's assistant came in, wondering, "Who could have sent an eight-year-old kid upstairs a few minutes ago to look for a forty-foot mule?"

Paul Pearlman, Washington's perennial handball champion, has a real tale of woe to unfold. It seems he followed a figure in a slinky black gown for ten blocks before he found out it was a Supreme Court justice.

Overworked girls in the Pentagon Building are circulating chain letters of their own:

"Fellow slaves! This is a plan to bring happiness and steak dinners to tired government working girls. It won't cost you a nickel. Simply send five copies of this letter to girls as under-privileged and neglected as yourself. Then tie up your boss and send him to the girl on the top of the list. When *your* name reaches the top, you will receive 12,938 bosses.

"Have faith! Don't break the chain! The last girl who did got her own boss back!"

New England

In his slightly biased *History of New England*, Will Cressy points out:

"New England consists of six states and Boston, which is frequently in an awful state."

"They do not 'till' the soil in New England. They blast it. The crops are planted in among the rocks with a beanshooter or a gun. They harvest them with search warrants."

"The Down-East Yankee has a keen gift of humor, because it is a gift."

"Statisticians have figured that, judging from the amount of furniture brought over in the *Mayflower*, the boat was slightly more than three miles long."

To which the late Fred Allen added, "Many typical New England seashore resorts are so dead, that the tide went out one day some years ago and never came back."

A poet on the *Old Farmers' Almanac* staff has a low opinion of Maine weather, if you can judge by the following:

> *Dirty days has September,*
> *April, June, and November.*
> *From January up to May*
> *It's pretty sure to rain each day.*
> *All the rest have thirty-one*
> *Without much chance of any sun*
> *And if one of them had two and thirty,*
> *They'd be just as wet and twice as dirty.*

In the old days of enormous country houses, there was one monster of a place in Lenox, Massachusetts, called "Shadowbrook." To show you how big it was, there's the story of the owner's son wiring from Yale, "Arriving this evening with crowd of seventy-six classmates." The owner wired back, "Sorry, but many guests already are here. Have room only for fifty."

It wasn't a very large motel and the smartest thing about it, apparently, was the live-wire bellboy. "What part of the country do you hail from?" asked an approving visitor. "Cape Cod, sir," said the bellboy. "I just knowed you was one of those shrewd Down-Easters," chuckled the visitor. "Only thing that surprises me is that you don't own the motel by this time." "There's one thing stopping me," explained the bellboy glumly. "The owner— he's from Cape Cod too."

Boston society folk, especially those living on or adjacent to Louisburg Square, dwell in a world of their own.

One old blue blood, for instance, eighty-five if she was a day, insisted on swimming at Bar Harbor far into September, though the ocean water by that time was absolutely freezing. Her friend saw her bobbing about in the surf one day when a big seal splashed right by her. When she finished her swim she was neither frightened nor even titillated by the unusual experience

—just very, very angry. "That Mr. Abernathy," she grumbled, "gets ruder every day. He swam right by me and never even said 'good morning.'"

Ted Weeks, editor of the *Atlantic Monthly* and authority on all matters pertaining to Boston, swears this happened. Two old Brahmins from Louisburg Square were dining in the Harvard Club and discussing the career of an old classmate who had defied tradition and gone down to Washington to assume a post in the Cabinet. "They say Bob is doing quite well," allowed the first Bostonian. "Making quite a reputation for himself." "I suppose he is," conceded the other grudgingly, "but purely in the national sense."

"Harvard graduates," observed Clip Amory, "are a conservative lot. Twenty years after a Harvard man has left the campus, you can tell by his suit he's from Cambridge." "Sure," agreed a Yale alumnus nearby, "because it's the same suit."

A group of hidebound old blue bloods in Boston were invited to a formal garden party one day this summer, and were startled to discover that the host, who had acquired a New Hampshire wild-animal farm without their being told about it (a sin in itself), had brought a few beasties down with him to help entertain his guests. One of the beasties, for instance, was a baby elephant! John Marquand relates that the most conservative and dignified of the guests so far forgot himself as to essay a playful slap on the elephant's rump. Unfortunately he was not familiar with the toughness of an elephant's epidermis. Result: several broken blood vessels in his right hand. He had to wear his arm in a sling for weeks.

The South

Lewis Gannett, distinguished book reviewer for the New York *Herald Tribune* put down with a sigh the sixth long novel about the Civil War he had read in two weeks. "The old question of who really won the War between the States has been settled at last," he said. "Clearly, it was the National Association of Book Publishers!"

Nobel Prize-winning novelist William Faulkner, however, enters this demur from an unreconstructed rebel in Mississippi: "Confound it, suh, if the South had had that atom bomb, we'd have cleaned out them damyankees in two weeks flat!"

The late Joe Palmer told about a newly elected senator from Tennessee who was making his way through Kentucky at a time when horseback was the only mode of travel in those parts. He tarried for the night at a stately plantation near Harrodsburg, where he was offered some delicious home-brewed bourbon, served neat in a water glass.

The Tennessean inquired tactfully if his host was acquainted with a delicious concoction called a julep, and learning with surprise that it was unknown in that part of Kentucky, dispatched flunkies forthwith to pick some mint from the banks of a neighboring stream. He thereupon made some of the darndest juleps in the history of choice beverages.

This was in April. The senator came back that way again in October, but though the servants greeted him ecstatically, the master of the house failed to put in an appearance. "No, suh, he ain't here no mo'," reported the head servant mournfully. "He took to his bed right after yo' teached him to put grass in his whisky and jus' plain drunk hisself to death."

Marion Montgomery passes along a story about the old family retainer of the president of a small college down South. The prexy's wife discovered that a cherished friend was moving into the neighborhood and asked the family retainer to go over and help her get moved in properly.

The retainer, her mission accomplished, returned to announce emphatically, "I ain't nevah goin' there no more. Dem folks just ain't quality. Dat friend of yours eben washes her own windows."

"But, Lucy," protested the prexy's wife, "you've seen me wash my windows too."

"Yes'm," admitted the retainer, "but dat woman knows *how*."

Reports an English visitor to Charleston, South Carolina: "On my way to the hotel, I decided to pick up a couple of American shirts, so I told my taxi driver to stop at the first haberdashery he encountered. 'Yes, sir,' said the driver, but when we were stopped by a red light, inquired, 'What was that you said, boss?' 'A haberdashery,' I repeated. 'Yes, sir,' he agreed again, 'a haberdashery it is.' We rattled along a couple of blocks and then he stopped once more. 'Listen, boss,' he assured me. 'With me there's no use beating round the bush. What is it you want? Liquor—or women?' "

In Red Springs, North Carolina, Flora Perry, librarian of the exclusive Flora McDonald College for the cream of Southern womanhood, noticed that an old Negro in the beautiful gardens always was on the job a full hour before any of his fellows. It was no urge to better his position in life, he hastened to explain to Miss Perry. "No, *ma'am*," he continued. "I just likes to breathe air early before other folks have a chance to be sniffin' off'n it."

Pastor Johnson preached long and earnestly about Jonah and the whale at an old colored Baptist church in Mississippi but made little impression on Sister Abernethy. On her way home, she scoffed, "What's so wonderful 'bout dat Jonah spendin' three days in de stummick of a whale? Mah husban' spent longer dan dat in de stummick of an alligator." "Sure 'nough?" asked an incredulous stranger in town. "How long would you say?" Sister Abernethy did some hasty calculating, then announced, "It's goin' on three years now."

The late Lyle Saxon was slaving over a manuscript on the

plantation of a friend outside Baton Rouge one day when the old mammy who kept his quarters in order inquired, "How come, Mr. Saxon, you spend all yo' workin' hours peckin' away at dat typewriter 'stead of bein' out huntin' and golfin' wid yo' friends?" "Because I'm an author, Mammy," explained Saxon. "Writing books is my business. This is my fifth I'm working on now. Right here on the shelf are the other four I've written."

Mammy's face was a picture of commiseration. "You poor soul," she clucked. "You never sold a one of dem, did you?"

Carl Carmer tells about a great big husky farm hand on an Alabama plantation who had a fantastic reputation with every lady within a radius of thirty miles. One day his boss said, "Mose, I'd like for you to visit my friend Colonel Parker's place over in Louisiana. He's got seventy-three gals working for him and nary one man, and I told him you'd be just the man to remedy a situation like that." "Just how far from here," inquired Mose, "is that place of Colonel Parker's?" "Two hundred and forty-two miles," said the boss. "Anything you say," declared Mose dubiously, "but that's a mighty big distance to travel for just one day's work!"

Colonel Worthington appeared on the veranda of his Alabama mansion and announced emphatically, "There are two things, suh, we don't stand for in the sovereign state of Alabama. One is sectional prejudices and the other is damn Yankees."

Miss Jeannie-Mae Beaufort, belle of a Mississippi town, was walking to the beauty shop when she became aware that she was being followed. For a time she pretended not to notice, but finally, becoming really perturbed, she wheeled to face the offender. To her surprise, it was gallant old Colonel Trombley, the town's only authentic military hero.

The colonel was in no way flustered. "Good morning to you, Miss Jeannie-Mae," he said with a flourish of his fedora. "I've been having a debate with myself for six blocks: whether to catch up with you and enjoy the repartee, or linger behind and enjoy the view."

A Northerner insulted a South Carolina bartender by asking anxiously, "Are you quite sure you know how to mix a very dry martini?" The bartender gave him a withering look and drawled, "Mister, ah been mixin' martinis heah fo' nine yeahs—an' in that time ah've used exactly two bottles of vermouth!"

Time was when only millionaires sneaked off to Florida and California when the snow began to fly. Today everybody's doing it. They tell of a meeting, for instance, that took place on the sands of Miami Beach between the wives of two rival cutters in the cloak-and-suit industry. "I'm here for the whole winter," boasted one. "Four months solid! And you?" "Five weeks, I'm afraid," was the answer, "is all I can manage this year." "Tsk! Tsk!" clucked the first with mock sympathy. "So your husband isn't working again?"

In Miami Beach, the aging author of a half dozen inspirational novels turned up with a ravishing if gaboring miss in tow, explaining she was his "niece." The niece walked out on him three days later, disillusioned with the literary life. "Not only did he lie to me about the size of his yacht," she complained to newsman Jack Kofoed, "but he made me do the rowing."

A successful young lady designer of men's sportswear, vacationing at Daytona Beach, was delighted to see a stalwart youth approach, sporting a pair of print bathing trunks she had originated. Becoming conscious of her stare, he flushed slightly, and asked, "Have we met somewhere?" "I never saw you in my life," chuckled the young lady. "I just have designs on you."

The Florida real-estate boom in the twenties provided shoe-string operators and gold brickers a field day the like of which they've never enjoyed since. At its height—just before the boom was lowered—any subdivision that cost less than five million (all on paper) was regarded as smalltime stuff.

Kenneth Roberts tells of one impressive group who engaged a sign painter to erect a billboard proclaiming, "A five-million-dollar hotel and golf course will be erected on this spot." Unfortunately, the impressive group couldn't raise the eighteen dollars to pay for the sign, so the painter carted it away and sold it to another bunch of capitalists on the next beach.

"How much," asked Mr. Lapidus, "is that new hotel at Miami Beach?"

"I'll tell you, Joe, how to estimate your bill," advised a friend who had just flown back to New York. "Guess the highest you can imagine—then add 25 per cent! I myself pulled a boner when I asked for a forty-dollar suite. They handed me a Hershey Bar.

"There's a seven-piece orchestra in the men's room! That was too much even for a big spender like Jack Benny. He said a pianist and violinist would be plenty.

"The barbershop looks so elegant, I didn't dare go in until I had shaved in my room. All the signs are in French. Nobody understands what they mean, but it adds class. And in every room they have wall-to-wall carpeting!"

"So what," interrupted Lapidus. "New York hotels have that too."

His friend demanded, *"On the ceilings?"*

Comes the end of summer and residents along the Atlantic seaboard start watching anxiously for hurricane warnings, ready to batten down all hatches if the big winds begin to blow. In early fall the hurricanes—furious winds swirling counterclockwise over a diameter of fifty to three hundred miles—sweep up from the West Indies. Most of them spend their force harmlessly at sea, but occasionally they are diverted over Florida and up through New England.

That spells trouble—and plenty of it. A 1938 hurricane, for

instance, left about five hundred deaths and a quarter of a billion dollars' worth of damage in its wake.

One "native son" in Florida refused to be discouraged when a hurricane carried his whole house away. He rebuilt on the old foundations, maintaining stoutly, "This is the world's greatest spot—especially when it's standing still."

They have "big blows" in Oklahoma too. Legend has it that one "twister" blew a farmer off his buckboard, and pinned him flatter than a pancake to the side of the barn. Relatives scraped him off, but while they were carting him into the house, another gust blew him out of the wheelbarrow and back into natural shape.

Why do vicious hurricanes bear lovely girls' names, with no Tom, Dick, or Harry having the ghost of a chance to get into the act? It all started in 1941, when a University of California professor named George Stewart wrote a rousing novel called *Storm*. An immediate best seller and still widely read in a reprint edition, *Storm* tells how a minuscule weather disturbance off the coast of Japan could develop into a raging torrent by the time it swept across the U.S.

A junior meteorologist in Stewart's novel called the particular storm he was tracing after a girl he knew: "Maria." U. S. Weather Bureau operatives followed suit. So did military personnel in World War II. The practice was made official in 1953. Now the names of hurricanes are solemnly chosen at the beginning of each year by the big brass. It was hurricanes "Carol" and "Edna" that caused such devastation in the late summer of 1954.

Most of the public approves of designating hurricanes by girls' names, though malcontents still clamor for other systems, such as numbers (1,2,3), letters (A,B,C), animals (Antelope, Bear, Coyote), and Lord knows what else.

Movie star Zsa Zsa Gabor (or her press agent) also demurred at the selection of "Zelda" for the tag end of a recent line-up. "Zelda indeed," she pouted. "Why not Zsa Zsa? Anyhow, by the time they reach 'Z' there won't be any wind left. For next year, I demand that they start the list backward."

Texas

At a dinner party down South, Peter Lind Hayes refereed a hassle between a proud daughter of Kentucky and an equally proud son of Texas. The fur—and the boasts—flew in all directions.

"Why, we have so much solid gold stored in Kentucky," concluded the young lady, "we could build a wall of the stuff, ten feet high and four feet thick, clear around the borders of Texas."

The Texan smiled tolerantly. "Go right ahead and build it, honey," he urged, "and if we like it, we'll buy it!"

It's tough to get the last word in with a Texan, regardless of the circumstances. Jerry Coleman, for instance, back in big-league baseball after a distinguished tour of duty as a pilot in Korea, tells about a group of GI's over there who came upon a remarkably small horse tethered to a post.

"Gosh all hemlock," said one soldier, "I'll bet that's the smallest horse in the whole wide world."

"You're crazy," contradicted a recruit from Texas. "In the Lone-Star State, man, we got horses that's as little as two of that one!"

A Texas zillionaire decided to bestow a modest gift of $500,000 upon a university not far from Houston. One newspaper, however, made a slight mistake in its report of the bequest. It said that the gift was five million.

Fortunately, the zillionaire and the owner of the paper are friends. So there was not too much anger in the voice of the zillionaire when he phoned.

"I don't suppose I can make a liar out of that sheet of yours," he grumbled. "Since you said so, I'll make the gift five million this time. But confound it: don't let this happen again!"

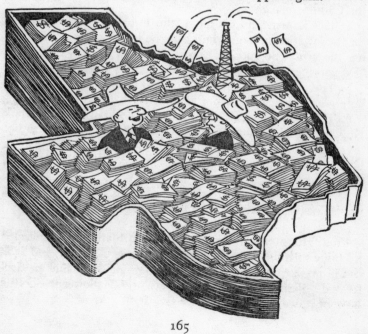

Another tycoon from Texas drove his air-conditioned limousine up to New York, but rebelled at paying a fifty-cent toll to cross the George Washington Bridge. "Son," he informed the attendant, "I never carry anything less than a $500 bill. *How much do you want for the bridge?*"

No collection of stories about Texas is considered official unless it includes at least two of these time-honored stand-bys:

1. The Texas governor who decided to collect miniatures and announced, "I'm agoin' to start with Rhode Island." (Alternate: the kid from San Antone who was put out in the final round of a spelling bee. He couldn't spell S-M-A-L-L.)

2. The oilman from Tyler, Texas, who got his first look at the Eiffel Tower and conceded, "Right purty. How many barrels does it produce?"

3. The Dallas school kids who sing, "The butcher, the baker, the Cadillac maker."

4. The farmer who consulted the Lubbock weather bureau for the latest reports on a hurricane he had heard was threatening the area. "Be specific," ordered the harassed weatherman. "Do you mean the eastbound or the westbound hurricane?"

5. The old judge in Pecos who recalled the day he gave "an ornery hoss thief twenty-four years to leave Texas."

6. The Houstonian who was having a cocktail atop the Mark Hopkins Hotel in San Francisco. "How do you like that sunset over the Golden Gate?" enthused his host. The Texan made a mighty effort to be polite. "It's really not bad," he conceded, "for a small town."

7. The luckiest Texan of them all. His fifty thousand head of prize blue-ribbon cattle suddenly started gushing oil!

From Houston a husband returned to Flatbush and dazzled his bride with the gift of three sable coats, two Jaguars, and $30,-000 in tax-exempt bonds. "It's really nothing, lambkin," he deprecated. "Remember I was in Texas over Halloween. For the heck of it, we spent an hour playing trick or treat."

Deep in the part of Texas near Waco, there's a town that boasts one of America's few remaining hand-set newspapers—a journal, furthermore, whose running battle with the demon rum has caused reverberations as far away as the Cork Club in Houston's Hotel Shamrock and the Bucket of Blood Saloon in Virginia City, Nevada. Here's one of the doughty editor's most recent blasts, which has become so popular that some people carry it around in their pockets in mimeographed form:

"If you must sully our community's fair name by guzzling liquor, why not start a saloon in your own home? Be the only customer and you won't have to buy a license.

"Give your wife twelve dollars to buy a gallon of whisky. There are one hundred and twenty-eight snorts in a gallon. If you pay your wife the prevailing exorbitant rate of forty cents a snort, in four days, when you've lapped up the gallon, your wife will have thirty-nine dollars and twenty cents to put in the bank, not to mention twelve dollars to start up in business again.

"If you can hang on in this fashion for ten years, before dying from D.T.'s, your wife will have approximately thirty-five thousand, seven hundred fifty dollars and fifty cents on deposit—enough to bury you respectably, bring up your children, buy a house and lot, marry a decent man—and forget she ever knew you!"

John Henry Faulk once roomed with a Texan who was deeply religious—but lazy as they come. He had a prayer framed right over his bed, so every night he could slide blissfully between the sheets, point to the prayer, and say, "Yep, them's my sentiments."

The West

Not long ago, the editors of the *Farmer-Stockman* printed a picture of a deserted farmhouse in a desolate, sand-swept field, then offered a prize for the best hundred-word essay on the disastrous effects of land erosion. A bright Indian lad from Oklahoma bagged the trophy with this graphic contribution:

"Picture show why white man crazy. Cut down trees. Make too big tepee. Plow hill, water wash. Wind blow soil. Grass gone. Door gone. Window gone. Squaw gone. Whole place gone to hell. No pig. No corn. No pony.

"Indian no plow land. Keep grass. Buffalo eat grass. Indian eat buffalo. Hide make plenty big tepee. Make moccasin. All time eat. Indian no hunt job. No work. No hitchhike. No ask relief. No build dam. No give dam.

"White man heap crazy."

The Indians out West finally were convinced the white men were plumb loco when they imported a herd of camels to the deserts of Arizona and California. That was back in 1856. Harlan D. Fowler tells the story in a book published by the Stanford University Press. The camels were the bright idea of the U. S. Army, when Jeff Davis was Secretary of War, and, until the railroads supplanted them, did quite a job hauling heavy freight across barren desert stretches.

In 1864, a wily promoter in Sacramento rounded up ten of the camels and staged a race on which white men wagered thousands. The Indians knew that nothing under the sun could make a camel run when he wasn't in the mood. The animals broke from the barrier briskly enough, but, as the Indians had predicted, soon lost interest and, while the gallery jeered, stopped dead in their tracks.

The race was won by a resourceful rider who abandoned his camel and crossed the finish line in triumph astride a spavined mule.

Giving a penny back on every empty beer can, surmised Orville Reed, could do more for the scenic beauty of America than three new national parks.

There is just one spot in the U.S.A. where it's possible for a person to stand in four states at the same time. Look at a map and you'll see that it's at the southwestern tip of Colorado, with New Mexico to the south, Utah to the west, and Arizona to the southwest. (This is the kind of knowledge that wins thousand-dollar jackpots in TV quiz programs!)

Arizona is one state where most of the citizens are a little smarter than the average. They have to be, a man in Phoenix explained to me, because they've got Californians bang up next to them on one side and Texans mighty close to them on the other —not to mention city slickers like author Bud Kelland, architect Frank Lloyd Wright, columnist Westbrook Pegler and publisher Ed Meredith in their midst every winter. Wright is the man who once defined a New Yorker as "an Arizonian with an ulcer."

Arizona's population is soaring percentagewise faster than any other state, since new and needed underground water supplies were developed a few years ago. Where water exists, the natives tell you, "All you've got to do is plant a seed, spit on it—and duck." Newcomers are pouring in so fast that the latest census revealed an increase of over 50 per cent in ten short years!

The spanking new airport at Phoenix cost seven million dollars—and looks it. It's a far cry from an old field nearby where Clark Gable some years ago made a picture about the then fledgling Air Force.

They gave him his part when he appeared for the first day's shooting. He read the trite lines with mounting dismay, then begged, "Have a heart, boys. Don't make me go up in a script like this!"

Since Palm Springs and adjacent California desert land have become a favorite vacation spot for Hollywood's "elite," some hundred miles to the westward, less spectacular visitors from other parts of the country blow in expecting almost anything to happen—and it often does.

Instead of "getting away from it all," the movie folk generally bring it with them. None of their didos, however, seem to startle the casual tourist more than a pamphlet freely distributed at all shops and roadside barbecues. It is called *The Sex Life of the Date.*

It is a strange fact that a date-palm grove is very much like a sultan's harem, with one "male" tree supporting as many as seventy "female" trees. The latter carry clusters of flowers that look lovely, but are for some reason repellent to bees and other insects. The date trees require, therefore, man's help in the rite of pollination.

Then they produce a fruit so dainty it carries a parasol during the ripening season, so sweet it is called "the candy that grows on trees," so nourishing that millions of desert dwellers, from biblical times to the present, have made it the principal item of their daily diet.

This information proved particularly surprising to one famous motion-picture producer. "A sex life for dates!" he echoed unbelievingly. "I always thought they grew on fig trees!"

An old soldiers' organization held its annual powwow in sunny San Diego this year, with headquarters at the commodious U. S. Grant Hotel. One veteran from Alabama found himself in something of a dilemma. "I cain't send mah friends a picture post card even," he wailed. "If they all saw the name of the hotel ah'm patronizin', they'd run me out of the county when ah came home!"

Bob Campbell has preserved a typical weather report from a tourist-conscious resort in southern California: "Rain and heavy winds all yesterday and today. Continued fair tomorrow."

Just before Goodwin Knight took office in Sacramento as governor of California, he found himself aboard a train with a group of lunatics being carted off to an asylum. The guard was counting them off. "One, two, three, four," when he stumbled into Goodie Knight. "Who are you?" demanded the guard. Knight drew himself up and announced proudly, "You are addressing the next governor of California." "Okay," said the guard. "Get in line. Five, six, seven, eight . . ."

When the Shriners convened in Los Angeles one year, a main boulevard was roped off for their climactic parade, and only official cars, prominently marked "Potentate," "Past Potentate," and the like, were permitted to use the thoroughfare for hours preceding the big march. One smart lawyer, anxious to avoid a detour that would make him thirty minutes late for his golf game, devised a sign for his car that got him right through the police barrier and enabled him to sail majestically up the empty boulevard. His sign proclaimed: "Past Participle!"

California boosters take a dim view of tall claims made by their neighbors in Texas. "That's why I'm so anxious for Alaska to win statehood," explained a California politician to me recently. "It will make Texas only the *second* largest state!

"I suppose you know what our flag will look like if they make Hawaii a state?" continued the politician. "Forty-eight stars and a pineapple!"

When a new lighthouse was erected on a dangerous shore off a wild stretch of coast in the Northwest, a couple of Eskimos appointed themselves "sidewalk superintendents." They studied every detail of construction and, when the lighthouse began functioning, were on hand day and night to watch operations. Then a heavy fog blew in. The light revolved and the foghorn tooted continuously. One Eskimo turned triumphantly to the other. "I told you white igloo builder big bum," he exulted. "Light shine, bell ding-dong, horn woo-woo, but fog come rolling in just the same."

CHAPTER FOURTEEN

KEEP MOVING

Automobiles

A kindly Cadillac owner spied the driver of an old Model-T Ford
in difficulties at a roadside and offered to tow him to the nearest
garage. Along the way, he forgot all about his tow, and ran his
speed up to ninety miles an hour with the Ford careening madly
in his wake. A state trooper set out in pursuit, but was soon outdistanced. He phoned a side-kick twenty miles ahead and warned,
"Get the driver of a green Cadillac coming your way. I'll bet he's
doing a hundred." "Okay," was the reply. "And that isn't all,"
added the first trooper. "I don't expect you to believe me, but

there's a loon in a Model-T Ford right behind that Cadillac, blowing his horn like crazy and trying to pass."

"I hear you picked up another beautiful girl this evening," said one motorist enviously to another. "How on earth do you do it?" "Simplest thing in the world," boasted the successful Romeo. "A mere case of winkin', blinkin', and nod."

"What is the thing I'm most anxious to get out of my new car?" grinned a businessman in answer to an advertising expert's question. "That's easy! My seventeen-year-old son!"

One of the big automobile companies had just unveiled its new models for the year, and the Long Island distributor cunningly displayed the most expensive one in his beautifully decorated showroom to its fullest advantage. An insurance underwriter was one of many whose power of resistance was broken down completely. He walked in, made out a check, and announced, "I want that one in the window." "Splendid," enthused the salesman. "Do you want to drive it home immediately or shall we deliver it?" "Just leave it where it is," requested the buyer. "I'll never find such a fine parking space for it again!"

Two taxis banged into one another in front of the CBS Building on Fifty-second Street. "Wottzamatter?" hollered the driver of one. "Ya blind?" The other promptly countered, "Blind? I hit ya, didn't I?"

Fifty years ago, when an automobile still made people come running blocks to gape and horses shy in their traces, Colonel H. Nelson Jackson made the first transcontinental motor tour in history. He set out from San Francisco on May 23, 1903, and wound up on Fifth Avenue, New York, exactly sixty-three days later, after a series of adventures that included mudholes, unbridged mountain streams, and journeys across untracked and uncharted desert wastes.

One of Colonel Jackson's most unnecessary detours was near Marysville, California, when a girl's misdirection sent him on a fifty-mile wild-goose chase. After he had retraced the ground, he asked the girl, "Why did you send us the wrong way?" "It was so my paw and maw could get a look at you," she told him shamelessly. "They never seen an automobile. And if you're aiming to go clear to New York, a few more miles ain't going to hurt you none!"

Lady Drivers

How quickly can a joke get round the whole U.S.A.?

A Boston columnist, with some space to fill, made up a story about a motorist whose car stalled on the Merritt Parkway. He stopped a lady driver and asked her to give him a push, telling her, "You'll have to get up to about thirty-five miles an hour to really get me rolling." He thereupon climbed into his jalopy, took the wheel, and waited for the push. It was a bit tardy in coming, so he stole a look behind him. There was the lady—bearing down on him at thirty-five miles an hour! "The damage to the man's car," concluded the imaginative columnist, "was approximately three hundred dollars."

Well, there wasn't too much real news that day, and the Associated Press sent the story out over its wires. Result: about five hundred newspapers printed it as gospel, and about fourteen radio and TV comics made it famous inside of a single day from Connecticut to Oregon!

The State Farm Mutual Automobile Insurance Company, of Bloomington, Illinois, has a terrific jolt in store for complacent male drivers who explain every mishap on the open road with a condescending, "I'll bet there was a woman at the wheel!"

Vice-President Tom Morrill writes me, "In the past three years, housewives have ranked twenty-eighth best in a list of sixty-four occupational classes in the safe handling of private passenger cars—and we have the statistics to prove it."

Morrill pours salt into male wounds by adding that auto salesmen trail in thirty-second place, doctors in thirty-ninth, truck drivers in forty-third, lawyers in fiftieth, the clergy (whose minds obviously are on higher things) in fifty-fifth, and traveling salesmen and students near the end of the pack in sixty-first and sixty-second places respectively.

The only cheering note I can find in these doleful tidings is in the standing of editors, reporters, and photographers: twenty-sixth.

I'll have to take Mr. Morrill's word for it that lady drivers have become more proficient than was their wont, but their tongues certainly get sharper all the time.

Take the case of the reckless speeder who was hauled before a judge in a Los Angeles traffic court recently.

The judge delivered quite a sermon, but the lady driver wasn't having any of it.

"Aren't you the eloquent one?" she sneered. "I'll bet you can recite Lincoln's Gettysburg Address by heart, too."

"I'm proud to say I can," admitted the judge, "and I hereby fine you fourscore and seven bucks."

A Boston policeman waved a lady motorist over to the curb and complained, "Madam, why have you no red light on the rear of your car?" "Officer," she answered angrily, "it is not that kind of a car."

"Our new power brakes are out of this world," a salesman for the Indestructible Eight told a prospective lady customer. "Now with that equipment, instead of running over a victim, you can stop squarely on top of him."

Vic Flanders, of Norfolk, Virginia, writes that his wife insisted upon taking driving lessons despite his strenuous objections. The first day she was alone at the wheel, he spotted her at a distance of three blocks wobbling uncertainly toward their residence. He rushed inside, double-locked the door, ran up three flights of stairs to his private study, and took refuge under the desk. "It wasn't any use," he admits. "She got me anyhow."

Mr. Flanders adds that, despite the snapshot enclosed with his letter, his car is not a foreign make—when his wife got through with it the steering wheel was on the right side.

M. Kadison, the millionaire broker, is another roads scholar who seems to be in trouble as soon as his wife takes the wheel. One day she complained, "Just look how close to us that lunatic ahead is driving!" Another time she explained her erratic steering with "I washed the car a couple of hours ago, and now I can't do a thing with it."

After smacking head on into a parked moving van, she announced with some satisfaction, "This is one time I've beaten that fifty-dollar-deductible clause, anyhow!"

One kind of driver who is a perpetual menace is the lady gadabout who plasters stickers all over a car from every hamlet, waterfall, and nutburger stand visited en route. Charles Mabie, in New Orleans, has a neighbor who goes in heavily for such stickers. Notes Mr. Mabie:

> *She's been around, it's evident*
> *From all those stickers showing,*
> *But due to flaunting where she's been,*
> *She can't see where she's going!*

Aviation

A veteran pilot on one of the transcontinental air lines discovered early in his career that one gentlemen's washroom on a plane carrying over sixty passengers poses certain problems. He has solved them for himself very neatly, however. Now, whenever he wishes to wash up, he just lights up the panel reading "Kindly fasten all seat belts," gives the customers half a minute to comply—then saunters majestically to the convenience.

The hostess on a stratocruiser was saying good-by to the passengers at the end of the flight, when her eyes suddenly glazed with horror, and she grabbed by the arm one gent whose pants had fallen around his shoes. "*Mister* Goppelheimer," she said severely, "it was your *safety belt* I told you to unfasten."

Another passenger who experienced seat-belt trouble was a Montana cowboy. He just would not fasten his safety belt. "Missy," he informed the stewardess firmly, "for nigh on twenty years I've rode everything I ever mounted, and I don't aim to be saddle-tied at this stage of the game. Let 'er buck! I'll ride 'er!"

The pilot of a new jet plane was winging over the Berkshires and pointed out a pleasant valley to his second in command. "See that spot?" he demanded. "When I was a barefoot kid I used to sit in a flat-bottom rowboat down there, fishing. Every time a plane flew by, I'd look up and dream I was piloting it. Now I look down and dream I'm fishing!"

In the flight kitchen of United Airlines in Chicago, they estimate that passengers travel approximately 25 miles while they toy with their appetizer, 110 miles while they eat the main course, 40 miles for the salad, and 55 more during dessert. In other words, a single dinner goes a long ways—230 miles!

The publication of Charles Lindbergh's *The Spirit of St. Louis* calls to mind a story that was popular in publishing circles just after Lindbergh had completed his epoch-making flight to Paris. George Palmer Putnam was smart enough to sign him up for a "quickie" book about his exploit, and the hastily written *We* became a great best seller overnight. Lindbergh, shy and reserved, wouldn't let his publisher become overfriendly. "In fact," recalled Mr. Putnam, "I couldn't get the time of day out of him until I came round with his first royalty check. It was for an even hundred thousand dollars. This will unbend him, I told myself. I was partly right too. He glanced at the check, smiled briefly, and commented, 'On this basis, you can come around more often.'"

Dr. Morris Fishbein knows a man in the luggage business who has a unique system for enjoying his vacation. "I drive out to the airport," he said. "Just to see the planes take off and arrive?" asked Dr. Fishbein. "Nah," scoffed the luggage man. "Who cares about planes? But I get genuine pleasure from seeing the redcaps scuff up the suitcases."

A huge air liner, with all sixty seats occupied, zoomed over the state insane asylum, and the pilot burst into loud laughter. "What's so funny?" demanded the hostess. "I was just thinking," replied the pilot, "what a commotion there'll be in that joint when they discover I've escaped!"

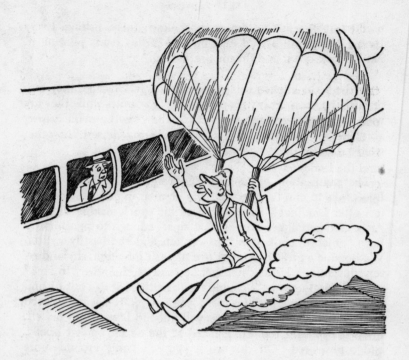

Mr. Gordon was dreaming of a play with two characters and one set that would run for eight thousand consecutive performances—while on a plane making a routine flight from New York to Chicago. Suddenly he looked up to see a parachutist drift past his window. "Care to join me?" hollered the parachutist. "Think I'm nuts?" responded Mr. Gordon. "I'm staying right here." "Have it your way," conceded the parachutist. "I'm your pilot."

General Jimmy Doolittle shared a seat in a transatlantic passenger plane with a young fellow who had been in the parachute troops throughout World War II. As the plane prepared to land at Paris, Doolittle noted that the paratrooper grew increasingly nervous. "What's the matter, my boy," scoffed the general. "Forgotten that you've been in a thousand planes before?"

"It isn't that, General," said the paratrooper earnestly. "This is the first time I've ever landed!"

George Jessel flew out to the Nevada desert, firmly convinced that after years of effort he finally had lined up a job for his Cousin Max—in the H-bomb tests. At the last minute, however, officials decided to use goats.

Georgie also reported the singular case of the flying saucer that landed in a dairy farm. The weird occupants poured out, and the leader leveled a new-fangled shooting iron at the nearest cow. "No stalling now," barked the leader. "Take us to your president!"

Railroads

A mentally disturbed patient was discharged as cured by an expert and given a job as gateman at a railroad intersection where traffic was not very heavy. There were, in fact, only two trains a day. One, up from the south, sped past the crossing precisely at noon each day; the other, bound from east to west, rattled by thirty minutes later. The new gateman waved at the engineers of the two trains each day and spent the rest of the time in peaceful contemplation. So did an old man named Heimerdinger who came down every morning to keep him company.

One day the gateman's phone rang. The train from the south, reported a dispatcher down the line, was a half hour late. "Take the necessary precautions," he warned. "I will," promised the gateman.

Hurrying from the booth, he pulled Mr. Heimerdinger to his feet and suggested, "I think it will be safer watching from the top of the hill today. And keep your eyes peeled too—because at twelve-thirty on the dot there's going to be the gosh-darnedest train wreck you ever saw in your life!"

Colonel Sam Fordyce, president of the Cotton Belt Railroad, was once on an inspection trip when his special train came to a grinding halt. Stepping out on the platform, the colonel found a gun jabbed into his ribs, while a gruff voice commanded, "Stick 'em up!"

The colonel recognized the voice. It was that of an old two-by-four bandit named Shang Doland, whom the colonel had saved from jail on two previous occasions. "Why, Shang," said the colonel softly. "Ain't you ashamed to come over on the Cotton Belt and try to rob a road as poor as this one? Don't you know that folks with big bank rolls never ride the Cotton Belt? Why don't you go over and hold up the Iron Mountain?"

The bandit was truly abashed. He pulled off his mask and said, "Colonel, I never would have held up this here special if I'd known it was yourn." He rounded up his accomplices, and off they galloped into the night. He took the colonel's advice, too. Couple of nights later he and his boys held up a northbound Iron Mountain train out of Texarkana, and got away with the haul of a lifetime.

A historian for the New York Central Railroad asserts that it was at Montrose, New York, back in 1870, that the line tried out the first device that enabled locomotives to pick up water without stopping. Employees soon referred to the process as "jerking water," and consequently Montrose became known as a "jerk-water" town. Today, of course, a jerk-water town is any pleasant little place where somebody you don't like happens to live.

Jim Barnes recalls a day when multimillionaire J. P. Morgan had to interrupt an Adirondack vacation to resolve a sudden crisis in Wall Street. He telegraphed the president of the New York Central Railroad that the ten twenty-four train was to be flagged for him at Paul Smith's station.

Arrived at the station, Mr. Morgan noted that the one man on duty had his feet planted unconcernedly on his desk, and was

reading a sports gazette. "How about getting up and flagging that ten twenty-four like you've been ordered?" thundered J. P. "Not me," said the unconcerned railroad employee.

So J. P. dug up a red flag and waved it furiously at the oncoming train. After it had ground to a stop, he discovered that Paul Smith's was a regular scheduled stop for the ten twenty-four.

A New England miss, visiting in Richmond, asked an outstanding citizen of those parts, "What sort of plant is a Virginia creeper?" Sadly he replied, "It is not a plant, miss. It's a railroad."

An old settler from Arkansas vows that his paw once decided to commit suicide, so he lay down on the tracks three miles ahead of the fastest express train in the state—and starved to death before it got there.

The engineer of this express, incidentally, made one unscheduled stop every day to pick up a dozen fresh-laid eggs from his cousin, who ran a farm ninety miles north of Little Rock. One day his cousin hailed him with the usual, "Hi, Cousin Abernathy," but this time added, "Ye'll have to keep them passengers waitin' a few minutes extry today. I got eleven eggs so far, but one hen is on the nest now, and that twelfth one ought to be along right soon."

In Wall Street they're telling about the commuter who saw the gate to the four-fifty train slam in his face, but was consoled to note that a darling little blonde had missed the train too. "What say we spend the time until the six thirty-one together?" he proposed. "Delighted," said she. "Let's go up to my place. It's cool and quiet, and I'll fix you a better drink than they serve in this neighborhood!"

Eventually the commuter arrived home, feeling no pain. "Well," said his wife, "what's the alibi this time?"

"No alibi," he protested. "I missed my train, that's all. But a darling little blonde let me idle the hours of waiting away in her duplex apartment."

"Ha, ha," jeered his wife. "Some dreamer! Now tell me who you played cards with—and how much you lost."

Commuters on the Long Island and New Haven railroads will lend a particularly sympathetic ear to a tale unwound by Robert J. Casey in his new book, *Chicago Medium Rare*. A trainload of passengers aboard a Northwestern Elevated Express was suddenly stranded at the Addison Street station. Seems the motorman heard a wild burst of cheering from the Cubs' baseball park as he brought his train to a stop and, unable to resist the temptation, unhooked his control, opened the door, and hotfooted it for the bleachers, where he arrived for the climax of a wild seventh-inning rally. The elevated line, meanwhile, was tied up for forty-five minutes while the management sought frantically to dig up a new motorman who cared only for the White Sox.

"So all right, things are going to pot," answered a commuter to a fellow who occupied a seat with him on the eight twenty-eight, and never stopped kicking about conditions from White Plains to Grand Central Station. "Why don't you write your congressman?" "What good would *that* do?" countered the kicker. "*I'm* my congressman."

CHAPTER FIFTEEN

LIMERICK LANE

Limerick is a lively Irish town on the banks of the River Shannon, just west of Tipperary, but if you as much as hint that its proud citizens have anything to do with the persistently popular five-line verse form that bears the name of their birthplace, any one of them is likely as not to tear you limb from limberick.

In case you're interested, the limerick form actually was popularized some years ago by the English artist and humorist, Edward Lear. He composed dozens of them—very clever too—for *The Book of Nonsense*, then, when he realized what he had started, grabbed a steamer and fled to Greece to get away from it all.

A quick survey of the specimens that follow will make his panic all too understandable.

    1. *At a bullfight in sunny Madrid*
       A tourist went clear off his lid.
       He made straight for the bull
       While the crowd yelled, "The fool
       Will go home on a slab"—and he did.

    2. *There was a young belle of old Natchez*
       Whose garments were always in patchez.
       When comment arose
       On the state of her clothes
       She drawled, "When ah itchez, ah scratchez."

3. There are plenty of people in Md.
   Who think that their state is a Fd.
   It seems odd to find
   That they don't seem to mind
   That Wis., not Md., is Dd.

4. A venerable dame in Nic'raguar
   Had her back hair nipped off by a jaguar.
   The lady gasped, "Ah,"
   The jaguar, "Bah,
   What a false, artificial old haguar!"

5. A lady who rules Fort Montgomery
   Says the wearing of clothes is mere mummery.
   She has frequently tea'd in
   The costume of Eden,
   Appearing delightfully summery.

6. There once was a lady named Psyche
   Whose love was a fellow named Yche.
   But the thing about Yche
   That the girl didn't lyche
   Was his beard, which was dreadfully pspyche.

7. A jolly old Southern colonel
   Has a humorous sense most infolonel.
   He amuses his folks
   By laughing at jokes
   That appear in the Ladies Home Jolonel.

8. A certain young pate who was addle
   Rode a horse alleged to be saddle,
   But his gust which was dis
   For his haps which were mis
   Sent him back to his lack which was Cadil.

9. A budget I knew who was flutter
   Lived the life of a fly which was butter.
   But ker which was po
   And girls that were show
   Turned him into a snipe that was gutter.

10. A nice patch of golds that were mari
    Belonged to a dan who was harri.
    When cals who were ras
    Filled their kets that were bas,
    She put up a cade that was barri.

11. Two eager and dashing young beaux
    Were held up and robbed of their cleaux.
    While the weather is hot
    They won't miss a lot,
    But what will they do when it sneaux?

12. A naughty old colonel in Butte
    Had a habit his friends thought was cutte.
    He'd slip off to Spokane
    And proceed from the train
    To a house of distinct ill reputte.

13. There once lived a teacher named Dodd
    With manners arresting and odd.
    He said, "If you please,
    Spell my name with three D's,"
    Though one was sufficient for God.

14. A gent with a drooping mustache
    Chewed some hair out while eating his hache.
    The phrases profane
    That he shrieked in his pain
    We shall represent here with a dache.

15. There was a young lady from Lynn
    Who happened to sit on a pynn.
    But to add to her contour
    She'd stuck so much ontour
    The point didn't puncture the skynn.

16. A doughty young private of Leeds
    Rashly swallowed six packets of seeds.
    In a month, silly ass,
    He was covered with grass,
    And he couldn't sit down for the weeds.

17. There was a young girl from St. Paul
    Wore a newspaper dress to a ball.
    But the dress caught on fire
    And burned her entire
    Front page—sporting section—and all.

18. While watching a game of croquet
    A lady got caught in the wuet.
    She was struck in the eye
    By a ball that went beye
    So she wears a glass orb to this duet.

19. There was a young girl in the choir
    Whose voice went up hoir and hoir,
    Till one Sunday night
    It vanished from sight
    And they found it next day in the spoir.

20. The kings of Peru were the Incas
    Who got to be known as big drincas.
    They worshiped the sun
    And had lots of fun,
    But the peasants all thought they were stincas.

21. A rascal far gone in lechery
    Lured maids to their doom by his treachery.
    He invited them in
    For the purpose of sin
    Though he said 'twas to look at his etchery.

22. A strip-tease named Cubbard in Kansas
    Said, "Mine's a routine that entrances."
    But when censors got there
    Miss Cubbard was bare
    She explained, "I don't know where my fans is."

23. A near-sighted fellow named Walter
    Led a glamorized lass to the altar.
    A beauty he thought her
    Till some soap and hot water
    Made her look like the Rock of Gibraltar.

24. There once was a scholar named Fressor
    Whose knowledge grew lessor and lessor.
    It at last grew so small
    He knew nothing at all,
    And today he's a college professor!

25. A student from dear old Bryn Mawr
    Committed a dreadful faux pas
    She loosened a stay
    In her new décolleté
    Exposing her je ne sais quoi.

It was in a Limerick saloon, incidentally, that a broth of a lad, decidedly under the influence, objected violently when the barkeep would serve him no more drinks. "I'll have yez all know," he hollered, "that I'm the featherweight champion of the Imerald Isle." "Be you now?" replied the barkeep grimly. "Well, one more peep out of you, me lad, and out you go—feathers and all."

CHAPTER SIXTEEN

THE LONG ARM OF THE LAW

There are lots of folks who subscribe to the theory that a lawyer's sole motto is "Let us have fees." I'm not one of them. I've noticed that the people who complain loudest about lawyers' fees are the ones who are bothering them oftenest to extricate them from some mess into which they've plunged themselves.

Legal lights have become used to abuse. Even Shakespeare, in *King Henry* VI, proposed, "The first thing we do, let's kill all the lawyers." And Lloyd Lewis told about a bleak, wintry night when General Ulysses S. Grant strode into a tavern in Galena, Illinois. It was during the court session, and a passel of lawyers was huddling about the fire. One of them noticed Grant and commented, "Here's a stranger, gentlemen, and by the looks of him, I'd say he's traveled through hell itself."

"I have," agreed Grant.

The lawyer chuckled and demanded, "How did you find things there?"

"Just like here," admitted Grant. "Lawyers all closest to the fire."

Adlai Stevenson, who returned to practice of the law when certain of his plans miscarried in 1952, is one legal light whose sense of humor never has deserted him. In 1937, for instance, while still a private citizen, he built a fine house just outside Lake Forest, Illinois, only to see it burn to the ground shortly after its completion. Stevenson was ruefully watching the debacle when a piece of flaming debris landed at his feet. He picked it up and lit his cigarette with it. "Anyhow," he told the fire chief, "I'm still getting some use out of the house!"

In 1911, the Wisconsin Supreme Court awarded the owner of a shy heifer named Martha the sum of seventy-five dollars for unwelcome attentions paid her by an errant bull. Justice Barnes, his voice quivering with emotion, explained the decision as follows: "This plebeian bull, lowly born and nameless, had aspirations far beyond his humble station in life, and forced his society on adolescent, unsophisticated Martha—contrary to provisions of Section 1482, Statutes of 1898. The sinister birth of the hybrid calf that resulted from the union was ineligible to become a candidate for pink ribbons at county fairs, and was sold in the end to a Chicago butcher for a low price."

Under the circumstances, seventy-five dollars seemed like a very light penalty—but, at least, justice prevailed and outraged virtue in Wisconsin did not go unavenged.

A rather melancholy story comes by way of Boston. A successful and formidable old jurist lingered over the breakfast table reading his *Law Review,* with his wife sitting silently across the table from him—just as she had done every weekday morning for the past thirty-seven years. Seized by a sudden daredevil impulse, she spoke up. "Henry," is what she said, "is there anything interesting in the *Law Review* this morning?" The jurist frowned and answered gruffly, "Don't be silly!"

William McDermott, extolling the merits of simple psychology, cites the case of a woman who came to the family counselor, declaring, "I hate my husband! I not only want to divorce him, but I want to make things as tough for him as I possibly can."

"I know just how you should proceed," the old counselor assured her. "Start showering him with compliments and indulging his every whim. Then, just when he knows how much he needs you—you start divorce proceedings. You'll fracture him!"

The wife decided this was sound advice. Six months later the counselor met her at a dinner and asked, "Are you still following my suggestion?" "I am," said the wife. "Then how about filing your divorce papers?" pursued the counselor. "Are you out of your head?" countered the wife indignantly. "We're divinely happy! I love him with all my heart!"

George Allen tells how a lawyer friend of his accomplished the acquittal of a notorious purveyor of moonshine whisky in West Virginia some years ago. The lawyer, obviously destined for big things in Washington, pointed dramatically at his bleary-eyed, crimson-beaked client and exclaimed, "Look at him, gentlemen of the jury. Can any one of you possibly believe that if this defendant ever got his hands on a bottle of hard likker he'd sell it?" The jury voted for acquittal without leaving the box.

Another George Allen story concerns the day early in his own career at the bar, when he settled a twenty-thousand-dollar lawsuit for thirty-five dollars. "Your honor," he told the judge, "I'm just in no mood to quibble."

Steve Allen knows a girl who has a Supreme Court figure: no appeal!

The judge frowned when he looked at the defendant and demanded, "Haven't I seen that face of yours before?" "Indeed you have, your honor," said the defendant hopefully. "I gave your son violin lessons last winter."

"Ah, yes," recalled the judge. "Twenty years!"

Accused in court of waltzing off with a motorist's tool kit, the defendant maintained stoutly that he'd taken it only as a joke. "How far," asked the judge gently, "did you carry that kit?" "Just over to my home," answered the defendant. "About four blocks." "Thirty days," snapped his honor, "for carrying the joke too far."

The witness was a starlet who didn't care how much of her understandably famous chassis was exposed to the jury. As her dress crept higher and higher, the prosecuting attorney cried, "Point of order, your honor! I've just thought of something!" "Of course you have," said his honor sympathetically. "So has every other man in this courtroom!"

An absent-minded attorney rose to defend a client, and, intent on winding up the proceedings promptly and reaching the country club, got off on the wrong foot.

"This man on trial, gentlemen of the jury," he bumbled, "bears the reputation of being the most unconscionable and depraved scoundrel in the state . . ."

An assistant whispered frantically, "That's your client you're talking about."

Without one second's hesitation, the lawyer continued smoothly, ". . . but what outstanding citizen ever lived who has not been vilified and slandered by envious contemporaries?"

The terrified citizen assured the police lieutenant he had been felled in the dark outside his back door by an unknown assailant.

A rookie cop was dispatched to the scene, returned in due course with a big lump on his forehead and a woebegone look on his face.

"I solved the case," he reported. "Quick work," complimented the lieutenant. "How did you accomplish it?" The rookie cop explained, "I stepped on the rake too."

An upstate police commissioner staunchly defends the practice of abandoning license plates on the front of cars, and confining them to the back of automobiles. "Remember," he adds, "that nine out of ten pinches are made from the rear."

A gang of robbers, out to make a killing, broke into a home for old actors by mistake. The retired, supposedly decrepit Thespians put up such a battle, the robbers were happy to make their escape. Bruised and bloody, they re-formed ranks at the gang hangout. "It ain't too bad," philosophized one. "We got twenty-two dollars between us." The leader silenced him with a glance and snarled, "I told you lugs to steer clear of actors. We had twenty-four when we broke in!"

Some thoughtful friend on the Coast sent John Straley a clock recently. When the post-office officials in New York heard the ticking, they suspected a bomb plot, and threw the package into a bucket of water. It didn't help the timepiece any, but Straley refuses to part with it. He explains it's probably the only clock in the world where every hour on the hour the cuckoo comes out and gargles.

Scheduled to die in the chair the following morning, with not a mourner in sight, a notorious killer, in line with the im-memorial custom, was allowed to order anything he wanted for his last dinner. The huge scowling desperado smacked his lips, and demanded cream of mushroom soup, mushroom patty, three portions of mushrooms under glass, and, for a dessert to top things off, a succulent mushroom pudding.

To the surprised warden the doomed man explained, "All my life I've loved mushrooms—but was convinced I'd get poisonous toadstools by mistake. Tonight's the first time I don't have to be afraid to eat them."

Do you think all motorcycle cops are heartless monsters? They tell of one up New England way who bagged two speeding cars at the same time, ordered the drivers to pull up at the side of the road. The lead car had a dazzlingly pretty girl at the wheel, and the appreciative young man in the second car whispered, "Go easy on her, bud," as the cop strode by, summons book in hand. A few moments later the girl drove off, and the cop approached the young man. He handed him a slip of paper. It contained the girl's telephone number. "Get going," he ordered, "and no more of that sixty-five-miles-an-hour stuff, or you'll never live to use this!"

CHAPTER SEVENTEEN

LOVE AND MARRIAGE

A very pretty girl in Altoona, Pennsylvania, had a persistent but
unwanted suitor in New York. When she refused to see him any
longer, he resorted to an intensive mail campaign, sending her

a special-delivery letter twice a day for forty-seven days. On the forty-eighth day his strategy produced results. The girl eloped with the mailman.

Wilfred was notoriously bashful in the presence of the opposite sex, so his parents were pleased but surprised when he announced he was headed downtown to see a girl. He was back, however, within the hour.

"You're home mighty early, son," observed his mother. "Didn't you see her?"

"Sure did," enthused Wilfred, "and if I hadn't ducked down an alley she'd have seen me!"

Young Spooner, fortified by two stiff drinks, asked for the hand of crusty old Mr. Walker's only daughter. "Take her," snorted Walker. "I'm sure you're not making enough to support her—but, on the other hand, neither am I!"

Nobody ever expected that the Nuthalls' gangling, ambitionless young son would ever amount to a darn, but on the day he was nineteen, he staggered the neighborhood—his parents most of all—by getting the daughter of the richest man in town to say she'd be his. The wedding actually took place, too, causing skeptics to lose a couple of injudicious bets, and the lad slipped a ring on his betrothed's finger, mumbling, "With all my worldly goods I thee endow." "Well," whispered one of the skeptics, "there goes young Nuthall's bicycle!"

The office vamp reported, "I went out with a millionaire from Detroit last night, and what do you think he gave me? Five hundred dollars!" "Zowie," jeered the girl at the next desk. "That's the first time I heard of a $498 tip!"

The entire course of a young man's secret love affair was revealed to his mother when she came upon a sheaf of letters from the girl and noted this sequence of salutations:

Dear Mr. Carmichael
Dear Bill
Bill Dear
Dearest Bill
You Wonderful Guy
My Own Sensational Lover
You Wonderful Guy
Dearest Bill
Bill Dear
Dear Bill
Dear Mr. Carmichael

A young blonde who spent hours every day before a mirror faithfully apeing the mannerisms of Marilyn Monroe mournfully reported to a school chum, "Every time I pass a group of boys in front of the drugstore you should just hear the loud whistle —but darn it, the boys never whistle back."

Art Carney tells one of those stories about the smart young brother who always was underfoot when his pretty sister wanted to pitch a little woo with her boy friend. To get rid of him one afternoon the b.f. suggested, "Why don't you go down to the street, Willie, and count the men who are wearing red hats. I'll give you a quarter for every one that goes by." To the surprise of both lovebirds, Willie, usually very cagey, fell in with this suggestion. Fifteen minutes later, however, they heard his triumphant voice from below. "I don't know how you two are doing up there," he hollered, "but my ship is about to come in. Here comes the Shriners' parade!"

"I hear," said an aspiring young model to her roommate, "that your fiancé is doing settlement work." "Yes," agreed the roommate sadly. "His creditors caught up with him."

A daughter explained to her ma, "I can't marry that handsome young millionaire after all. I just found out he doesn't believe in hell!" "Don't let that stop you, gal," ordered Ma. "You just marry him—and we'll convince him!"

John Barrymore, who had good reason to know as much about the rocky road of love as he did about acting, remarked ruefully one evening, "Experience is what you have left after you have completely forgotten her name."

When Johnny Baxter proposed to little Wynnie Sukes, she resolved to become the perfect mate and learn to do everything he could do. First came the problem of driving his convertible. She signed for a full course of instruction, but what with all the prenuptial parties and hubbub, was barely able to merit a beginner's permit by the time she tripped down the aisle.

The wedding over, the toasts drunk, the bridal bouquet thrown, Johnny and Wynnie chugged off in a shower of rice. Ten minutes later, however, everybody was amazed to see Wynnie come tearing madly back into the house. "What's the matter?" cried the guests. "Oh dear," wailed Wynnie. "I almost spoiled everything. I drove off without my beginner's permit!"

A Mr. Floogle in South Bend had a brand-new washing machine that went on the fritz. Mr. Floogle had bent over to probe deep into the mechanism of the machine when Mrs. Floogle entered and turned on the switch. There was a whirr, and Mr. Floogle's legs shot up into the air. Mrs. Floogle watched him threshing wildly about and observed happily, "Fine, Sam! You've got it working again!"

In the Aga Khan's memoirs, he recalls a journey to Paris he made with one Sir George Greaves. "Tell me," said the Aga Khan, "is Lady Greaves accompanying you?" Sir George answered coldly, "When I go to a banquet, I don't take a ham sandwich in my pocket!"

One of the stories that, judging by the number of times it's been submitted, must be among the most popular extant, concerns the old man explaining the secret of seventy years of serene, fight-free married life. "Driving home from our honeymoon," is the old man's story, "my mare stumbled. 'That's once,' I noted. Then it stumbled again. I said grimly, 'That's twice.' When that mare stumbled a third time, I just naturally pulled out my gun and shot that mare dead. My new wife got mighty riled about all this and bawled me out plenty. I just sat there quiet till she ran down. Then I said, 'That's once!' Son, I ain't had a bit of trouble with her since."

Rosita Quarles's summary of the difference between lovers and husbands: day and night.

"How long are you going to let your wife henpeck you?" sneered the companion of a typical Mr. Milquetoast. "How's for reasserting your mastery of your own home?"

Milquetoast strode into his apartment and hollered, "What time's dinner?" "Seven-thirty, like always," answered his wife without thinking, but she recoiled when he announced, "Nothing doing! Tonight it's seven sharp. And I want a steak, not that canned slop you usually serve me. And put out my dinner jacket. I'm going to take that little blonde in my office out dancing."

Mrs. Milquetoast froze with astonishment. Drunk with power, her husband continued, "And when I'm ready to have my black tie fixed in a neat little bow, do you know who's going to tie it?"

Mrs. Milquetoast recovered her voice. "I certainly do," she announced grimly. "The man from the Riverside Funeral Parlor."

Ten husbands who are more to be pitied than censored:

1. The husband who discovered that, though his wife sure could dish it out, she couldn't cook it.

2. The husband whose wife told him to pull in his stomach—after he already had.

3. The husband who returned for credit a book entitled *How*

to Be Master in Your Own Home, explaining sheepishly, "My wife won't let me keep it."

4. The husband whose wife made him drink thirty cups of coffee a day to cure his dreadful snoring. After six months she boasted, "He never snores at all any more. He just percolates."

5. The husband who was caught shaving at the border of Central Park Lake. A cop protested, "Haven't you got a bathroom of your own?" "I certainly have," answered the husband bitterly. "I also have a wife and four daughters."

6. The husband whose neighbor boasted, "I got a cute little cocker puppy for my wife this morning." "Gosh," sighed the husband, "I wish I could make a trade like that."

7. The husband whose son, a freshman at college, reported, "I've landed my first part in a varsity show. I play a man who's been married for twenty years." "Good work, son," enthused Father. "Keep this up and first thing you know they'll be giving you a speaking part."

8. The husband who brought his boss home for dinner, explaining, "You're about to meet the finest little helpmate, the swellest cook, the best little housekeeper a man ever had—that is, of course, if she's home."

9. The husband whose wife was so concerned about his happiness that she hired three detectives to discover the reason for it.

10. The husband who reported this division of his income: 40 per cent for food, 30 per cent for shelter, and 50 per cent for his wife's clothing and amusement. "But that makes 120 per cent," protested his accountant. "You don't have to tell me," sighed the husband. "I know it."

Two successful Chicago businessmen, who hadn't met since they were classmates in a little southern Illinois schoolhouse, met in the Loop one afternoon, and after the usual wistful reminiscences, one persuaded the other to try "potluck" for dinner at his home. "Potluck" wasn't very good that night. An unco-operative and bored wife served up some cold ham and a can of preserved peaches and disappeared huffily toward her bedroom. The host gulped down his last bite of peach and boomed, "Well, Joe, now that you've broken bread at my house you'll have to ask me to dine at yours some time soon." "Not a bad idea," agreed Joe sourly. "How about tonight?"

It was the morning after Father's Day, and editor Norman Cousins, parent of four, was sipping a cup of coffee thoughtfully. "Did they give you anything for Father's Day?" asked a member of the staff. "They did," admitted Cousins. "They gave me all the bills from Mother's Day."

The team of Pedro and Pancho had been inseparable since boyhood, but the day came when Pedro took unto himself a blushing bride. The affair had blossomed so suddenly that Pancho never even met the girl before the evening of the wedding. There was a great feast for the occasion, and the tequila flowed like water. The guests waxed happier and happier. In the midst of the uproar, however, Pedro suddenly discovered that both his friend Pancho and his lovely bride were missing. He instituted a private search, and soon discovered them locked in each other's arms in the bridal chamber. Pedro reappeared at the party in a paroxysm of laughter. "Come look," he demanded. "That fool Pancho so drunk he think he's me!"

While Mrs. Erskine vacationed in the Adirondacks, Mr. Erskine turned their Park Avenue apartment into something of a club for his male friends, with one poker game setting some kind of endurance record by lasting from Friday evening clear through to Monday morning. Mrs. Erskine surveyed the wreckage rather grimly when she returned home, but less than twenty-four hours later she was able to report to her sister, "Well, I've swept out every nook and crony."

"My darling," murmured a husband to his bride of twenty years, "as I always tell anyone who will listen, you have the face of a saint." Under his breath he added, "A Saint Bernard."

Eddie Cantor goes a long way back for his story of the housewife who protested, "I don't like this apartment, Joe. There are no curtains in the bathroom, so every time I take a bath, the neighbors can see me." "That's all right, Rachel," soothed her husband. "When the neighbors see you, *they'll* buy the curtains."

A harassed young bride served her husband only a plateful of graham crackers for dinner. "And I had such a lovely meal planned," she wailed. "But when the steak started to burn and fell into the lemon pie, I had to throw the tomato soup on them to put out the fire!"

Sticking her head into Mrs. Rodgers' East Hampton bungalow, a neighbor asked solicitously, "How's old Morty feeling this morning?" "He can't complain," said Mrs. Rodgers. "Land's sake," clucked the neighbor, "I had no idea he was *that* sick!"

The *Wall Street Journal*, undertaking something of a Kinsey investigation of its own, has determined that a man's relationship with the opposite sex can be divided roughly into seven stages:

1. Whaaa! I want my mama!
2. G'wan, beat it. We don't want any old girl playing with us.
3. Gee, Myrtle, you're beautiful!
4. If you don't marry me, I'll shoot myself.
5. Go on home to your mother. See if I give a darn.
6. She's considerably younger than I am, Alice, I'll admit, but she understands me.
7. Kitchy-kitchy-koo! Did you hear that, Alice? She said "Grandpa!"

The classified-ad section of an Ohio newspaper betrayed an odd desire on the part of one reader. He sought an old-fashioned wooden potato masher, explaining, "I want it for my mother-in-law." It turned out that absolutely nobody in the community had a wooden potato masher he wanted to part with, but one helpful reader wrote, "A wire potato masher will suffice nicely for your mother-in-law. Just hit her a little harder!"

Mr. Goodman was the kind of husband who believed he was entitled to a night off every week. What's more, he sold Mrs. Goodman on the proposition. So every Wednesday, regular as clockwork, he pedaled off by himself. Only one Wednesday, he neglected to come back home. For seven years he was among the missing. Then, one Wednesday afternoon, he suddenly reappeared. His wife, overjoyed, began calling all her friends. "Hey," protested Mr. Goodman, "whassa big idea?" "I thought I'd whip up a little welcome-home party for you this evening," she explained. "What?" roared Mr. Goodman. "On my night out?"

One friend listened to another explain his difficulties with his wife, most of which resulted from staying out nights. He said that he had spent one whole Saturday oiling the garage door to keep it quiet, had put graphite in all the locks, and had perfected a system for silent home-coming and entrance into the bedroom, but there she was, whether he was drunk or sober, and no matter what time—blazing away at him. He invariably got mad, spoiled his whole night, and felt terrible the next day—and this was one of those days.

The patient friend explained that he had the wrong system and that his was better—worked nine times out of ten. He said, "Drunk or sober, no matter what time, I slam into the driveway with the horn blowing and the brakes shrieking, bump into the back of the garage, slam the doors with all my might, fall into the front door of the house, and slam that too. Then I stumble upstairs, kick my shoes around, get my clothes off, and step into the bedroom, turn on all the lights, and yell, 'Move over, dear, here I come.' Nine times out of ten she pretends she's asleep."

An attractive young honeymoon couple boarded a train for Niagara Falls, and indulged in the traditional billing and cooing. Suddenly, however, the baffled bride found herself hurling hateful insults at her husband, with his rejoinders matching hers in bitterness and venom.

And then she discovered a total stranger sitting next to her in the drawing room. "How did you get in here?" she gasped. "Who are you?"

The stranger answered softly, "I'm ten years from now."

CHAPTER EIGHTEEN

THE PRINTED WORD

Author, Author!

"Be brief," was George Bernard Shaw's unfailing advice to aspiring writers. I was walking down the Embankment in London with him one day when a young writer held out his hand and announced, "My name is Rothschild, Mr. Shaw." Shaw, without so much as breaking his stride, answered, "Good-by, Mr. Rothschild.

"That," he told me with some satisfaction when we were out of earshot of poor Mr. Rothschild, "is *brevity.*"

Brevity is not always so simple to attain. The French author Pascal P.S.'d to a friend, "I have made this letter rather long because I have not had time to make it shorter." Woodrow

Wilson once remarked that it would take him two weeks to prepare a ten-minute speech, one week for a speech of an hour. Asked how long he would need to prepare a two-hour speech, he replied, "That I can do—right now."

Arnold Bennett once visited Shaw in his apartment overlooking the Thames Embankment in London and expressed surprise that not a single vase of flowers was in evidence. "I thought you were so fond of flowers," chided Bennett. "I am," responded Shaw abruptly. "I'm very fond of children too. But I don't cut off their heads and stick them in pots about the house."

Gabriel Pascal, the late motion-picture magnate, recalls one of his early dealings with Mr. Shaw. Shaw, it appeared, wanted eight thousand dollars for the screen rights to one of his lesser plays. "I'll give you four thousand," was Pascal's cabled reply. "You must have misunderstood my original demand," protested Shaw (collect). "What I asked was eighty thousand, not eight." Pascal answered promptly, "Excuse error. I'll give you forty thousand!"

Erich Remarque, author of *All Quiet on the Western Front* and *Arch of Triumph,* tells about a cousin of the same name who paced a hospital corridor awaiting the arrival of his first-born. A nurse finally ended his anxiety by informing him he was the father of an eight-pound boy. A few moments later she was back to say, "You now have another son." The father had not been expecting twins. He stammered, "That last Remarque is uncalled for!"

Hale and hearty at the age of eighty, George Moore, the famous Irish novelist, startled everybody by his continuing clarity of thought and physical well-being. "To what do you attribute your great good health in your eightieth year?" asked a reporter. Moore replied cheerfully, "It's because I never smoked, drank, or touched a girl—until I was eleven years old."

Harry Kurnitz, mystery writer and Hollywood bigwig, was in London one summer with Moss Hart and Kitty Carlisle (Mrs. Hart in private life), and it was this trio that prevailed upon novelist Edna Ferber, rather against her intuitive judgment, to embark upon an excursion boat bound up the River Thames. The day was hot, the small boat was overcrowded, and the captain, a pasty-faced youth of about twenty with an unlighted cigarette glued to his lips, unprepossessing, to say the least. The boat wasn't fifty yards from its mooring place when it got stuck in the mud, where it remained three solid hours until derisive urchins on the shore began skimming pebbles at the marooned excursionists. Miss Ferber then turned to Hart with a martyred expression and sighed, "And now, dear Moss, they're stoning us." Dear Moss tried to bribe a passing oarsman to remove his party and row it ashore, but the pasty-faced captain roared, " 'Ere now, there'll be no desertions from this ship. These currents are dangerous." The only other diversion before they all returned safely to port came when Mr. Kurnitz buried his head in his hands and groaned, "I never should have shot that albatross." Miss Ferber promises to confine future maritime ventures to the *Queen Elizabeth* and the *United States*.

A well-known literary figure on the West Coast recently made headlines with a spectacular suicide gesture. The fact that it obviously was designed to be unsuccessful brought to mind a famous lady friend of the late Robert Benchley. She made so many abortive attempts to do away with herself that Benchley finally told her, "You'll have to cut this sort of thing out, my dear. It's ruining your health!"

Hostesses who went in for literary parlor games never got very far when Robert Benchley was around. In a piece called "Ladies Wild," Mr. Benchley confessed, "In the exclusive set (no diphtheria allowed) in which I travel, I am known as a heel in the matter of parlor games. I will drink with the ladies, wrassle with them, and leer at them, but when they bring out the bundles of pencils and the pads of paper and start putting down all the things they can think of beginning with 'W,' or enumerating each other's bad qualities (no hard-feeling results, mind you—just life-long enmity), I tiptoe noisily out of the room and say, 'The hell with you.'

"For this reason, I am not usually included in any little game that may be planned in advance. If they foresee an evening of 'Consequences' coming over them, they whisper, 'Get Benchley out of the house.' For, I forgot to tell you, not only am I a non-participant in parlor games but I am a militant non-participant. I heckle from the sidelines. I throw stones and spit at the players. Hence the nickname, 'Sweet Old Bob,' or sometimes just the initials."

In his foreword to *The Benchley Roundup*, a selection of Robert Benchley's funniest pieces, his son Nathaniel recalls: "One time, during World War II an Air Force sergeant accosted my father in a bar and announced, 'I might as well tell you I don't like your work.' Benchley replied that he had moments of doubt himself. The sergeant then explained that he had hitched a ride from Africa to Italy on a cargo plane, and that the only available sleeping space had been on bags full of overseas editions of Benchley's books. By the time they passed Sicily, he said, he was so stiff and sore he hoped never to even hear the name of Benchley again. 'Try it yourself sometime,' he concluded. 'That stuff isn't so hilarious when you have to sleep on it.'"

Frank Sullivan, the Socrates of Saratoga, met a disturbed young lady who complained that she could never live, or even tarry briefly, on an island. "Islands," she said, "give me claustrophobia." Father Sullivan, who has learned by experience that the surest way to calm a phobia-ridden friend is to trot out phobias of your own, told her, "I know exactly how you feel. I have somewhat the same trouble." "You get uneasy on islands too?" she asked eagerly. "Not islands exactly," Sullivan admitted gravely. "I'm uneasy on continents."

The young lady seemed comforted.

Frank Sullivan boasts, incidentally, that he remains a rebel to the bitter end. He always sails, for instance, under true colors instead of false, leaves no stone turned, and, when angry, never dreams of hitting the ceiling. He hits the floor—and just lies there screaming. He carries a bag around with him, letting cats into it, and when he casts discretion it certainly isn't to the winds. "You might also mention," he concludes, "that I do not cast any pearls before swine, either. I save *my* pearls to cast before pretty girls. The reaction is far more gratifying." On my own, I'll mention that Frank Sullivan remains, year in and year out, one of the greatest and most consistent humorists in America.

One of the most popular American humorists a hundred years ago was Josh Billings—(real name, Henry Wheeler Shaw [1818–85])—who wowed the populace with his homely philosophy, deliberately misspelled. Josh began his career as an auctioneer in Poughkeepsie, but made the big time with gems like the following:

"Konsider a postage stamp: it sticks tew the job til the goods is delivered."

"It's better to know nothing than to know what ain't so."

"The wheel that squeaks loudest is the one that gets the grease."

"A sekret ceases tew be a secret if once it's confided. It is like a dollar bill: once broken it's never a dollar again."

"Love is like the measles: we kan't have it bad but oncet, and the later in life we have it, the tuffer it goes with us."

Cut from the same cloth was the droll commentary of Kim Hubbard (1868–1930), who, some seventy years later, made the towns of Gnawbone, Bear Wallow, and Weedpatch Hill famous the country over.

Hubbard created the character "Abe Martin," a single-gallused

cracker-barrel philosopher not unlike Herb Shriner—with a dash
of George Gobel thrown in for good measure.

It was Kim Hubbard who coined the oft-quoted, "What the
country needs is a good five-cent cigar," though V. P. Tom
Marshall usually gets the credit. Other Hubbard observations:

"A restaurant waiter allus lays your check on the table upside
down so you won't choke t'death."

"Nothin' makes a poet as mad as a late spring."

"A warnin' is all the average American needs t'make him take
a chance."

"The hardest thing t'stop is a temporary chairman."

"Speakin' of the high cost o' courtin', who remembers when
all a fella needed wuz a narrow buggy an' a sack o' red cinammon
drops?"

Wall Street was buzzing the other day with the story of a slap-
happy hostess at a cocktail party who collared a bewildered author to tell him, "I read your book as a magazine serial, in book
form, and as a condensation, and now I've seen it in the movies
and on television. Frankly, Mr. Ingold, just what the hell are
you trying to say?"

At the same party, an authoress whose tongue is feared on
three continents was heard assuring an old, old friend, "Enjoy
yourself while you can, my dear. After all, you only live nine
times."

Author Ben Hecht takes a very dim view of celebrities. "A
roomful of them," he writes in his autobiography, A *Child of
the Century*, "depresses me, possibly because I have learned at
first hand the wretched things that make a celebrity—the pain
of almost constant defeat, the arrows of a thousand critics forever
sticking out of your rump, the fact that your name has become
a magnet for irritation, malice, or calumny. And worst of all,
the fact that a celebrity cannot, like luckier folk, drop out of

sight when he is ripened with age. He must stay on the vine and rot—for all to see and disdain."

Budd Schulberg, who writes wonderful books, but drives his publisher crazy by never delivering them on time (I know, because I'm the publisher!), explained his technique to reporter Ed Wallace. "First," said Budd, "I clean the typewriter. Then I go through my shelves and return all borrowed books. Then I play with my three children. Then, if it's warm, I go for a swim. Then I find some friends to have a drink with. By then, it's time to clean the typewriter again."

And that's why Schulberg's books are so few and far between. But they're worth waiting for!

A well-known but improvident author was toiling over a new novel when there came a ring on his doorbell. His caller proved to be a comely young woman who announced, "I represent the Federated Community Charity Fund." "You've arrived in the nick of time," enthused the author. "I'm starving."

James Branch Cabell, whose novel *Jurgen* was considered very daring stuff back in the 1920's, likes to tell of a note he received from a rabid fan some years later. "Dear Mr. Cabell," it began. "I have chosen you as my favorite author. Please write to me immediately and tell me why."

When F. Scott Fitzgerald's novel, *The Beautiful and Damned*, was published, everybody asked his wife Zelda how closely the heroine was modeled after her own career. "It seems to me," replied Mrs. Fitzgerald after some thought, "that on one page I recognized a portion of an old diary of mine which disappeared shortly after my marriage, and also scraps of letters which sound to me vaguely familiar. In fact, Mr. Fitzgerald—I believe that is how he spells his name—seems to believe that plagiarism begins at home."

An author in Kankakee found himself in something of a predicament recently. A magazine accepted a short poem and sent him a check for thirty-five dollars. The only man who could identify him at the bank, however, was his liquor dealer—whom he owed a hundred!

Agatha Christie, famous writer of detective stories, returned to London after a long visit to Bagdad with her husband, a renowned archaeologist. Asked how a woman with great creative talent felt about being married to a student whose eyes were turned always to antiquities, Miss Christie replied warmly, "An archaeologist is the best husband any woman can get. Just consider: the older she gets, the more he is interested in her!"

There was a time when John Gunther and his beautiful wife, Jane, in their interminable search for the "inside" of some place or other, arrived in Tokyo, Japan. They had been in primitive villages for a month and were therefore specially delighted to find a bath attached to their new hotel room. It was a highly polished wooden tub already filled to the brim with boiling hot water. "They must roast elephants in here," commented Jane, and sought a "cold" faucet to bring down the water's temperature.

There was none to be found, so she finally gritted her teeth and inched her way tortuously into the tub, where she enjoyed a veritable picnic. When she climbed out (red as a lobster), she summoned an attendant to mop up. It was then that the Gunthers discovered that Jane had used the week's bath water for the entire hotel. Each guest, explained the indignant manager, was supposed to take only a pitcher full of the steaming hot water for sponging-off purposes.

It cost Mr. Gunther twenty-five dollars to pay for the emptying and refilling of the tub. I presume he charged it off to research.

If you ever hope to get along with an author, there is one

thing you must understand from the outset. Every word that he sets down on paper automatically becomes a priceless gem, and the merest suggestion that he alter or condense his text is an unforgivable insult. Nor is this an occupational disease acquired after long apprenticeship. It manifests itself at an appallingly early stage of a writer's career.

When my son Jonathan, for instance, was eight years old, he and a favorite classmate named Judy Goetz (whose parents fashioned the dramatic versions of *The Heiress* and *The Immoralist*) were assigned to write a play. Jon had captured a live frog the week previous and this was very much in the minds of the collaborators when they set about composing their play.

The next day Jonny was home with a cold. Judy stormed in about five, crying. "That teacher has rewritten our whole first scene!" "Wha-a-at?" roared Jonny. "She can't get away with it!"

"Let me see this scene that your unfeeling teacher has desecrated," I suggested.

The manuscript was handed over to me, and I now give you, in its original and unabridged form, the scene as Judy and Jonny wrote it:

The curtain rises. A frog is on the center of the stage.
Frog: I don't think I'll go to school today. *Curtain.*

The World of Books

There is a man in New England, supposedly sound of mind and body, who has devoted virtually his entire life and fortune to a collection of recognized classics in unrecognized languages. His treasures include *Uncle Tom's Cabin* in Ukrainian, *Ben Hur* in Hebrew, and *Hamlet* in Hindustani.

Another collector seeks only first editions of books Abraham Lincoln was known to have read in his leisure hours.

A third buys volumes printed on black paper. No other color interests him.

A fourth seeks odd-shaped volumes: round, heart-shaped, fashioned after fruits and animals.

A fifth's sole craving is for books left unfinished because of their authors' untimely deaths—titles like Dickens' *Mystery of Edwin Drood*, Stevenson's *Weir of Hemiston*, and Hawthorne's *Dr. Grimshawe's Secret*.

These and other odd fish from the sea of literature are catalogued and dissected in bibliophile Walter Blumenthal's sprightly *Bookmen's Bedlam*, a Rutgers University Press publication. In its pages you will learn about the smallest, the largest, and the darndest books in all the world.

Smallest book: An edition of Omar Khayyam published in 1933 in Worcester, Massachusetts. Each copy, bound in full crimson morocco, weighs only a third of a carat. The whole edition of 150 would fit in an old-fashioned watchcase.

Largest book: Up the River Nile at Thebes, in the Temple of Rameses II. Its "pages" are walls 138 feet wide—"an ancient chronicle of triumph that has defied obliteration for more than three thousand years."

Most secure book: Bishop Lyndwood's *The Provinciale*, which, according to his will, was chained "for all time" to St. Stephen's Chapel, Westminster, to serve as the standard text of his work and discourage effectively both borrowers and abridgers.

An Englishman, Augustine Birrell, ordered a nineteen-volume set of the works of Hannah More buried deep in his garden. "The books take up too much room on my shelves," he explained, "and they are just as likely to be dug up from the garden as to be picked out for reading up here."

His countrywoman, Lady Gough, insured immortality among the literati by forbidding in her library the placing of books by male authors alongside those by female authors—unless, of course, they were married.

Mr. Blumenthal also claims to have unearthed the longest and shortest plays ever published. The longest, he says, is called *The Spanish Bawd* and runs a mere twenty-one acts. The shortest is Tristan Bernard's *The Exile*, and concerns a mountaineer and an exile. Here is the complete text:

Exile: Whoever you are, have pity on a hunted man. There is a price on my head.
Mountaineer: How much?

The revival of Sherlock Holmes by A. Conan Doyle's son, Adrian, and John Dixon Carr, is a source of deep satisfaction to the rank and file of detective-story addicts, and even the exacting members of the Baker Street Irregulars have reacted favorably. Discrepancies they have discovered, but theirs is an allegiance best expressed in the lines composed by Conan Doyle's brother-in-law (himself the creator of Raffles), Mr. E. W. Hornung:

> *Tho' he might be more humble,*
> *There's no Police like Holmes.*

In Great Britain, furthermore, they've launched a comic strip involving the intrepid Sherlock and his faithful Dr. Watson. It is carried in the *Evening Standard,* and in that sheet's letters column there recently appeared the following: "I rejoice to see the decline of that cursed interfering fellow Holmes to a mere comic-strip feature on a rather obscure page." The letter was signed, "Yours joyfully, Professor Moriarty."

The publishers of the Modern Library received a note from a young lady in Arkansas, which read, "I enjoyed your publication, *Les Miserables,* very much indeed, but would you mind telling me which character is supposed to be Les?"

Another reprint publisher received this fan letter from a satisfied customer: "Your book, *How to Win Friends and Influence People* ought to be read by every private in the Army. A week after I finished it, I got promoted to corporal. P.S. Have you got any books on sex technique?"

In a big marble mansion just off Fifth Avenue dwells the mother of a prominent publisher. She's so old that her family has been worrying about her keeping the place going all by herself. Her son, in fact, called in a high-priced analyst (one of his authors) and said, "Mama's taken to puttering about the kitchen. I want you to question her and tell me of her mental condition, but please be quite sure she doesn't know you're probing her mind."

"Trust me," the analyst assured him. "If you've read my book, I don't have to tell you I know exactly how to proceed in cases of this sort."

He found Mama happily engaged in roasting a leg of lamb and soon had her babbling away unreservedly. When he deemed the moment ripe, he suddenly held up a spoon and asked, "Mama, what's this?" "A spoon, of course," she replied. Then he held up a fork, which she identified just as readily. Finally he held up a knife. "And this, Mama: what's this?" he inquired.

Mama crinkled her tired old eyes, cocked her head to one side, and asked mildly, "A phallic symbol, maybe?"

In London, Peter Windsor encountered a man who had read a Charlotte Brontë novel eight times—obviously the perfect octo-Jane-Eyrian.

Commentator Sam Himmell, in *Printing News*, indicated that a lot of the tears shed over vanishing village smithies might have been saved for more deserving unfortunates. There are still 18,-215 blacksmith shops in the U.S., but only 7,368 bookstores!

At the last booksellers' convention in Atlantic City, a disconsolate purveyor of priceless literature sat in a hotel lobby, his head heavily bandaged and a pair of crutches across his knee. To a solicitous confrere he explained, "I fell out of a window."

"Obviously," commiserated the confrere, "you will be out of commission for the balance of the convention—so how's for slipping me the phone number of the little blond authoress you had draped over your arm the first evening we were in session?"

"With pleasure," agreed the bookseller, "but if a man answers the phone, I suggest that you hang up. It's probably the scoundrel who threw me out of the window."

Alan Green, discoursing on the importance of a novelist's engaging his readers' interests with his very first paragraph, cites two detective-story writers who remembered their lesson almost too well.

The first opened his book as follows:

"Was it necessary," asked the judge, leaning over the bench, "to produce this entire lake in evidence?"

Number Two came through with:

"It was nearly midnight before they had scraped Uncle Harry off the dining-room table."

A lady in Chicago sued for divorce recently. "I love detective stories," she told the judge, "and Field's automatically sends me every new one published. My husband gets hold of them first and writes the name of the murderer on top of page one!"

It appears the judge also liked whodunits. "Your husband obviously is a fiend," he ordained. "Divorce granted."

In Hollywood, William P. Dudley bought a limited edition of the works of Shakespeare from a temporarily impoverished Thespian, who assured him, "Parting with this treasure grieves me more than I can say. Each night before retiring I spent at least an hour reading and rereading the immortal bard's plays." When Mr. Dudley examined the set in his home, he found that none of the pages had been cut! "An unopened Shakespeare!" he thought to himself. "That's the uncuttest kind of all!"

Book-trade journals often ask publishers to supply summaries of forthcoming novels in "thirty-five words or less." Julien Dedman, of Scribner's, says that, had this practice been in vogue in the golden age of Athens, a preview of the *Odyssey* probably would have read something like this: "Strange goings-on in murky waters off the coast of Greece. Several wanton murders by a character named Ulysses. When he finally returns home, he rubs out the suitor of his wife, who was planning to divorce him for desertion."

Unhappiest librarian on record was the little man who set out to catalogue every volume in a famous English library. Because of his build, he had to raise the height of his chair by sitting on one fat volume.

When he completed his magnum opus, the index had only one glaring error—he forgot to include the single volume he had been sitting on for thirty years!

A student bought a desk dictionary from Bob Campbell's U.C.L.A. shop, reported later, "It's interesting—but I wish it didn't change the subject so often."

There's a bookseller up near White Plains who, convinced he never could support a wife and a Jaguar on the wages of a purveyor of the immortals, studied medicine in his spare time. He finally won his doctor's degree, and hung out his shingle next door to the bookshop. His first patient was a beautiful, beautiful girl (Westchester County is full of them). She complained of a stomach-ache. Our brand-new doctor examined the troubled area with a keen appreciation, then asked innocently, "Now do you mind if I browse around a little?"

Powers of the Press

When Horace Greeley made his famous pronouncement, "Go West, young man, and grow up with the country," he was not merely indulging in campaign oratory. He followed his own advice. Determined to push through his campaign for a transcontinental railroad, the great journalist set out by stagecoach in 1859 from Missouri, was deposited on the rolling prairie when a herd of buffalo stampeded the stage horses and overturned the coach, capsized again in the Sweetwater River where he lost a trunkful of manuscripts, persuaded Brigham Young to grant him a far-reaching interview in Salt Lake City, and wound up finally in a mad dash over precipice-bordering Sierra roads to Placerville, in the center of the California gold rush country.

According to the legend, Greeley was expected to speak in Placerville at seven in the evening, and the driver was instructed to get him there in time—or else. They set out at such breakneck speed that Greeley first cried, "I don't care if we arrive a bit late," then amended his statement to, "I don't care if we never get there at all." A final bump sent his head clear through the roof of the coach. The driver simply hollered, "Why don't you hang on to your seat, Horace?" scattered a welcoming brass band in nine directions, and arrived at the Carey House at one minute before seven. Greeley regained consciousness at one minute after nine.

By 1861, when Mark Twain covered the same territory, the story of Horace Greeley's wild ride into Placerville had become so familiar that Twain vowed he heard it "ninety-two times in eight days, flavored with every aroma including whisky, brandy, beer, cologne, sozodont, tobacco, garlic, onions, and grasshoppers." One guide promised to withhold it, but, says Twain, "in trying to retain the anecdote in his system he overstrained himself and expired in my arms."

A San Antonio newspaper featured this ad in its classified columns recently: "Wanted, big executive, from twenty-two to eighty. To sit with feet on desk from ten to four-thirty and watch other people work. Must be willing to play golf every other afternoon. Salary to start: $500 a week. We don't have this job open, you understand. We just thought we'd like to see in print what everybody is applying for."

There's a city editor on one of the Chicago papers who misuses words in a fashion with which no Hollywood producer possibly could compete. A reporter asked, "How much do you want me to write on that fire?" The editor answered, "About half a paragraph." He told his staff another time, "Here's our new policy. Do it if you can, but if you can't, don't worry. After all, it's mandatory." His top effort for the year, however, was, "They tell me we're printing too many old platitudes lately. Let's get rid of those old platitudes, boys, and go out and find some new ones."

When Ward Morehouse, now one of New York's best-known commentators on theatrical affairs, first broke into the newspaper field, he landed a job on the Savannah *Press*. For the princely wage of nine dollars a week he did city-news odds and ends and wrote a sports column under the pseudonym of "J. Alexander Finn." One day he picked an all-Savannah scholastic football team and was rash enough to omit the name of a stalwart named Bubber Bryson. Bubber did not take kindly to this discrimination. In fact, he sent a member of his retinue down to the *Press* office to beat the bejabbers out of young Morehouse. The editor in chief surveyed the damage to Ward's cherubic countenance and beamed. "This is a mighty fine thing to happen, boy! Shows your column's being read!"

There was a journalist in Chicago named Perlstein who suddenly changed his name to Paris. The latter, he explained, he now knew, as a result of careful investigation, had been the correct family name all the time. This gave author Emmett Dedmon the opportunity to tell all and sundry, "The last time I saw Paris —he was Perlstein!"

Pierre Lazareff, editor of the Paris newspaper, *Ce Soir*, summed up the life of a journalist in one sentence for a college class recently: "A journalist spends the first half of his career writing about things he doesn't understand, and the second half concealing the fact that he understands them only too well!"

Oh-so-true words from Bill Vaughan, of the Kansas City *Star*: "A favorite refuge of politicians, when caught in a crack, is to claim that they were misquoted in the press, and the chances are ten to one that they were. That is, they were misquoted in that the reporter cleaned up their rhetoric, supplied the missing verbs, and made sure that their predicates agreed in some gen'l way with their subjects.

"The nastiest thing a reporter could do to a politician would be to quote him absolutely accurately down to every uh, or, well, you see, that is, and so on."

John Wheeler, chairman of North American Newspaper Alliance, told fellow Sigma Chis of an early experience of Brother Kent Cooper of the Associated Press. When Kent was in his swaddling clothes, he played a fiddle in a theater orchestra near Indianapolis. The great Victor Herbert breezed into town, and Kent bagged an interview with him.

While Herbert chatted with Cooper, he hummed the beginning of a catchy melody, then paused to slip off one of his stiff, detachable cuffs and wrote the notes thereon. "May I have it?" asked Cooper eagerly. "You may copy it," said Herbert, "but I can't give it to you. After all, I can't arrive in Chicago with one shirt cuff."

Cooper kept his copy of the four bars Herbert had jotted down. He heard them many times over in the years to come. They were the opening notes of what was to be Victor Herbert's crowning composition—"Kiss Me Again" from *Mlle. Modiste*.

Richard Conte, assigned the role of a newspaper reporter in an upcoming motion picture, determined not to play it in the stereotyped, ridiculous manner followed slavishly by countless predecessors. To remind himself of his vow, he pasted this set of rules on his dressing-room mirror:

1. *No cigarette dangling from right side of lower lip.*
2. *No hat perched far back on head.*
3. *No loosened collar, and tie pulled far to one side.*
4. *No worn trench coat with turned-up collar.*
5. *No press card tucked in hat band.*
6. *No use of any of these phrases: "Stop the presses!"; "I have a scoop"; "Here's your headline!"; "Gimme rewrite"; "Tear out the front page!"*

Editor Sam Day tells a story of a cranky old head of a Philadelphia paper who liked to dash off his own lead editorials. He

finished one in a white heat and slapped it into the copy basket
with a great flourish. The managing ed, unfortunately, didn't
know what he was talking about, and the boss had to admit, once
he was challenged, that neither did he. Finally he decided,
"Print it as is. It'll make them think, anyhow!"

Joe Patterson, one of the great newspapermen of all time, confessed to an interviewer, "I built the popularity of my paper on
legs. When we got the circulation, we put stockings on the legs."

Early in his journalistic career, columnist Bob Considine toiled
for "Cissy" Patterson on the Washington *Times-Herald*. Shortly
after he left to seek greater fame in Manhattan, she phoned him
to report that she had just had a whopper of a fight with her
brother, Captain Joe Patterson, over a piece he had authored,
and wanted Considine to ghost-write a full-page answer she proposed to run over her signature in the *Times-Herald*. Bob banged
out a honey and air-mailed it to her. She phoned the next day
and enthused, "It's exactly what I wanted, Bob, and I insist on
paying you for it. How much do you want?" "Shucks," deprecated Bob, "I don't want anything at all. I did it for an old
friend." "No, no," said Cissy. "Let's settle it this way. What did
you get for your last article in *Cosmopolitan?*" "Seven hundred
and fifty bucks," answered Considine, "but that hasn't anything
to do with this. I beg you to forget all about it."

Two days later he got a check from Mrs. Patterson for five
hundred dollars with a note in longhand attached that read,
"Dear Bob: I called *Cosmopolitan.*"

The cream of America's journalistic fraternity was assembled
at Las Vegas for a series of highly publicized atomic-bomb tests,
but heavy winds necessitated one delay after another. The cream
did not take kindly to the postponements. "They don't seem to
realize whom they've kept waiting," was their implied attitude.

About the fifth long afternoon, the youngest reporter in the crowd pointed to a red, setting sun and inquired, "That's the west over there, isn't it?"

A bored veteran yawned elaborately and assured him, "If it isn't, son, you've just scored the biggest scoop since the Johnstown Flood!"

Bill Nichols, of *This Week* magazine, describes a publisher as "a man who goes around with a worried look on his assistants' faces."

Advice from Richard Carlson to neophytes aiming for *The New Yorker:* "Write with *Collier's* in mind—then chop off the last two paragraphs."

Jim Thurber, reminiscing about his early days on *The New Yorker* magazine, says, "Editor Harold Ross gave me a job because he convinced himself I was an old pal of E. B. White. I tried to tell him I had met White for the first time on the way in to his office, but he wouldn't listen. I thought I was hired to be a writer, but for three weeks all I did was sign slips of paper they thrust under my nose. Finally, I asked, 'What am I signing here, anyhow?' 'That,' said my secretary, 'is the pay roll.' That's when I found Ross had made me managing editor. When I asked him why, he said firmly, 'Because everybody starts at the bottom here.' It took me eight years of solid writing to persuade Ross to make somebody else his confounded managing editor."

In *The Reporter*, Bill Mauldin confided the formula whereby Harold Ross, late and great editor of *The New Yorker*, managed to stay off radio programs. "I'm a profane *** by nature," he explained, "and whenever one of those *** round tables or something called up, I'd say, 'Hell, yes. I'll be glad to sit in on your *** panel, or whatever the *** you call it!' The word soon got around that I couldn't draw a breath without cussing and the *** hucksters never bothered me again."

227

An alert *Fortune* reporter spotted a very special classified ad the other day, inserted by an optimistic lady from Salzburg, Austria. "For sale," it proclaimed. "Palatial mansion in historic Salzburg. One hundred rooms, twenty-eight fountains, acres of courtyard. Price: one million dollars."

Here's how *Fortune's* house organ sized up the incident. The ad, it asserted, had been shipped in "uber der transom" by a "furuckte Frau who had been gestucken mit a weissen Elephant on her Hande." Her chances of getting out from under, it continued, were negligible, since "a million dollars heute is a lot of coconutten for ein Haus." In the old days, of course, sighed the *Fortune* sage, subscribers used to buy yachts and castles without "batting ein Auge," but there's a new order in vogue today, and that sort of extravagance is "raus forever"—or strictly "Keine Dice."

The personnel manager of a big paperback-book publishing outfit keeps a bowl of goldfish on his desk. "No, I don't give a damn about goldfish," he explains. "I just like to have something around here that opens its mouth without asking for a raise."

Most reassuring to timid souls who believe that the literary life of America is about to be snuffed out by television, is the revelation of what book publishers were fretting about back in the 1890's. Trolley cars, believe it or not, were what these short-sighted fellows foresaw as the ruination of the book business— trolley cars and tandem bicycles! "When young people," groaned one agitated publisher in 1894, "prefer bouncing down to Coney Island and back on a dangerously speeding trolley, to curling up in the library with a good novel, what in the world are we coming to?"

After the trolley and bicycle scares, of course, it was cheap automobiles, then movies, then radio that were going to sound the death knell of the book business. Television is only the latest of an endless series of bugaboos. But, as I repeat every time I get the chance, nothing—absolutely nothing—will ever take the place—or give the infinite satisfaction—of a really good book.

CHAPTER NINETEEN

THE PUN-AMERICAN CONFERENCE

The time having come to mete out some pun-ishment, we might as well begin with the singular story of a relative and name-sake of Syngman Rhee, doughty President of South Korea, who came to America to learn the magazine business and enlisted under the banner of Mr. Luce's *Life* magazine. Off on his very first assignment, he succeeded in getting lost completely, and it took New York's best private eyes to track him down.

When they finally spotted him in a Third Avenue café, one cried in relief, "Ah, sweet Mr. Rhee, of *Life*, at last I've found you."

A high Soviet commissar named Rudolph Mozoltoff was walking down a Moscow street with two friends—a man and his wife —when a drop of moisture settled on his blouse. "It's raining," he announced through his beard. "You're wrong," said the wife. "It's snowing." "Oh no," insisted her husband. "Rudolph, the Red, knows rain, dear."

An anthropologist in darkest Africa encountered one tribe whose dexterity with spears astounded him. The chief's aim was particularly unerring. When the anthropologist produced a half dollar from his tunic, the chief speared it from a distance of fifty yards. He achieved the same result with a quarter.

"Now," proposed the delighted scientist, "let's see if you can score another bull's-eye on this ten-cent piece." The chief demurred. "These tired old eyes of mine aren't what they used to be," he confessed. "Mind if I let my kid brother try it?"

With that, he cupped his lips and bellowed, "Brother, can you spear a dime?"

George Ansbarry tells about a twelve-year-old boy who was passionately devoted to his stamp album until the kid next door began collecting stamps, too. "He buys every stamp I do," the twelve-year-old complained to his father, "and has taken all the fun out of it for me. I'm quitting." "Don't be a fool, my boy," counseled the father. "You seem to forget that imitation is the sincerest form of philately."

There are any number of pun-icious characters in Peter De Vries' novel, *The Tunnel of Love*. One thinks a seersucker is a man who spends all his money on fortunetellers. A second keeps asking his analyst, "Have I told you about my aberration?" A third—my favorite—calls his place Moot Point (because there's a legal difficulty about the right of way), and, when asked if he ever heard of a dance called the czardas, asks dubiously, "That's by Hoagy Carmichael, isn't it?"

The captain of an undermanned sailing ship was offered a consignment of hardened convicts during the Napoleonic Wars. "Nothing doing," protested the wily captain. "Too many crooks spoil the sloop."

Jane Cannon's improbable story concerns a young miss who wanted to have her hair bobbed, but lacked the cash demanded by the town's only beautician. "My paw owns the biggest orchard in these parts," the girl reminded the beautician. "How's for letting me pay you in apples?" "Listen, toots," was the indignant reply, "I stopped bobbing for apples when I was twelve years old."

You will now kindly imagine that it is an unseasonably hot day in the spring of 1606, and that William Shakespeare and a friend from his Globe Theater staff are bent on a swim at a British beach resort. They're wearing last year's regalia, of course, and Shakespeare suddenly suspects that moths have been feeding on the back of his bathing trunks. "Wouldst investigate?" he asks his friend.

The friend makes a thorough, if unobtrusive, inspection, then reports cheerfully, "No holes, Bard."

An Irish literary critic was singing the blues, suffering, he explained, from a severe attack of new-writus. "You'd be happier," a supposed friend assured him, "if you'd just read Joyce and Synge."

And critic Jack O'Brian, upon hearing that the famous Dublin poet, George Russell (known universally as "AE"), had lost his temper in a debate, wrote, "You mean that AE's Irish rose."

That's what I think he wrote, anyhow. His pun-manship is not too legible.

Dick Rodgers, who obviously should stick to his inspired song writing, wagers that you can't list four islands whose names are complete questions.

The answers—and I advise you to start running before you give them to anybody—are: Hawaii? Jamaica? Samoa? and S'*tate*n Island?

Libby Noble, of Los Angeles, has an uncle who loves wandering to the far corners of the earth. He is known as the roamin'est Noble of them all. . . . Henry Allen, also of Los Angeles, is going to confine *his* traveling this year to a trip to Kansas City, believing that Missouri loves company.

A mighty North African potentate was wont to while away many a pleasant evening appreciating the gyrations of a native dancing belle named Bubbles. One night, however, a booking agent persuaded him to try Sari, a new importation from Paree. The potentate was so displeased with the substitution, he muttered the North African equivalent of "Phooey," phoned the agent, and announced curtly, "Sari wrong number."

The scene now shifts to Saudi Arabia, where according to Ken Suslick, of Chicago, an Arab sheik fell off the merry-go-round of a carnival and was promptly gobbled up by the second of three hungry sheep grazing nearby. (Sheep always graze in threes in those parts, it seems.)

The owner of the carnival, angry at losing a cash customer in this distressing fashion, seized the offending animal and exclaimed, "Middle lamb, you've had a dizzy Bey."

In the fair city of Rochester, New York, Howard Hosmer would have you believe that a young couple received from Australian friends a crated, two-month-old rary as a gift. The rary, not unlike a kangaroo in looks and habits, was cute as all get out, but its appetite was enormous and, as it matured, it showed every sign of eating the couple out of house and home.

The Rochester zoo had all the raries it wanted at the moment, and the young couple reluctantly decided to do away with their Australian beastie altogether. The husband knew a country road that skirted a steep bluff overlooking the Genesee River gorge, and, borrowing a dump truck for the purpose, dropped the animal over the edge.

Too late, the animal realized his fate. His last reproachful words, as he plunged into space, were, "It's a long way to tip a rary."

In England, a scamp named Sam Rollins became so expert in counterfeiting small coins that he avoided detection for years. Scotland Yard, however, finally caught up with him. On his way to jail, Rollins asked his captor disconsolately, "How did you track me down?" The Scotland Yard man, obviously a night-club devotee of Joe E. Lewis, hummed softly, "Sam, You Made de Pence Too Long."

Another counterfeiter's proud boast was, "I'm an expert with the bad mintin' racket."

The late Oliver Herford once visited a prominent nose and throat specialist, and found himself in the midst of a group of sinus patients who had had their treatments and were pulling themselves together in the waiting room. "They have come to cough," observed Mr. Herford, "but remained to spray."

Have you happened u-pun:

1. The chap at Coney Island who makes a pretty penny by being a habitué? He stands by a scale on the boardwalk, chanting to passers-by, "Habitué 168, habitué 184 . . ."

2. The young man in white who passed a pretty girl in a Los Angeles hospital corridor? He cauterize and winked. She interne winked back. (They were both attending a limping patient, who kept complaining, "My heel is Achille-ing me.")

3. The bridge game at the White House where a daring Eisenhower finesse failed and he went down two tricks? It was one of the few times anybody ever set a president.

4. The beautiful young lady who tugged constantly at her dress and wiggled uncomfortably? Obviously, a chafing dish!

5. The member of a Sanitation Department who was asked where he first had met his bride-to-be? Softly he hummed, " 'Twas on a pile of debris that I found her."

6. The disk jockey who lived on spins and needles? He won an Academy Award with his old plaque magic.

7. The maiden of sixteen who ne'er had been kissed? Summed up Bergen Evans: "A lass and a lack."

8. The big steel magnate who altered his will eleven times in two years? Obviously, a fresh heir fiend.

9. The two scoundrels in Casablanca who fleeced the town's

richest citizen? As they made off with the boodle, they muttered, "We must do this Moor often."

10. The Irishman who told his chiropodist, "Me fate is in your hands"?

11. The baker who perfected a new variety of doughnut? He calls it the "Phyfe." Soon, he hopes, every lover of antiques will be dunking Phyfes.

12. The postman who cut a big hole in the bottom of his pouch? His motto was, "The mail *must* go through!"

13. The harem-scarem heiress who invaded a Tunisian seraglio? She demanded a parlor, Bedouin, and bath.

14. The trusty at a state-prison farm? He routed the warden from his bed, shouting, "There's a character outside attaching an airplane propeller to his old jalopy. I think he's preparing to fly the coupe."

A butcher in the Bronx got along swimmingly with every tenant in his building except a mysterious swami who occupied the third-floor rear. How that butcher and swami loathed each other!

One evening, however, the swami found that his cupboard was bare and was forced to patronize his enemy's shop. "Give me a pound of liver," he ordered of a clerk. The butcher beckoned the clerk to the rear of the establishment. "Here's our chance to put one over on that fraud," he exulted. Then, pointing to his clerk's thumb, he sang, "Weigh down upon the swami's liver."

That same swami had a cousin who, understandably enough, was a whirling dervish in the Ringling Circus. One day an uncommonly handsome damsel picked up this dervish and took him out for a row on the lake in Central Park.

Suddenly the boat tilted, and the damsel quavered to her companion, "I'm afraid I've lost my oar, Derv."

Bruce Rogers, the famous typographer, traveled all the way from Danbury to tell me about a woman who enters bank, (1) greets the cashier, (2) declares she's in the bank's debt, (3) gives him the money, (4) says good-by, and (5) is grabbed at the door when the cashier shouts that her money is counterfeit—all in characters from Shakespeare: Othello, Cassio, Desdemona, Iago, and Caesar.

Writes Jerry Nedwick of Chicago, "Knowing how you like good corn" (where did he get a notion like that?), "I'm passing on an old vaudeville routine used by Harry Vokes and Hap Ward way back in 1902:

" 'Where did you get those pants?' 'Pantsylvania.'

'The coat?'	'North Dacoata.'
'The vest?'	'Vest Virginia.'
'The collar?'	'Collarado.'
'The hat?'	'Manhattan.'
'The shirt?'	'A fellow gave it to me.' "

Elizabeth Behymer, of Dallas, was in court when a drunk was handed a stiff fine and reprimanded by the judge. The drunk suddenly cussed out the court and made a break for freedom. He was apprehended and fined once more, with his honor pointing out, "Had you been chaste and refined, you'd never have been chased and re-fined!"

In my opinion, that judge was in contempt himself.

There's a pun concerning cats, too, but you have to know a little French (very little) to appreciate it. Seems there were three cats riding on a barge in the Seine when a river steamer rammed into it and sent it to the bottom.

The headlines in Paris papers the following morning read, "Un, Deux, Trois, Cats Sank."

A gardener attached to Buckingham Palace, chronicles writer Lee Rogow, stole a chair belonging to Queen Elizabeth and hid it in his greenhouse. He was speedily apprehended and sen-

237

tenced to reading nothing but puns for ten years, an obvious vindication of the old maxim that people who live in glass houses shouldn't stow thrones.

Stout sea captain Peter Swanstrum (he says the crew is always having fun at his expanse) lost a sailor overboard in a storm and saw him swallowed by a whale. The resourceful captain took after the whale in a rowboat and, by judicious handling of an oar, managed to beat the tar out of him.

A special maestro was hired to conduct a concert of music by Bach and Mozart. In rehearsal he pushed the civic orchestra so intensely, he became known as a Bach Suite driver.

Clifton Fadiman, the pun-loving rover, has selected for special mention a few outstanding examples of the ancient art. He heads his list with Groucho Marx's irr-elephant hunting tale. In Africa, he grumbled, he found the tusks too firmly rooted, but in Alabama, of course, Tuscaloosa. Then there was the time George S. Kaufman got tangled up with the word "euphemism." He finally extricated himself by declaring, "Euphemism and I'm for youse'm."

Louis Untermeyer characterized composers plagiarizing from Debussy as "Debussybodies." Christopher Fry noted that a silver-tongued but opportunistic orator was "coruscating on thin ice." Max Beerbohm declined to be lured into a hike to the summit of a Swiss Alp. "Put me down," he said firmly, "as an anti-climb Max."

Fadiman himself, steering a party of friends to a little Italian restaurant he had praised to the skies, suddenly discovered he had misplaced the proprietor's card. "We'll have to go elsewhere," mourned Fadiman. "I seem to have lost my Spaghettis-burg address!"

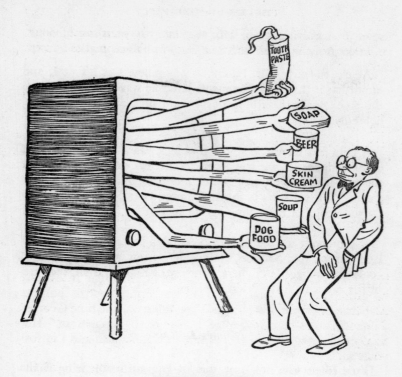

CHAPTER TWENTY

SOMETHING IN THE AIR

A really dyed-in-the-wool television addict these days, maintains Weare Holbrook, must be properly attuned to nose appeal. Mr. Holbrook valiantly kept his set turned up for one entire evening, and found his olfactory apparatus exposed to the following:

8:00 *A coffee with that delicious aroma.*
8:15 *A cigarette with that satisfying flavor.*
8:30 *A toothpaste that keeps your mouth "kissing sweet."*
9:00 *A bread with that home-baked fragrance.*
10:00 *A cigar with that rich Havana filler.*

239

10:30 A *shaving lotion with that tangy he-man scent.*
11:00 A *cedar chest with that built-in balsam breeze.*

At eleven-thirty, Mr. Holbrook was relieved at his post, and rumor has it that, some moments later, he was strolling through the stock yards, breathing deeply and pounding his chest delightedly.

A man in a television studio told Jack Paar, "My wife falls for every commercial she's exposed to. Before retiring each night she uses four face creams, two chin creams, and even one elbow cream." "I'll bet she's beautiful," mused Paar, "but tell me: how do you keep her from slipping out of bed?"

If somebody walked up and demanded the real first names of Red Barber, Red Skelton, Skitch Henderson, and Bing Crosby, could you oblige? Well, here, courtesy of Frank Farrell, they are, in the order named: Walter, Richard, Lyle, and Harry.

Allen's Sallies

Fred Allen was not only one of the authentic wits of the American theater but a generous, unassuming, and inspiring gentleman whose like will not soon be seen again. The half hours I spent with him in the dressing room every Sunday evening before we went on for "What's My Line?" will be among the memories I will cherish always.

Fred Allen's real name was John Florence Sullivan; he borrowed the "Fred Allen" from an agent when he broke into vaudeville after World War I with what he called, "The world's worst juggling act." A placard on stage read, "Mr. Allen is quite deaf. If you care to applaud, please do so loudly." Fred wore a suit obviously too big for him. "I had it made in Jersey City," he explained to his audience. "I'm a bigger man there than I am here."

His first chance to utter words on a stage came when he assumed the role of a Wise Man in a Christmas play at his Sunday school. The words were, "Myrrh is mine, its bitter perfume breathes a life of gathering gloom." Fred was six at the time.

Fred Allen's famous feud with Jack Benny was for stage purposes only. In private life they were firm and fast friends. At a Friars' dinner in honor of Benny, Fred's speech, by common consent, was the highlight of a memorable evening. "When Jack signed his new contract with CBS," confided Allen, "he was told he could have everything he wanted. To his everlasting credit, be it said he never took advantage of this. He left them the basement of their building at 485 Madison Avenue." Concerning

Benny's talent as a violin virtuoso, Allen added, "Jack is the only fiddler who makes you feel the strings would sound better back in the cat."

John Crosby recalls a day when Benny was appearing on the Paramount stage and Allen heckled him from a front-row seat. The audience was laughing so hard that Jack finally waved a twenty-dollar bill and offered it to anyone who could top Allen's last gag. Instantly, Allen was on his feet, topped his own sally with a better one—and claimed the twenty dollars!

Typical Fred Allen creations who reappeared in the pages of his nostalgic book, *Treadmill to Oblivion*, included the only armless sculptor in the world (he put the chisel in his mouth and his wife hit him on the back of the head with a mallet); Professor Gulpo, who swallowed umbrellas (he was putting something away for a rainy day); and an uncle who brought his goldfish to the aquarium every year for a two-week romp. One day, however, Uncle fell into the tank himself, and they couldn't tell him from the other fish. Finally, they threw a picture of Allen's aunt into the water—and when one of the fish recognized it and tried to escape from the tank, they grabbed him. For twenty years, claims Fred, his mother in Boston kept a light burning in the window for him. When he came home she gave him a royal welcome and a gas bill for $729.

Fred disposed of network executives with a caustic "If the United States can get along with one vice-president, I don't know why NBC needs twenty-six." Of his agent, he remarked, "He gets 10 per cent of everything I get except my blinding headaches."

One of his happiest conceptions was the Allen Relaxation Society, designed for tired businessmen whose doctors had prescribed a long rest, but who didn't have time to follow orders. Allen supplied substitutes to take the relaxation for these brilliant tycoons, thereby leaving them free to overwork themselves to death or their hearts' content.

"We took care of one magnate," recalled Fred, "whose doctor warned him to go off with his wife for a long, health-restoring cruise. We produced a man who not only took the cruise for him, overate for him, undertipped for him, and got seasick for him, but flirted so shamelessly with a cute blonde for him that his wife went into a huff all the way from Cherbourg to Juan-les-Pins."

One morning, Janet Kern sportingly printed in her column a letter from a reader lambasting her savagely—also ungrammatically—for daring to criticize a remark Fred had thoughtlessly made on "What's My Line?" Fred wrote consolingly, "Dear Janet; isn't it strange that people learn to hate before they learn to spell?"

Very few important comedians laugh at other important comedians. Very few, in fact, even bother to listen. A great exception is Jack Benny. George Burns and Danny Kaye can reduce him to helpless mirth merely by opening their mouths. In fact Jack not only laughs at his confreres, but cues them into repeating their best stories.

It was at his insistence that Jesse Block, of the famous team of Block and Sully, told us of their appearance at the London Palladium, where Miss Sully suddenly discovered that her necklace was missing. "Don't worry," soothed Block. "There are no gangsters over here. All we have to do is summon Scotland Yard."

In due course, exactly the kind of character they were expecting turned up from the Yard—complete with walrus mustache, derby, rolled umbrella, and black notebook. They heard nothing from him for twenty-four hours. Then Block was told he was calling. "What did I tell you?" he exulted.

When he returned to the dressing room, Miss Sully demanded, "Has he found my necklace?"

"On the contrary," answered Block glumly. "He's lost his umbrella."

Steve Allen, droll TV star, says that if you'll listen attentively enough you'll discover that a comedian always starts his next story with "And seriously," after the last one has laid an egg. "And seriously," he adds, "we've been packing the rafters at our own show. Of course there haven't been many people in the seats, but we sure are packing those rafters!"

When but a babe, recalls George Burns, his ma paid a nurse-girl a dollar a day to wheel him around the park in his buggy—and he's been pushed for money ever since.

William Archibald Spooner was an Anglican clergyman and educator who became the dean of New College, Oxford, in 1876, a post which he occupied with distinction for thirteen years. What his students remembered with the greatest delight, however, was an unfortunate predilection for transposing the letters or sounds in two or more words.

For example, he startled one audience with, "Kinquering congs their titles take," told another, "Our chapel desperately needs funds with which to refurbish these beery wenches."

The official word in all dictionaries for such mix-ups always was "metathesis," but the dean erred so frequently in this direction that "Spoonerism" took its place, and is now accepted by scholars without question as definitive. (In China, of course, it's called a slip of the Tong.)

With announcers on the air working under continuous pressure, the wonder is they scramble words so seldom. But the best of them have perpetrated some "fluffs" that will be remembered for years.

Really smart announcers have learned never to attempt correcting a Spoonerism. Woe befell the unfortunate commentator who hailed "Hoobert Hever," then hurriedly bumbled on, "I mean 'Hervie Hoober.'" Another fellow got tangled up in "Visit your nearest 'A and Poo Feed Store.'" A third referred to "My dear friends, the Duck and Doochess of Windsor." Bill Leonard, evidently mindful of the ups and downs in an actor's career, once introduced Joe E. Brown as "currently starving in *Harry*." And a top reader of commercials is still trying to live down his prize Spoonerism: "For that extra thrill, try Buppert's Reer."

Two radio announcers got their tongues twisted with unfortunate consequences recently. One, speaking of a fragile movie star, declared, "Her breath will take your beauty away." The second attributed a news flash to "respected White House souses."

Today people actually are making a hobby of collecting TV bloopers. Some of the more glaring errors—including many no self-respecting publisher would print—have even been immortalized on a series of fast-selling phonograph records.

By common agreement, the TV master of ceremonies who won this year's award for the prize boner was the hapless soul who asked a small boy three times, in increasingly urgent tones, to name "the cereal you love to eat every morning, sonny." Sonny finally broke his silence by pointing out to the M.C.—and the coast-to-coast TV audience, "You're hurting my arm, mister."

It served the moderator of one of radio's innumerable quiz shows right! His jack-pot question was "Can you name the difference between amnesia and magnesia?" The audience howled with joy when the contestant, after a moment's deep deliberation, hazarded, "The fellow with amnesia has no idea where he's going."

A sportscaster was giving his all to a wrestling show in Knoxville, Tennessee, recently when the cops asked him to interrupt his rhapsody long enough to make an announcement. A 1955 Buick was parked illegally outside the arena, blocking all traffic. The sportscaster read aloud the model, make, and license number, with all the proper flourishes—then realized it was his own car!

On an unrehearsed TV show, a loquacious gob threw the M.C. off stride by maintaining that his girl had the most beautiful legs in the world. "How do you know?" ventured the M.C. The gob said, "I counted them."

With panel shows and quiz programs featured ever more prominently on TV, the spotlight has focused on Mark Goodson and Bill Todman, the ingenious young pair who concocted a half dozen and more of the most successful examples of the art. "What's My Line" is theirs, for instance, and so are "I've Got a Secret" and "Two for the Money." Somebody once saw a table with four empty chairs grouped around it and quipped, "If Goodson sees this, he'll have a new TV show by six this evening!" Another day, Bill Todman let a heavy chair slip out of his grasp. "Careful, Bill," admonished Goodman Ace, "or you'll lose your script."

When she appears on the panel of "What's My Line?"—or any of the many other television shows in which she stars— Arlene Frances invariably wears around her neck a gold chain and beautiful diamond-encrusted heart. One day she received a call from a young lady who explained that her boss had noticed the heart, loved it, and was anxious to get a replica to give his wife as an anniversary gift. Arlene, because she is a warm, generous girl, went to considerable trouble to arrange a meeting between the boss and the jeweler who had fashioned the heart for her, and the boss got his replica in due time and at a reasonable price.

A week later the secretary phoned Arlene Frances again. Her boss, she explained, was so grateful for her interest that he was sending one of his products to her as a gift. Arlene said "Thank you," without ever inquiring what the product was. The next morning she found out. The boss was one of the heads of the Dodge Motor Company. His gift—a shiny new Dodge sedan— was standing in front of her apartment house when she stepped out into the sunshine of Park Avenue.

Did you know that the principal radio announcer who told the nation the sad details of the funeral procession of Franklin D. Roosevelt in Washington was Arthur Godfrey? Godfrey tells of the man who took a taxi from a hotel, bound for Union Station, and instructed his driver to pull up while he, followed by the driver, alighted to watch the solemn procession file by. The two men stood bareheaded and mournful for a long time, then resumed the drive to the station. There the passenger asked, "What do I owe you?" "Two bits," said the driver. "Your meter must be out of kilter," said the passenger. "We must have been standing out there an hour at least." The driver reminded him, "Mister, he was my President too."

Groucho Marx met an honest-to-goodness bullfighter south of the border and asked him, "How many bulls do you figure you've met?" "At least two hundred, señor," smirked the bullfighter. "You must be the envy of every cow in Mexico," marveled Groucho.

An amateur radio ham went delirious with excitement when he caught a newscast straight from Moscow on his set. "Our great athlete, Ivan Skvitch," the announcer was booming, "has just smashed all existing world's records for the two-hundred-yard dash, the mile run, the five-mile run, and the hundred-mile run, overcoming such formidable obstacles as a blizzard, a range of mountains, and complete lack of water." There was a moment's silence, and then the announcer continued in more subdued tones, "Unfortunately, Ivan Skvitch's fantastic performance was in vain. He was captured and brought back to Russia."

John O'Hara, distinguished author of *Ten North Frederick* and *A Rage to Live*, has rallied to the defense of television. In his provocative column in *Collier's* he told of a friend whose sprawling household includes children by his first marriage, children by his present wife, and stepchildren whom his wife brought with her. There are, roughly, ten children in all.

"Before we bought a TV set," this friend assured O'Hara, "this place used to be a madhouse. Kids all over the house. But then we installed the set in our cellar. Now the kids spend their lives there, and once a week we throw them a couple of fish heads, and everybody's happy."

CHAPTER TWENTY-ONE

IT'S ONLY A GAME . . .

Baseball

Say Hey Willie Mays's "autobiography," *Born to Play Ball*, really was written by Charlie Einstein, who dogged the center fielder's footsteps faithfully for weeks, trying to assemble enough facts to justify a $3.50 price tag on the book. The first draft completed, Einstein contacted Willie on the phone, where, according to the always-accurate Harvey Breit, the following conversation ensued: Einstein: "Hi, Willie, this is Charlie Einstein." Mays: "Who?"

Einstein: "Charlie Einstein. You know—the fellow who wrote the book." Mays: "What book?" Curtain . . .

Another distinguished literary light from baseball circles, Casey Stengel, was persuaded to attend a performance of George Abbott's musical production, *Damn Yankees*, which is an adaptation of Douglass Wallop's sprightly (and wishful-thinking) novel, *The Year the Yankees Lost the Pennant*. Asked how he liked the show, Casey drew himself up in the best and haughtiest George Jean Nathan manner and declared, "I ain't gonna comment about a guy which made $100,000 writin' how my club lost."

Catcher Dixie Howell was chasing a foul pop one night at the Montreal ball park. It was headed right over the home team's dugout, and one of the players not in the game jumped out and grabbed Howell to prevent his falling down the step. Dixie ended up hanging onto the roof of the dugout while the ball bounced way up in the air.

"Did you see how high that ball bounced when it landed on the concrete?" demanded Howell.

"Concrete, hell," said his teammate. "It landed right on my head!"

Two rooters at a ball game were so engrossed in the contest that neither wanted to take time out to march back to the refreshment bar for hot dogs—and there wasn't a vendor in sight. They finally bribed a kid nearby to go for them, giving him forty-five cents and saying, "Buy a dog for yourself at the same time."

The kid came back with thirty cents change for them, explaining, "They only had *my* hot dog left."

Stan Musial, champion batter of the National League, is aptly described by Joe Garagiola, catcher on a rival team, but close friend of Musial's in the off season. "Stan," broods Garagiola, "comes sauntering up to the plate and asks me how my family's making out. Before I can answer him, he's on third base."

Charlie Grimm is equally renowned as a big-league baseball manager and a left-handed banjo player. He was acting in the former capacity in Chicago a few seasons ago, with no conspicuous success. In fact, his Cubs were floundering in last place, when one day a scout rushed into the clubhouse in great excitement to report, "Charlie, I just saw a kid in a sand-lot game fan twenty-seven batters in a row. He had such baffling curves and blinding speed that nobody even got a foul off him till two were out in the ninth. Should I sign him up?" "You're balmy," Grimm told him, strumming idly on his banjo. "It's hitters we need right now. Sign the fellow who got the foul off him."

Lou Boudreau, manager of the Boston Red Sox, snorts with disgust at recurrent rumors that there have been occasional clashes of temperament between him and his star operative, Ted Williams. Boudreau dismisses the rumors with a single sentence that might be tacked up over the desk of every big-league manager in baseball: "Any manager who can't get along with a .400 hitter ought to have his head examined."

Frank Graham tells this story about a typical, dyed-in-the-wool Brooklyn Dodgers fan. Gil Hodges, in the throes of a slump, stepped up to bat in the fourth inning. "Git dat bum outta dere," yelled the fan. "He can't hit his way outta a paper bag!" Toots Shor, sitting behind the fan, warned, "Lay off that Hodges. He's a pal of mine." "Okay," conceded the fan reluctantly, "but tell me, mister, how many udder bums on dis team is pals of yours too?" "Well," figured Toots, "there's Campanella, and Snider, and Erskine, and Jackie Robinson, to name only a few." "Holy mackerel," said the fan. "Lemme outta here, mister. You ain't gonna stop *me* from enjoyin' dis game!"

How many United States Presidents are real baseball fans,

and how many simply put on an act to win friends and influence voters? Sam Himmell has done some diligent research along these lines and comes up with the following. Abraham Lincoln was actually playing baseball when a committee came to his home to inform him he had been nominated for the presidency. William Howard Taft was a confirmed baseball fanatic; it was he who originated the now-standard procedure whereby the President opens every pennant race by tossing out the first ball at the Washington stadium (F.D.R. threw out more first balls, of course, than all the others combined; if practice makes perfect, he could have qualified for a job on the Senators' first-string mound staff!).

It was Benjamin Harrison, twenty-third President of the U.S., who tagged the New York club of the National League with its nickname, "The Giants."

The most avid fan among Presidents was Woodrow Wilson, the most apathetic, Calvin Coolidge. Harry Truman once yearned to be a professional ballplayer, but couldn't quite make the grade. William McKinley, on the other hand, turned down what was in those days a fabulous offer, from a big-league scout, to pursue his political career.

When Casey Stengel signed his first contract to manage the New York Yankees, Jimmy Cannon took him over to Toots Shor's celebrated bistro for a celebration of sorts. The ebullient Mr. Shor promptly produced a pencil and proved by mathematics that Casey's team was a shoo-in to cop the pennant. At closing time Stengel pulled off the tablecloth upon which Mr. Shor had made his computations and started to stuff it in his pocket. "Hey," roared Toots, "whassa idea of trying to bust up my joint?" "I just won my first pennant on that tablecloth," explained Stengel, "and I'd like to keep it as a souvenir."

In seventeen years as a stellar pitcher in the American League, "Lefty" Gomez of the Yankees didn't exactly knock down the fences with his bat. In fact, he averaged about four scratch sin-

253

gles a season. One day he closed his eyes, took a hefty swing and, to everybody's amazement, including his own, smacked a solid triple to left center. Poised on third, the triumphant "Lefty" boasted to Coach Art Fletcher, "Hey, Art, I think I can steal home." Fletcher shuddered, and begged, "It's taken you four months to get this far: don't blow it!"

Yogi Berra, the great catcher of the New York Yankees, is famous, too, for some of the classic remarks he makes far from the baseball diamond. He was describing, for instance, the deep friendship that exists between two other infielders on the team and summed it all up by insisting, "Why, they was as close as Damon and Runyon!"

Milton Berle discovered Tallulah Bankhead rooted to a radio in her dressing room one day, screaming her head off for the New York Giants. "Gosh," exclaimed Miltie, "I didn't realize you were so interested in the national pastime." "Dahling," snapped Tallulah, "I *am* the national pastime."

Incidentally, Tallulah wanted some new recipes for her chef to try. She called her favorite bookseller and ordered two copies of Fanny Farmer's Boston Red Sox Cookbook!

Leo Durocher, ex-manager of the New York Giants, is—or was —probably the most accomplished needler—or "bench jockey"— in big-league baseball today. He could get antagonists so angry with a couple of sarcastic barbs that they forgot all about the business at hand and actually came charging at him in the dug-out to do him bodily injury.

A few springs back the Giants were playing a preseason ex-hibition game at West Point. The cadet corps began to ride Leo as he paced up and down the coaching box at third base. "Hey, Durocher," roared one leather-lunged upperclassman, "how did a runt like you ever sneak into the big leagues?" Leo, they say, silenced the uproar with a single retort. He just hollered back, "My congressman appointed me!"

The New York Giants once had a deaf-and-dumb pitching star popularly known as Dummy Taylor. Taylor thought it was safe to tell umpire Hank O'Day exactly what he thought of him with his fingers, but unfortunately, O'Day knew the sign language too. The episode cost Taylor a five-day suspension and a hundred-dollar fine. Another arbiter once cleared the whole Red Sox bench, including Coach Heinie Wagner. "I didn't say a single word," protested Wagner. "That's possible," admitted the red-faced ump, "but I know what you was thinking, and I didn't like it. Git!"

Entire pennant races have hinged on one tough decision by a harassed umpire. In 1908, Hank O'Day called Fred Merkle out for failing to touch second on a hit that ostensibly had beaten the Cubs, and the Giants lost the championship by that one game. The Brooklyn Dodgers, too, feel that a single wrong decision at the plate by umpire Dascoli in a late-September game in Boston cost them the 1951 championship. In both instances, of course, the umps simply were "calling them as they saw them."

Jerry Bruck is readying a novel about a baseball umpire named Gibbon, for publication about the time the new season opens. This Gibbon loses his glasses during a twilight game at Ebbets Field, spends the rest of his life in a futile search for them, and finally plunges to his death from the second tier of a grandstand in Kansas City. The title, of course, will be *The Decline and Fall of the Roaming Umpire.*

Umpire Bill Guthrie is responsible for two of the classic rejoinders in big-league baseball history. He told one batter who was kicking up an unholy rumpus about a called third strike, "Pipe down, son, and nobody but you and me and the catcher will know you can't see any more." And to another indignant athlete who had tossed his bat into the air in protest, Guthrie announced, "If dat bat comes down, mister, youse is outta da game!"

Riddle from Jim Albright: If two gals fortify themselves with a bottle of hooch, hie themselves to the ball park, and get magnificently plastered, what inning is it, and how many men are on base? Answer: It's the last of the fifth, and the bags are loaded.

Every once in a while some rawboned rookie from the hills turns up at a big-league training camp to evoke inevitable comparisons with Ring Lardner's famous "busher"—and to become the butt of endless practical jokes dreamed up by other members of the squad. One spotted a sign reading "Billiards" above a tavern entrance and actually asked, "What in tarnation is billiards?" A veteran on the team narrowly averted swallowing his chew of tobacco and answered, "Don't tell me you never had a slug of billiards, son! Best drink in the world! Guaranteed to put hair on your chest!"

The rookie was led into the tavern, and the veteran, with an elaborate wink to the barkeep, announced, "Give this lad a glass of the best brand of billiards in the joint." The barkeep scooped up a tall glass of soapy water from the sink, added a slug of gin, and slid the vile concoction across the bar. The rookie managed to down it, grimaced, and murmured weakly, "Them billiards is a powerful drink, all right, but did any of you fellers ever notice how much it tastes like dishwater?"

Laraine Day contributes the story about an elementary-school teacher who told his class to jot down the names of the nine men who, in their opinion, were the greatest in American history.

Everybody completed his list but ten-year-old Jerry, who sat with his brow furrowed, chewing on his pencil. "What's the trouble, Jerry?" inquired the teacher. "Can't you think of nine outstanding Americans?" "I've got eight, all right," answered Jerry, "but what I still need is a second baseman."

Golf

"Slamming Sammy" Snead, one of the all-time greats of golfdom, is an old buddy of another outstanding athlete, Ted Williams, outfielder of the Boston Red Sox. Ted invited Snead to sit on the Red Sox bench for a big game against the New York Yankees, and led his teammates in needling the golf star. Baseball, was the tenor of the remarks, was a man's game: tough, demanding, and complex. "Any old goof could hit a defenseless golf ball." But what about connecting with a baseball that was propelled toward the plate at blinding speed by a smart tricky pitcher? Snead took all the ribbing with perfect good nature, finally drawled, "Maybe all you boys say is true, but there's one thing in golf: when we hit a foul ball, we've gotta get out there and play it."

I don't think I ever saw a story sweep across the nation as quickly as the one about the man who interrupted a match-deciding putt on the eighteenth green, to stand respectfully, hat in hand, while a funeral cortege rumbled by on the road behind him. Then he sank his putt. "Congratulations," said his opponent grudgingly. "It took iron nerve not to let that funeral procession fluster you into missing your putt!"

"It wasn't easy," admitted the victor. "On Saturday we would have been married twenty-five years!"

There was a near tragedy at the water hole of the Century Club in Westchester last fall. An irate golfer plunked one new ball into the pond and threw his driver after it. When a second

ball landed in the same spot, he threw in his whole bag of clubs. Then his caddy made a grave mistake. He laughed. So the golfer threw in the caddy.

Ben Hogan, all-time golfing great, was foiled by fate one day when he tried to give a duffer the thrill of a lifetime. Ben and a friend were playing a practice round. They had just holed out on a short three-par hole whose green was partially surrounded by trees and traps when suddenly, out of nowhere, a ball plopped down and trickled within two inches of the cup.

Hogan playfully tapped the ball in, and when a red-faced player came puffing from the direction of the deepest trap, held out his hand and said, "Mister, you're in for the biggest kick you ever got out of golf. Just look in that cup." The player followed directions and then hollered to a partner still hidden from view, "Hey, Joe, whaddya know! I sank it for a seven!"

In Hollywood, actor John Payne had to grow a beard for one of his swashbuckling Western roles. With a three-week growth of foliage concealing his manly features, John essayed a round of golf on the toughest course in town and drove one ball into a deep sand trap. A member of a foursome on an adjoining fairway investigated the cause of the interesting language emanating from the trap. He watched John blasting away, then noted his whiskers flapping in the afternoon breeze.

"Good heavens, Payne," he asked, "how long have you been in this trap?"

George Burns, of Burns and Allen, playing golf on a strange course, studied the lie of his ball and asked the caddie, "What club would you use here?" "A number eight," said the caddie without hesitation. So Burns used a number eight, hit a perfect shot—and found himself still forty yards short of the pin. "That's a full spoon shot," he announced to the caddie angrily. "Why did you tell me you'd use a number eight?" "Because," explained the caddie, "that's the only club I've got."

It is estimated that a prominent attorney in our town has now taken golf lessons from thirty-seven different pros in the past four years. "I can't understand it," he wailed in the locker room one day. "Despite all the lessons, I played worse last year than the year before, and the year before it was worse than the year before that." "How are you doing now?" asked his friend, Dr. Morris Fishbein. "You shouldn't have asked," said the attorney sadly. "Already I'm playing next year's game."

A mild earthquake once settled a championship golf match in Arizona. A contestant had to sink a long putt on the eighteenth green for a win, but his ball stopped on the lip of the cup. He resigned himself to a play-off of the tie the following morning.

Just then the earth trembled, however, the ball plopped into the cup, and there being nothing in the rule book to the contrary, he was declared the new champion. His opponent had one more stroke too—apoplectic.

The last word on the royal and ancient game of golf was passed by two wealthy Chinese merchants of San Francisco, who were invited to spend a day at a country club outside of Berkeley and saw, for the first time, a couple of duffers trying to hack their way out of a sand trap. "Wouldn't you think," observed Ah Sing, "that men as rich as that could get servants to perform such arduous and unpleasant labor for them?"

Published by the Coats & Clark's Sales Corporation, located at 430 Park Avenue, New York 22, is a long-needed schedule of the going rates for (1) listening to stroke-by-stroke descriptions of interminable matches, (2) sympathizing with habitual victims of "lucky" and "unethical" opponents, and (3) helping to condemn rascally caddies who forget to hold pins, rake traps, and demur at searching for balls in the deep woods because of poison ivy or rattlesnakes.

Staying awake during recitals of this sort is difficult work, and it's high time it was properly compensated!

Hackers on the golf links will rejoice at the announcement that the Motorola Corporation is experimenting with an electronic ball. It is equipped with miniature batteries and a tiny transmitter which sends a radio-frequency signal strong enough to be picked up by a portable receiver in the pocket of the golfer.

Gone will be those dreary searches for lost balls! The duffer can whack one a hundred yards into the deepest rough and, by simply turning his receiver in the proper direction, recover what Charles Morton would call "his elusive white pellet" without a moment's delay.

Daniel E. Noble, vice-president of Motorola, warns that this revolutionary golf ball, unfortunately, has been developed for demonstration purposes only, so far.

May it be perfected in time to help an earnest but inept golfer in Hollywood who had his first chance to break 125 a few Sundays ago—but had to sink a ten-foot putt to accomplish the feat! Trembling with excitement, he crawled around the green for five minutes studying each blade of grass in the path of the ball, then fluttered a handkerchief to determine the exact direction of the wind.

Finally he appealed to a companion, Bob Sterling, who shoots in the low seventies. "How should I putt this, Bob?" he asked. Sterling answered, "Keep it low!"

Football

History records that in 1916 a young lieutenant, just graduated from West Point, was summoned from his post at Fort Sam Houston to coach the football team of a nearby school named St. Mary's. The coach, one Dwight D. Eisenhower, found the spirit at the school willing, but the material sparse. Desperately seeking reinforcements for the skimpy squad of eighteen, he suddenly spotted a husky specimen crossing the campus. "Look here, young fellow," he called sharply. "Why the heck aren't you out to play football for your Alma Mater?" The husky specimen replied, "Lieutenant, I'll have you know I'm the principal of this school."

Rotund and rollicking Herman Hickman, once all-American guard from Tennessee, then line coach of the greatest teams ever turned out at Army, then head coach at Yale, has, alas, quit active participation in football. He now does his all from press box and sound stage.

Solvent but sedentary, Herman the Erudite has wasted away to a mere 290 pounds—just small enough to fit in his entirety on a twenty-one-inch screen. When he was eating at government expense at the Point, Herman hit a high of 320, and there was talk of splitting him three for one.

In his youth Herman aspired to a career in the law. At the age of seven he was already sending for catalogues of legal tomes. At ten he was reading—and memorizing—them. When he graduated from college in 1932, however, jobs were nonexistent in law

offices and just about everywhere else. Herman became a wrestler for a time—the only pro in that sport ever admitted, says Jimmy Cannon, to the human race. Then he turned to coaching gridiron squads.

Competent football players were few and far between when Hickman finally landed at Yale. Some friends from his home town of Johnson City, Tennessee, decided to help him out and, for a birthday present, brought him a burly, barrel-chested tackle named Apidoupolos, who tossed the varsity squad around like a set of ninepins at his first scrimmage. "He's terrific," conceded Hickman, "but can he satisfy Yale's entrance requirements? For example, how's his Greek?"

"He *is* Greek," explained the friends. "It's his English we're worrying about."

In December 1952, Herman Hickman got lost in the hills of eastern Tennessee. "Mighty embarrassing, losing my way in practically my home territory," he told a mountaineer. "Home territory, my foot," scoffed the mountaineer. "You look like a big fat Yankee to me."

Herman convinced him, however, and the mollified mountaineer asked, "Who won that election last month?"

Herman knew that this section was solidly Republican, so he said, "You'll be glad to know that Ike Eisenhower sailed in. But don't you take any newspapers around here?"

"We take 'em," nodded the mountaineer grimly, "but the durn Democrats won't read 'em to us."

The trusting citizens of an Indiana town found out what happens if you elect a veteran football referee to the post of police commissioner. The very day he assumed office he arrested the community's outstanding strip-teaser. His charge: her back was illegally in motion.

Neal O'Hara tells about the football coach who started a brand-new backfield for the final quarter of a game safely won, consisting of Osscowinsinski, Yablanowicz, Palleofontack, and Bacjewobonwich. "Are they any good?" asked an old grad on the bench. "Heck no," barked the coach, "but, boy, will I pay back a score I owe a couple of those smart-aleck newspaper sports writers!"

Herman Massin tells of a time Lou Little, well-loved coach of the perennially undermanned Columbia football team, suggested to Frank Leahy, then at Notre Dame, "Suppose my Lions are playing Michigan State. We kick off and State returns the ball to our five. On the next play they pull the shift you invented. Wouldn't you say that shift was designed to pull my team offside?"

Leahy replied thoughtfully, "All I can say, Lou, is that if your team kicked off to Michigan State, and they returned the ball only to your five-yard line, your defense certainly must be improving."

Guided Muscles

A much-beaten pugilist announced his intention to retire from the ring, but his manager, sensing the loss of a fair-to-middling meal ticket, sought to dissuade him. "This ain't no time to quit, Spike," he protested, "just when you're beginning to improve. I've been noticin' right along that in every fight lately you come to much quicker!"

"The first lesson to remember in the gentle art of self-defense," advises Steve Allen, "is to keep your glasses on."

Fight managers aren't what they used to be now that television has entered the act, maintains Budd Schulberg. They used to yell, "Don't forget to duck, kid." Now they exhort, "Don't let him get away with that! He's trying to keep your back turned to the camera again!"

When a Brooklyn lad decided to become a professional pugilist, his mother was outraged and never ceased her lamentations —not even when he bagged the middleweight championship. "Now you're at the top," she begged him, "quit before it's too late. Promise you'll stop fighting right now." "But, Mama, you don't understand," the son protested. "I'm in the big money now that I'm champ. With TV and everything, I'm likely to gross a cool hundred thousand on my next bout." "A cool hundred thousand," gasped the mother. "My boy, promise me you'll stop fighting in nine or ten years."

The Idle Hour Athletic Club was putting on one of its better fixed fights, with the five-to-one favorite bribed in advance to let himself be knocked cold in the eighth round. The underdog, secure in the knowledge that he couldn't lose, let a couple of real punches loose and rattled every tooth in the favorite's head. "You dirty little double-crosser," hissed that gentleman in a clinch. "Just wait till I get you outside!"

Harry Ruby tells about the prize-fight manager whose inexperienced new middleweight was taking an unmerciful trimming in his first professional bout. Finally the manager propped up his unhappy charge and told him, "I don't care if it's bad luck or not—but this is the ninth round coming up, and, kid, you've got a no-hitter going!"

Fishing

In a Maine fishing camp, Hans Hinrichs, of New York, was served a beaker of orange juice whose flavor delighted him. "Emil," he asked his host, "where do you get your oranges? Never have I tasted such delicious juice." "In the little store down the road," answered Emil.

Mr. Hinrichs bought an entire crate on his way back to town. But when he sampled the juice, the taste definitely was not the same. He phoned Emil to register his disappointment. "I can't understand it," admitted Emil. "Your oranges are the same as ours. What gin did you use with them?"

At another fishing camp, deep in the Wisconsin woods, a group of vacationing city fellers dispatched an old guide once a week to canoe fifteen miles to the nearest village and back to collect newspapers and mail. When they checked out for the season, the old guide presented his bill. It read, "Three up and three down, at two dollars a went. Twelve dollars."

"Fishing is simplicity itself," explains Hamilton Clay, Jr. "All you have to do is get there yesterday when the fish were biting." One disciple of Izaak Walton picked the wrong day for sure. He was discovered by the father of a seven-year-old boy, pole discarded, hopping on one foot, caressing the other, and howling with anguish. "What happened?" demanded the father. "I guess it's my fault," said the seven-year-old. "This man told me he hadn't had a bite all morning—so I bit him."

If you'd like to hear about some of the darndest varieties of fish under the sun—or at least under the surface—Eugenie Clark's *Lady with a Spear* is the book for you. She tells about one fish that has double eyes, enabling it to see either in the air or in the water; another which, at full growth, is considerably less than one inch long; another that squirts poison at its enemies through a hypodermic-like syringe. Then there's the razor fish, which swims standing on its head, and, queerest of all, the pipe-fish, of which the male, believe it or not, has the babies!

One of the fishermen's favorite "tall tales" concerns the fellow who, impatient at his failure to pull in a single thing, impulsively dipped the minnow he was using as bait in a jug of moonshine and then lowered his line again. Seconds later he felt a strike and hauled in a huge sea bass, which was threshing about helplessly against the minnow, which had it by the throat and was choking it to death.

The parson, detained from his dearly loved weekly fishing expedition by a young couple who insisted upon being hitched immediately, regarded the bridegroom sourly, and inquired, "Do you promise to love, honor, and cherish this woman?" "I do," said the bridegroom fervently. "Good," boomed the parson, heading for the nearest exit. "Reel her in."

A fisherman in the Arabian Sea pulled in his net one day and found entangled therein a strange copper bottle with a golden seal. When he broke it open, a cloud of black smoke rushed out and turned into a monstrous genie. "I will revenge myself for my imprisonment in that bottle," roared the genie, "by killing everybody I see, and I will begin here and now with you."

The quick-thinking fisherman sneered, "Go ahead and kill me, you goon. Tear down that whole coastal range of mountains. And still I won't be convinced that a monster like you could be contained in that tiny bottle!"

"You won't, hey?" roared the genie. "Doubters like you *really* burn me up. Look at this, you twerp!"

Condensing himself in the twinkling of an eye, he poured himself back in the bottle. "Amazing!" chuckled the fisherman as he replaced the cork and threw the bottle back into the sea.

Hunting

Lest you think that hunting these days is a carefree and inexpensive diversion, Brother Bill Feather of Cleveland quotes these prices from a sports lovers' catalogue: "Duck shooter's parka: $55; Duckers' mittens: $10; Lambskin vest: $32; Alpaca-lined covert coat: $85; Paul Bunyan hunting boots: $38.70; Shotgun: $550; Sleeping bag: $98."

When Herb Wise, of Lengsfeld, goes duckhunting, however, he needs none of this highfalutin paraphernalia; just his trusty old double-barreled fowling piece. One day he took his nephew along to show how it was done. A solitary duck flew over the blind. "Down you go," chuckled Herb, and fired. The duck flew serenely on.

Herb scratched his head. "Son," he declared, "you are witnessing a miracle. There flies a dead duck!"

A prominent society physician was better equipped when he set out on a hunting trip, but he also returned empty-handed. "I didn't kill a thing today," he admitted. "That's the first time that's happened in years," said his unfeeling wife.

Some brand-new members of a hunting club were coming in from their first day's shooting. Since they were unused to handling guns, the casualty list was rather formidable. One had his hand in a sling, another was hopping on one foot, a third looked like the drummer boy in the old Revolutionary War picture. "Cheer up, fellows," urged an old member. "Judging by the bulge in your bag, you're not coming back empty-handed anyhow!" The one who was carrying the bag answered wearily, "That's our hunting dog!"

Joe Grizzly Bear, Indian scout at a hunting camp in the Black Hills, has a favorite picture. He carries it in his wallet, in fact. It shows a fat lady all togged up in fancy hunting clothes, with a smoking rifle in her hands, and a look of unholy glee on her face. "I must have hit something," she's exulting to her husband. "Just listen to that language!"

A party of hunters finally talked their faithful cook, old Mose, into going with them while they tracked down a huge grizzly. "All right, I'll go," he conceded reluctantly, "but if you gets wrestling with that bear and you looks round and don't see no-body, that's me."

In Colonel Weatherbee's Louisville trophy room there hangs a majestic moose head. A visitor's young daughter, fascinated by it, finally asked her father, "May I go into the next room and see the rest of it?"

One of the colonel's hunting forays produced no such imposing specimen. Blithely he sounded his moose-call horn, but no noble animal burst into the clearing. Instead, an army of mice scurried into view.

"Damnation," muttered the colonel. "I told my secretary to order a moose-call by mail, but, as usual, she made a typographical error!"

In Africa, three big-game hunters were resting by their campfire after a hard day in the jungle when one announced, "I'm restless. Think I'll go for a short hike before chow."

The other two didn't fret over his non-appearance for over an hour. Then one glanced at his watch and murmured, "Hmm! Wonder what's eating old Ernest?"

Racing

A race-track devotee of many years' standing, thoroughly versed in the lore and form sheets of horse racing, was astonished to note that two dear little old ladies picked the winner unfailingly in seven straight races—some of them fantastic long shots. Finally he whispered to them, "Divulge your system to me, ladies, and I'll show you how to pyramid your bets so you'll make a million." "There's really no trick to it," chuckled one of the little ladies happily. "We just bet on the ones with longest tails."

The late Joe Palmer had a prize story about a horse owner in Wyoming who showed up at a race meeting with an eight-year-old non-starter and put him in an important race. Since an eight-year-old maiden is hardly a betting attraction, he was off at $136.50 and galloped home first by a cool ten lengths. The stewards suspected dirty work at the crossroads and demanded of the owner, "Is this horse unsound?" "No, sir," asserted the owner. "Soundest horse you ever saw. Ankles like iron, and there ain't never been a pimple on him." "Well then," persisted a steward, "why haven't you raced him before?" "To tell the truth," said the owner sheepishly, "we couldn't ketch him till he was seven."

A racing habitué bought a broken-down filly in a claiming race. When he went to the paddock to examine it, he found it on its side, with two veterinary surgeons attending it. "Is my horse sick?" he asked. "She's not the picture of health," said the vets, "but we hope to pull her through." "But will I ever be able to race her?" persisted the habitué. "Chances are you will," one vet assured him, "and you'll probably beat her too!"

Two Jewish race-track addicts met on the way home from Belmont, and one began immediately to bemoan an unbroken streak of miserable luck. The other boasted, "Not me! I've gone right back to fundamentals. Every morning now I pray for fifteen minutes at the synagogue, and since I started not a day has gone by that I haven't picked at least two winners." "What have I got to lose?" said the unfortunate one. "I'll try your system."

Three weeks later they met again. "I followed your advice," began the steady loser. "Not only did I pray every morning, but every evening as well. All day Saturday I spent in the synagogue, too, not to mention a couple of holidays. And in all that time, believe me, not a single winner I picked." "I can't understand it," said his friend. "What synagogue did you pray in?" "The one on Grove Street," was the answer. "No wonder, you schmo," shouted the friend. "That's for trotters!"

Haggerty had had a miserable run of luck at the track and was down to his last ten-spot when, just before the last race, he happily caught sight of his parish priest anointing one of the horses entered therein. "With the holy father blessin' the craiture," reasoned Haggerty, "how kin he lose?" So he put the whole ten right on the nose to win.

There were eight horses in the race—and Haggerty's choice

finished eighth. A few days later he encountered the reverend gentleman on the street and grumbled, "It's been lettin' me down ye've done, that's what! I bet on a horse because ye stop to bless it, and begorra, it finishes last!" The priest told him sadly, "You should have more faith than that, my boy. I wasn't blessing that horse. I was giving him the last rites."

Gambling

A purveyor of lottery tickets always lay in wait for wealthy Baron Rothschild when he exited from a European spa, and tried to talk him into buying the equivalent of a fifty-cent chance. To get rid of him, Rothschild said one day, "Here's fifty francs. Pick out any one you want and don't bother me again." Some days later the ticket seller came up in great excitement and said, "The ticket I bought for you has won the grand prize—$250,000!"

"Well," said the baron, pleased in spite of himself, "I suppose I'll have to reward you. Which do you prefer: ten thousand dollars in cash, or three thousand dollars a year for the rest of your life?"

"I'll take the ten thousand," said the ticket seller without a moment's hesitation. "With your luck, I wouldn't live another six months!"

When the mighty Hoover Dam, harnessing the waters of the Colorado River, was completed in 1936, agricultural and industrial interest in the Southwest were protected for the first time from a recurring and devastating cycle of floods and droughts. Boom times ensued for southern California, Arizona, and Nevada, but nowhere were the results so immediate as in the town, twenty-six miles from the dam, called Las Vegas.

From a sleepy community of five thousand in 1925, Las Vegas has mushroomed into a feverish, brassy city of fifty thousand today, featuring high gambling, low taxation, easy marriage, and painlessly simple divorce. It has seven magnificent resort hotels

with more building—and virtually anything goes there, particularly a visitor's money.

Let's take the lush Sands Hotel as typical of this new vacation "paradise." The Sands, fronting the new and constantly expanding "Strip," cost four million dollars and it took the proprietors almost two full months of round-the-clock gambling by panting guests to recoup their investment. One gent who had lost three thousand dollars considered a sixteen-dollar charge for his room exorbitant. The benevolent desk clerk reduced it to fourteen dollars and the man went away happy.

Another guest—a lady whose lantern jaw won her the nickname of "Mme. Popeye"—held the dice for forty-five minutes. She made twenty-seven consecutive "passes" (sevens and elevens), but being a cautious soul, won only $132. Excited gamblers around her, however, backed her heavily, and her splurge cost the management $215,000.

Outside of the constantly crowded gaming rooms of the Sands, and other hostelries in its class, are lavish accommodations, elegant shops, and deserted swimming pools. For those who do not like fancy roulette or the galloping dominoes, there are slot machines in every nook and cranny.

I asked one busy lady, "Which way is it to the office of the Las

Vegas *Sun?*" Without breaking her rhythm (she couldn't lose her money fast enough at one machine, so was crouched over two), she answered: "Thirty slot machines straight ahead, then fourteen dice tables to the left."

Las Vegas night clubs don't care how much they pay their stars, figuring, no doubt, that the stars will probably lose their loot, and then some, right back at the gaming tables. At one time, luminaries like Bankhead, Lena Horne, Joe E. Lewis, and Melchior are likely to be appearing within the confines of a single mile along the "Strip."

To see them, you need only order a round of sodas for your entire party. The boys will get you on the way out. Joe E. Lewis ended his engagement by climbing atop a dice table and imploring, "Shoot any part of me." At the airport he added, "If I was alive today, I'd be a very sick man. But I'll be back to play Las Vegas again next year. I want to visit my money."

One of the characters who presides over the gambling activities in the Sands Hotel rejoices in the name of Sherlock Feldman. In his salad days, Sherlock was co-proprietor of a gambling casino in the Klondike, where they used chips made of ice. One night a lucky miner made twenty-two consecutive passes, with all his pals backing him to the hilt, and Sherlock's partner moaned, "They've broken the bank. We're ruined!" The resourceful Sherlock, however, merely turned up the furnace another fifteen degrees, and all the chips melted.

Another time, at the Sands, a patron who had taken a fearful shellacking wagered every last chip he had left, crying, "Shoot the works." He was so agitated that his upper false teeth fell out upon the table. Sherlock promptly planked down *his* lower plate and declared cheerfully, "You're faded."

Education is not neglected at Las Vegas. There's a new elementary school that Joe Lewis has christened P.S. 6-to-5. "How old are you?" Arlene Frances asked one of its cutest pupils. The little girl answered, "Four, the hard way."

Gambling parlors and slot machines are not the only hazards in Las Vegas with which to conjure. "Look out for the odd-shaped swimming pools too," warns Mel Torme. "They have a very high chorine content."

An officer of the law stopped short when he observed a man proceeding down Main Street clad only in a barrel. "Ah, ha," he exclaimed. "Been playing poker, eh?" "Not me," said the man in the barrel sadly. "But I just left six other fellows who were."

The man who was watching Mr. Guggenheimer play bridge was mildly puzzled when he failed to double an opponent's grand-slam bid although he held the ace of trumps in his hand. "A bit cautious, what?" he asked *sotto voce*. "Lordy," explained Mr. Guggenheimer, "I'd never dare double that lunatic. He redoubles at the drop of a hat!"

Indoor Sports

The wife of one of the forwards on the New York Rangers hockey team admitted, "It's really thrilling to be married to a big-time hockey star. Every time he comes home he looks like a different person."

Mrs. Nussbaum's and Mrs. Goldstein's first visit to a neighborhood bowling alley was not exactly a triumphal affair, but Mrs. Nussbaum derived a certain modicum of comfort from their performance. "I hope you noticed," she said on the way home, "that we didn't lose a single ball!"

Coaches all agree that something will have to be done about the height of basketball players. They've grown so tall and gangling on most squads, nobody under six feet is allowed to carry the towels and water bucket any more.

Players no longer shoot baskets; they drop in the ball while passing by, as though they were mailing a letter.

One Indiana team *averaged* six feet last season. Everybody was impressed except poet Carl Sandburg. "So what?" he pointed out. "Abe Lincoln was over six-three!"

Cartoonist Robert Day, six-six himself, depicts a guard who was so tall he merely had to stand under the basket with his head protruding therefrom. Enemy shots, of course, bounced harmlessly off his noggin.

No wonder his coach watched him, chuckling happily and enthusing, "Best darn guard in the country!"

Milton Berle rashly planked down a bet on William and Mary College near the close of the basketball season—and lost. "Dawgone it," he complained, "how was I to know they were going to let Mary play?"

From basketball-mad Indiana comes the story of two Scottish fans who attended a championship game. One was equipped with a pint, to which he resorted with increasing frequency—but alone. Meanwhile, he regaled his arid companion with tales of his own triumphs as a center on the Glasgow Globetrotters.

"Fifty per cent o' yer gab I can persuade myself to credit," grumbled the arid one at long last. "I can see ye're an unco' fine dribbler. But, mon—yer na gude at all at passin'!"

The Russian temperament is peculiarly suited to chess. They say that a Russian named Droskycharnoff invented the greatest defense in the history of the game. He grew whiskers so long that they hid all sixteen of his pieces.

When it came to self-confidence, another Russian chess champion named Bogolyubov took the cake. Asked the secret of his success in game after game, he explained calmly, "When I have the white pieces and move first, I win because I am white. When I have the black pieces, I win because I am Bogolyubov."

Sylvia Fine, Mrs. Danny Kaye in private life, tells the story of a West Coast chess master whose five-year-old son loved to watch him play, and even accompanied him to Sacramento for the state championship. At a crucial point in the final match, the father reached out to move a knight.

The five-year-old tugged urgently at his sleeve and whispered, "Papa, don't move the horse." The father reconsidered, suddenly discovered that the move he had contemplated would have cost him the match, reoriented his strategy, and ultimately triumphed.

On the way home he gazed proudly at his son and asked, "What made you warn me not to move the horse?" The boy explained simply, "He looked hungry."

CHAPTER TWENTY-TWO

TRAVEL IS SO BROADENING . . .

(Around the World in 28 Pages)

A Philadelphia socialite, returning home with his family from a two-month tour of Europe, was asked by reporters when his ship docked at Quarantine, "Did you see many signs of poverty abroad?" He answered bitterly, "Not only did I see signs of it, but I've brought some back with me."

The socialite's new English chauffeur was stopped by an immigration officer who explained, "We have a tip that you are smuggling in a quantity of pornographic literature." "It's a lie!" sputtered the chauffeur. "I haven't even got a pornograph!"

277

Sailing across the Atlantic aboard the *Queen Mary*, the traveler is apt to hear this story, intriguing even if it isn't true, about how the liner got its name:

Since time immemorial, Cunard ships always had names ending in "ia" and, in keeping with this tradition, the new addition to the fleet was scheduled to be called the *Queen Victoria*. When the Cunard chairman called on King George V, however, to acquaint him with this fact, and began by saying, "We're pleased to tell you our new liner will be named after one of Britain's greatest queens . . ." the King interrupted happily, "Good, good! Her Majesty, I know, will be simply delighted!"

So, the *Queen Mary* it became, and the good lady herself christened the ship as it slid down the ways.

The English

Riding up to London in a first-class railroad compartment with Winston Churchill, a man on the seat opposite stared at him for a full half hour, finally tapped him on the shoulder and inquired, "I say, would your name possibly be Churchill!" "It would," grunted the great "Winnie." "*Winston* Churchill?" persisted the stranger. "Right again," said Mr. C. The stranger slapped his hand on his knee and boomed, "Then I do believe we went to Harrow together in 1888!"

The late Harold Laski was dispatched one day to secure an interview with Winston Churchill. When he returned, his editor said, "Well, did you get in to see him?" "Not only did I get in," Laski assured the editor, "but I sat for two hours and listened to his thunderous and well-rehearsed improvisations."

Here's a story that highlights the special quality that makes the English different from all other folks. An elderly lady was riding down to London in a first-class railway compartment when she suddenly confided to the young lady across the aisle,

"I saw a splendid play the last time I visited London. Gielgud starred. He was superb. The direction and lighting also were perfect. Only fault with the play was the girl in the leading role. Marguerite Chapman I believe her name was. Shocking performance. I wonder how she got on to acting for a living in the first place."

The young lady's eyes flashed. "It may interest you to learn," she snapped, "that I happen to be Marguerite Chapman."

The elderly lady nodded. "Yes," she said softly, "I know."

Historians finally have discovered what Lord Godiva said to Lady Godiva when she returned from her famous ride. He was waiting at the door in a towering rage and demanded, "Where, exactly, have you been? Your horse got home two hours ago!"

And when a lovely young lady in waiting at King Arthur's Court sneaked into the castle, she whispered feelingly to Queen Guinevere, "What a knight!"

In Pierre Barton's lively *The Royal Family*, he recalls a sea trip Queen Victoria made to Ireland. The ship encountered dirty weather, and one monstrous wave almost knocked Her Majesty galley-west. Regaining her equilibrium with some difficulty, she commanded an attendant, "Go up to the bridge, give the admiral my compliments, and tell him he's not to let that happen again."

King George V, narrates Berton, was an avid stamp collector. A secretary commented one morning, "I see in the *Times* that some damn fool paid fourteen hundred pounds for a single stamp at a private sale yesterday." "I," retorted King George calmly, "was that damn fool."

In London, three Oxford professors of literature resisted the determined advance of a group of fancy ladies they encountered on Picadilly, then sought to find a phrase best describing them. The specialist in the Barchester novels voted for "A chapter of trollops." The Shakespearian scholar clung to "A flourish of strumpets." The collector of short stories carried the day, however, with "An anthology of pros."

Two crooked, but very formal, Londoners had shared the same cell in jail for over six years. One's reserve finally broke down and he assured the other, "No need to call me 'Number 855625' from now on, old chap. Henceforth, to you, I'm plain '855'!"

A wealthy Londoner sought to purchase an expensive American convertible car. "But, my dear fellow," expostulated the dealer, "we've been allotted only two of this model all year, and there are already one hundred seventy-four orders ahead of yours." "Too bad," murmured the Londoner, seemingly not too dismayed. As he left he ostentatiously tossed a large bundle of ten-pound notes into the trash basket.

The very next morning the precise model he was seeking was delivered to him. A few days later the dealer called him on the phone. "Those ten-pound notes," he roared, "are all counterfeit."

"Exactly," agreed the Londoner blandly. "That's why I threw them in the trash basket."

British pride in native products has not dimmed.

A London plutocrat was driving his fine new Rolls-Royce over the Alps when he heard a disquieting "twang." His front spring had broken.

He called the Rolls plant in London by long distance, and, in what seemed like no time flat, three gentlemen arrived by plane with a new spring—and off went the plutocrat on his interrupted jaunt.

Now comes the really interesting part of the story. After six months the plutocrat had received no bill from the Rolls people. Finally he appeared at the plant in person and asked that the records be checked for "the repair of a broken spring in Switzerland." After a brief delay the manager of the plant appeared in person, gazed at him rather reproachfully, and announced, "There must be some mistake, sir. There is no such *thing* as a broken spring on a Rolls-Royce."

Tom Driberg, Member of the British Parliament, is authority for the fact that several London "pubs" have taken to featuring a new drink they call "The Clothes Brush." When this concoction is served to a customer, the barman puts an actual stiff-bristled clothes brush beside it. The customer usually downs the drink in a single gulp, then falls flat on his face. A few minutes later he comes to, gravely brushes the dust off his clothes with the brush, pays his check, and goes about his business. Driberg avers further that in a Soho pub where he was watching the clothes-brush routine in its finest flowering, one customer, at least, had the strength of mind to order something else. "Just whip up something long and cold and full of gin," he commented. The man alongside him promptly volunteered, "Take my wife here."

The Scottish

A thrifty old Scot named MacCrindle stayed with a business associate in London and became deeply attached to the latter's black cocker spaniel. The dog returned his affection and kicked up such a fuss when MacCrindle was leaving that the Londoner insisted he be taken home as a gift.

"This is uncommon kind of ye," declared MacCrindle, "and as soon as I get back to Scotland, I'll be sending ye the biggest finest turkey ye ever did see."

Several months passed before MacCrindle ran into his English friend again. The latter remarked in passing, "By the way, that turkey you were going to send me never did arrive."

"I forgot to tell ye," replied MacCrindle. "The turkey got well."

On a lake steamer in Scotland, a lovely young girl fell overboard. The waters were very choppy, and the girl had already gone under twice when a middle-aged Scot, extremely well dressed, kerplonked into the lake and dragged the girl aboard the steamer. The girl's father threw his arms around the drenched Scotsman and enthused, "You're a great hero, sir. How can I ever repay you?" "Just tell me one thing," said the Scotsman grimly. "Who pushed me?"

Houdini, the wily escape artist, made one of his rare miscalculations when he fought his way free of a supposedly foolproof police straight jacket and heavy handcuffs from the top span of a big bridge in Scotland. The stunt was widely advertised, and a traffic-stopping throng was expected. Yet only a corporal's guard turned up. "Don't they like me here in Scotland?" the disappointed Houdini asked a city official. "They're crazy for you," was the reassuring reply. "But, mon, you performed on the wrong bridge. That's a toll bridge!"

McGregor lay breathing his last. He roused himself to whisper to the assemblage round his bedside, "Tannish owes me fifty pounds." "It's a great mind the man has," marveled his wife. "Clear as a bell to the very end." McGregor spoke again: "I believe I owe Sandy Mollinson a hundred pounds." "Ach, the poor mon," sobbed Mrs. McGregor. "Take no notice of his delirious meanderings!"

The song of a generous Scotchman:

> *Oh, I hand out cash with a lavish hand*
> *In a philanthropic fury.*
> *Ask, and I'll give to you fifty grand—*
> *That is, while I'm on the jury.*

An English commercial traveler found himself stranded for the weekend in a small Scottish town whose amusement list was limited, to say the least. In desperation, he asked the innkeeper, "What on earth can a poor soul do in this town after dark?" The innkeeper considered the query gravely, then replied, "I'm not sure, sir, but the fancy lady walks at eight!"

Another salesman, representing the Highland Kilt Company (he had a kilt complex), ran into a spell of dirty weather in the Midlands and notified headquarters, "Likely to be marooned here for several days. Wire instructions." Back came a telegram—collect—which read, "Begin summer vacation as of this morning."

Scotch joke variation Number 68414: Excavators in Aberdeen have come upon a Scottish penny dated 1588. A few feet away they then unearthed three skeletons, all on their hands and knees.

The Irish

Irish prerogatives, claims author Frank O'Connor, are in jeopardy. It was galling enough when he read in Variety that the music for the two St. Patrick's Day dances staged in Omaha last year was furnished, respectively, by Adolph Urbanovsky's Bohemian ensemble and Toothless Simon and his Five Cavities. But Frank really needed an outlet for his Eire escape when he picked up a fine old sturdy shillelagh and found brazenly stamped thereon, "Made in Japan"!

In an opening-round match for the duffers' booby prize at a Dublin golf club, says Frank, one Timothy O'Brien demanded of his opponent, "How many strokes would you be takin' on that last hole?" "Let me see now," mused the opponent with a fine show of concentration. "I'd say I took eight. No, 'twas only seven." "I'll put you down for nine, you spalpeen," announced O'Brien severely. "You'll recall there's a penalty of one stroke here for improvin' your lie!"

Mr. Doolan caught his old friend, the bartender at Moriarty's saloon, in an unguarded moment and begged, "Mike, me mother-in-law has gone to her just reward, and it's a ten spot I'm needin' to supply a wreath that will uphold the Doolan standards. Can ye advance me the ten?"

The bartender emptied his pockets and the cash register, but the combined total came to only nine dollars and thirty cents.

"That'll do for the moment," said Doolan hastily. "I'll take the other seventy cents in drinks."

During a tour of America, the distinguished Irish wit, speech maker, and parliamentarian, T. P. O'Connor—fondly known as "Tay Pay" to his constituents—was asked repeatedly, "What is the state of Ireland today?"

"Status quo," "Tay Pay" would reply cheerily. "In the South of Ireland we have the Catholics, and in the North the Protestants, and they're at each other's throats as usual all the time.

. . . If only they were haythen so they could live together loike Christians!"

Clancy sidled into the back of the Shamrock Bar and Grill with his right pocket bulging. "It's a stick o' dynamite I've got there," he confided. "I'm waiting for Finnegan. Every time he meets me he wallops me side and breaks me pipe. This time, begorra, he'll blow off his hand."

Maureen O'Hara, as fair a colleen as ever whipped up a blintz in County Cork, tells about an Irish sea captain who became temporarily confused on the bridge one day and narrowly averted ramming the admiral's flagship. A rash of signal flags broke out on the admiral's vessel. "It's a message for you, sir," an ensign told the befuddled captain. "It says, 'You blank blank landlubber, what the blank do you think you're doing with that blank blank tub of yours?'" "H-m-m-m," mused the captain. "Better take that down to the signal room and have it decoded immediately."

A candidate in the recent Irish elections displayed a candor some of our own politicians would do well to emulate. "All we ask," he declared from the platform, "is another two years to complete our program." "And what," demanded a voice from the rear, "*is* your program?" The candidate answered forcefully, "To stay in for another two years!"

The French

There once lived in France a whimsical couple who named their first-born son "Formidable." All his life, he was the butt of assorted jibes because of this ridiculous name, especially since he grew up to be a skinny unimposing wisp of a man.

Nevertheless, Formidable found himself a beautiful wife—the

catch of the town—and what's more, lived with her in utter tranquility for a full fifty-seven years.

At eighty-five, Formidable came to the end of the road. His dying request to his wife was, "Do not put that awful name of mine on my tombstone. It would prevent my resting in peace." Tearfully the wife promised, and was good as her word. His epitaph read simply: "Here lies a man whose wife was absolutely faithful to him for fifty-seven years."

And so every Frenchman who passes that grave exclaims, "*Regardez! C'est formidable!*"

Anatole Litvak tells an enchanting tale about a young Parisian who was wheeling his baby son's carriage through the Bois. The son was howling with rage. The Parisian contented himself with repeating softly, "Control yourself, Bernard. Just be calm, Bernard."

A child psychologist watched the scene approvingly and tapped the Parisian on the shoulder. "Congratulations, monsieur," he said warmly, "for keeping your temper so admirably. You know instinctively how to handle the little fellow. Gently does it! So he's named Bernard, eh?"

"Not at all," corrected the Parisian. "He's named André. *I'm* Bernard."

Author Harry Kurnitz achieved the impossible: he happened upon a restaurant in Paris where the food was positively terrible. What's more, the waiter cheerfully admitted the fact. "Monsieur would be wise," he whispered, "to get out of here fast. There's a really fine little restaurant right across the boulevard." "Are you sure?" asked Kurnitz. "Sure? *Certainement*," said the waiter vehemently. "I own it." Then he added, "This miserable place is where I find my customers."

The maître d'hôtel at one of those intimate side-street French restaurants assured Irwin Shaw that snails were the specialty of the house. "I know," sighed Shaw, "and you've got them dressed as waiters."

A Wall Street banker took his wife to Paris, where he closed a big bond deal. Final signing of the papers took longer than he had expected, so he called the Ritz Hotel and told the French maid, "Please tell madame to go to bed and wait for me." "*Bien,* monsieur," answered the maid, "but who shall I say called?"

An heir to millions, native of Cincinnati, was dining alone in Paris when he thought he detected a "come hither" look in the eyes of the prettiest girl he had ever seen. "She jumped into a cab," he told his friends when he returned to America, "and I jumped into another. 'Follow that girl,' I commanded. Down the Champs Élysées we raced, across the Seine, and up the Boulevard Raspail. When she alighted at a studio building in the heart of the Left Bank, I was only a few steps behind her. I caught her on the landing of her apartment, and with a happy sigh I never will forget, she melted into my arms." "What happened after that?" his friends asked breathlessly. The excitement died down in the heir's voice. "After that," he admitted, "it was just like Cincinnati."

An old French farmer was walking through his pasture with an American tourist and his eager-beaver wife. "I notice," said she eagerly, "that some of your cows have horns and some haven't. Why is that?" "There are three cases in which they lack horns," explained the farmer carefully. "Some are born without them, some are dehorned, and some have their horns knocked off fighting." "And what about that different-looking one over in the corner?" persisted the wife. "Ah," murmured the peasant. "That is case Number Four. That is a horse."

Two Americans met on the Champs Élysées on their first visit to Paris. "This sight-seeing sure takes a lot of time," grumbled one. "I've been here nearly four days and I still haven't visited the Louvre." Suggested the other, "Maybe it's the water."

Sacha Guitry, long-time favorite of the Paris theater, had a father, Lucien, who was equally famous in his day. Lucien, among other things, was noted for the perfection of his make-up for various of his starring roles. For example, he had a photo of Pasteur pasted on his mirror and, while visitors gaped, he would make up for the role, looking so *exactly* like the photo when he was finished that no one could detect any difference whatever. Nor was there any. For what the wily Guitry had done was to make himself up first as Pasteur, then have himself photographed—then substitute the result on his mirror in place of the original!

In Paris, Frank L. Rand was fortunate enough to be there or thereabouts when a lady tourist saw her sight-seeing group riding away in a bus without her. After frantically consulting her pocket English-French dictionary, she took off in pursuit, shouting, "Hey, garcon! Wait! Attendez! Stoppez at once! Je suis gauche derriere!"

Sunny Italy

Sunrise over St. Peter's and the Tiber, an Italian nobleman assured a beautiful young tourist from the States, was a memory of Rome she would cherish the rest of her life. "We will sit in my garden," he proposed, "and watch the dawn together." "But, Count," she protested, "what about the dew?" "My dear," said the count firmly, "when in Rome, dew as the Romans dew."

A lady from Indiana got her first view of the Colosseum, clutched her guide's arm, and gurgled, "It's perfect! Don't let them change a thing!"

The night Gina Lollobrigida was the mystery guest on "What's My Line?" panel moderator John Daly observed appreciatively, "There's one Roman who wasn't built in a day." Victor Borge estimated, "She's about five and a half feet tall—lying down on her back." Steve Allen had the last word. "Only two good things have come this way from Italy all season," he declared, "and Gina's got both of them."

Darkest Africa

Two shipwrecked Broadway characters, marooned on a dinky and deserted island off the coast of Africa for months, shrieked with joy when a bottle came floating in on the tide. With trembling hands one of the castaways extracted a note from the bottle. Then his face fell. "Nuts," he exclaimed. "It's from us!"

From an installation in the Sahara Desert, a big oil refinery got a letter complaining that the personnel's water rations were inadequate. The president pooh-poohed, "Those spoiled so-and-so's are always complaining they haven't enough water." "This time," answered his aide, "I think they mean it. Their postage stamp is attached with a pin."

Several telephone maintenance men were assigned to stretch a new line across a remote district in the Zulu country. A Zulu chief and his advisers watched the work in silence for a while, then the chief pointed out disgustedly, "White men damn fools. Put wire so high, livestock can walk right out under it."

An intrepid British sportsman invaded the African jungle in search of big game (he was driving a Jaguar, of course), but ran afoul of a blazing native insurrection. Whipping out his service revolver, he emptied all barrels point-blank at the enemy, returned to his base to report happily, "I guess I've just shot the last of the red-hot Maumaus!"

An Irish sailor wandered up the beach while his ship was anchored at an obscure African port, and was promptly captured by a band of cannibals.

Each day the fiends would prick his arm with a spear and drink some of his rich Hibernian blood. The day came when he could stand this no longer. Thrusting his lower jaw out at the chief, he hollered, "Kill me and eat me if ye will, ye heathen rascals, but this is positively the last day ye're going to stick me fer the drinks!"

In far off Nigeria, Africa, the owner of one of the few movie emporiums has found out exactly what his patrons want and, by golly, he gives it to them. On every Monday, Tuesday, and Friday, for the past six years, writes a magazine correspondent, he has packed them in with *King Kong*, and on Wednesdays, Thursdays, and Saturdays, he turns them away with *The Mark of Zorro*. It's on Sundays, however, that he really hits the jack pot with a double bill consisting of—you guessed it—*King Kong* and *The Mark of Zorro*.

One of the great cartoons of recent years was drawn by Ed Fisher for *The New Yorker* magazine. It shows a cannibal chieftain happily advising his assembled board of strategy: "Now here's the plan. We let word out that we're in a state of political ferment. Russia smells an opportunity and makes overtures. The West gets worried. *They* make overtures. Russia asks to send cultural ambassadors, and we let them. The West asks for equal representation, and we invite them. Then, when we've got them all here, we eat them."

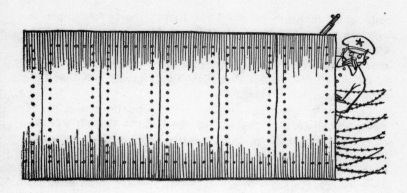

Behind the Iron Curtain

Here are two paragraphs about the Russians. Can you guess who wrote them?

"Let it be clearly understood that the Russian is a delightful person till he tucks in his shirt. As an Oriental he is charming. It is only when he insists upon being treated as the most easterly of Western peoples instead of the most westerly of Easterns that he becomes a racial anomaly extremely difficult to handle. The host never knows which side of his nature is going to turn up next."

". . . Asia is not going to be civilized after the methods of the West. There is too much of Asia and she is too old. You cannot reform a lady of many lovers, and Asia has been insatiable in her flirtations aforetime. She will never attend a Sunday school or learn to vote save with swords for tickets."

No, dear reader, the author was neither Winston Churchill nor John Foster Dulles, but Rudyard Kipling, in a story called "The Man Who Was," written way back in 1890!

During the Kremlin's abortive campaign to provide more consumer goods for the Russian people, one farmer got fed up with another set of empty promises and had the nerve to demand in an open meeting, "Where is the white flour and the new shoes Comrade Malenkov has been promising us?" "What is your name?" countered the visiting delegate. "Petrovsky," said the farmer. "Okay, Comrade Petrovsky, I will answer your question at our next open meeting."

The next meeting had scarcely gotten underway when there was a disturbance at the rear of the hall. "I know," said the delegate. "You want to know what's happened to the white flour and the new shoes."

"Not at all, Comrade," was the reply. "I want to know what's happened to Comrade Petrovsky."

Two strangers stopped to admire a handsome new automobile parked at a curb in Prague. "Beautiful model!" enthused one. "Another great triumph for Soviet initiative and ingenuity!" The other protested, "But that's an American car. Don't you know one when you see one?" "Of course I do," snapped the first stranger. "But I don't know *you!*"

A German in the Western Zone of Berlin, suspecting that letters to his son in Warsaw were being read by Communist operatives, declared in one, "I'm enclosing herewith a hair, which will fall out, no doubt, if some censor opens the envelope." The son replied, "Stop your foolish worries. The hair was still there when your letter arrived." The German now had all the information he wanted. He had not put a hair in the original letter.

Another German, in East Berlin, was assigned to labor in a factory which was supposed to ship parts for baby carriages back to Moscow. Having a baby himself, he resolved to pilfer enough parts to construct a carriage of his own. A fellow workman, aware of his scheme, asked him a few days later, "Well, have you got that carriage rolling yet?" The German scratched his head and said, "It's the most astonishing thing. I've got all the parts—but no matter how I assemble them, it comes out a machine gun!"

A story currently circulating in Budapest concerns two political prisoners who were trying to console one another before they went to trial. "If only I hadn't confessed," mourned one, "that I bought sugar on the black market." "That was a mistake," admitted the other. "Why did you confess that?" "What could I do?" was the answer. "The man who interrogated me was the one who had sold me the sugar."

"What a man, that Krubnovkivich!" enthused a Russian delegate to the U.N. "He invented radio, airplanes, and the electric light. In fact, I'd say he's almost as great a genius as Yibishiv."

The American looked puzzled. "Who was Yibishiv?" he asked.

"Ha," chortled the Russian. "Yibishiv invented Krubnovkivich!"

An alert factory worker in Budapest sidled up to the lady foreman and implored, "May I leave at the end of eleven and a half hours this evening instead of twelve, Madam Director? I'd like to go to the state opera."

"You may," decided the director. "I'm happy that our workers appreciate culture. But cut out that 'Madam Director' business. Now that we have been liberated, remember we are all comrades! By the way, what opera are you attending?"

"*Comrade Butterfly*," said the worker.

In the Soviet heaven, the Communist equivalent of St. Peter stopped one applicant at the gate (made of ersatz pearl) and demanded, "State your qualifications for entering here." "Well," said the applicant, ticking off the reasons on his fingers, "on earth my father was, first, a rich industrialist. Second, my mother came from a family of middle-class tradesmen. Me, I was a writer. And, finally, after inheriting a large sum of money, I married a baroness."

The Soviet St. Peter was choking with rage by this time. "And are those your only claims for entering the Soviet heaven?" he spluttered.

Meekly the applicant added one claim more. "I thought my name might help me," he murmured. "It's Karl Marx."

Oriental Flavor

A reporter known to Nunnally Johnson was present in Tokyo when a very small Jap was hanged for doing in several members of his family. The reporter's comment—heard all too distinctly by Mr. Johnson—was, "Oho, there's a little nip in the air this morning."

The Japs are great ones for imitating American and British products, but the labels they paste thereon are often dead giveaways. In Tokyo, for instance, a New York newspaperman delightedly displays a bottle of so-called "Scotch whisky" whose label proclaims, "These whisky is made from choicest grape, as by appointment to His Majesty King Elizabeth."

Chinese factory workers, to the accompaniment of city-wide fanfare, were accorded a rare treat in Communist-dominated Shanghai recently: an election with secret ballot to choose a new workers' committee! Each man, upon approaching the ballot box, was handed a sealed envelope and told to deposit same through the slot at the top of a cardboard box.

One rash worker flipped open the envelope and began to examine his ballot. "Hey," shouted a supervisor. "What do you think you're doing there?"

"I want to know who I'm voting for," explained the worker.

"You must be mad," decided the supervisor. "Don't you realize that the ballot is *secret?*"

An engaging Chinese myth concerns an artisan who, eager for wealth and fame, determined to cast a very special bell. Effort after effort proved fruitless however. There always was a flaw. Finally the artisan said, "Wealth and fame obviously are not for me. They're overrated anyhow. But before I quit, I shall cast one more bell—just for my own satisfaction and enjoyment."

The tone of this last bell was so glorious that people thrilled everywhere when they heard it. "Who cast this perfect bell?" they asked. And so the artisan became rich and famous.

Another oriental legend tells of a traveler who strayed from his caravan and was lost in a trackless wilderness of sand. Two days of aimless plodding left him exhausted and about to perish from thirst. Suddenly his eyes lit on what looked like a waterskin. Reaching it on his knees, he tore it open. Alas, it was only a bag of gleaming flawless pearls!

Hearts are no longer so light or life so bright in "dreamy Chinatown" on the tip of lower Manhattan since the families who stayed in the homeland were swallowed up by Communist hordes.

But the show must go on for out-of-town visitors who wouldn't dream of leaving New York without a sight-seeing tour of the missions and hostels on the Bowery, and the joss houses—carefully preserved replicas of Chinese temples—on Pell Street.

In one teashop every bus load of tourists is regaled with the story of old Loo Ching, the Chinese laundryman, who violated a fundamental law of his powerful Tong soon after his arrival in New York and was condemned to death in a secret conclave. American law permitted no violent carrying out of the sentence, so the Tong leaders simply decreed, "We pronounce Loo Ching a dead man."

From that moment on, not one soul spoke to Loo Ching or revealed the slightest awareness of his presence. Shopkeepers ignored his attempts to buy or beg food. Children turned the other way when he shuffled down the street. His room was rented to another and his belongings deposited in a back alley. Loo Ching spoke not one word of English and knew nothing of American ways.

So each day he grew thinner and more desperate, until finally his wasted body was found in the snow outside the teashop. His death sentence had been carried out.

Gallagher strolled into his favorite saloon and was rather surprised to find the floor strewn with rice. "What's this?" he exclaimed. "Had a wedding in here today?" "Naw," explained the barkeep. "I just knocked the stuffings out of a Commie Chinaman."

A San Franciscan had just decorated a grave in the public cemetery with a garland of roses when he noticed a venerable Chinaman placing a bowl of rice on a mound adjacent. "What time," whispered the American, "would you be expecting your friend to come up and eat that rice?" "About same time," answered the Chinaman, "yours comes up to smell the flowers."

Columnist Irving Hoffman, bound home from Hong Kong, visited Bombay, India, and was shown the city by a high police official. "Maybe you'd like to hear about the most dangerous political fanatic in the country," suggested the official. "At this very moment he's probably constructing a bomb to hurl into police headquarters. If you'd like to meet him in person, that, too, can be arranged. He's my brother-in-law."

Three salesmen who had dined sumptuously at a Chinese chop-suey emporium were now studying the "tell-your-fortune" slips of paper that are wrapped in a certain kind of crisp little Chinese cooky. The paper in the first man's cooky read, "You are about to embark upon a business venture that will net you millions." The second man's read, "You will soon meet a tempestuous redhead whom you will take on a long journey." Then the third man opened his little slip. This one read, "Help! I'm trapped in a Chinese bakery!"

"Hello, Hawaii"

Hawaii has become a movie maker's paradise. The natives have become so used to Hollywood shenanigans, in fact, that a Clark Gable or Hank Fonda can wander, entirely unmolested, the length of Kalakaua Avenue. *Time's* apt line about Esther Williams ("a lot of water has flowed over this dame") was duly appreciated by the Waikikeyhole set, but when the ravishing Esther appeared on the coral sands in person, she attracted no more attention than a local *wahine* waddling by in her shapeless *muu-muu*.

For uninitiated souls on the mainland, *wahine* means "woman," and a *muu-muu* is a garment patterned after the unflattering covering that appalled missionaries, some hundred years ago, hastily draped over native maidens who were blissfully ambulating with all their abundant charms fully exposed. One maiden is supposed to have flung the covering angrily hence. It landed on a cow, which registered even more vociferous indignation; hence the name, *muu-muu*. The missionaries, meanwhile, their purity assured, proceeded to do mighty well for them-

selves in a material way. Their descendants are the recognized aristocracy of the islands.

The recent eruption of Kilauea Volcano in Hawaii came as no surprise to natives of that area. Well they know that Pele, tempestuous and all-powerful red-haired fire goddess, after wanderings more extensive than Eleanor Roosevelt's, finally settled down to housekeeping in that volcano. Every now and then she is expected to flex her muscles to keep the franchise.

Madam Pele (Hawaiians pronounce her name "Paley," to conform with a Madison Avenue god of comparable stature at the Columbia Broadcasting Company) controls the warmth of the earth and the ocean currents, and woe betide anyone rash enough to thwart her desires!

In 1935, for instance, you are told solemnly, two American Army planes flew a dangerous mission over erupting Mauna Loa and, by pin-point bombing, diverted a flow of lava that imperiled Hilo City. Everybody knew that Pele would have her revenge. Sure enough, some months later these very planes collided in mid-air, and only one occupant parachuted to safety.

Furthermore, that survivor proved to be the single member of both crews who had not participated in the mission over Mauna Loa!

How, I asked, could one interpret the moods of Madam Pele and perhaps forestall her? The *kahunas* know, was the answer. The *kahunas* are a rough equivalent of the witch doctors in other civilizations.

There is at least one accredited *kahuna* in every sizable community, and even white residents (*haoles*) from the mainland soon learn to seek their counsel.

When U. S. Navy engineers constructed the first dry dock at Pearl Harbor, the story goes, they ignored the warning of *kahuna* that the site they had chosen was a graveyard for subjects of Madam Pele. What happened? When the scaffolding was removed, the dry dock collapsed (this fact, at least, can be verified), and imbedded in the bottom of the structure was found the skeleton of a whale.

Next time out, the Navy listened carefully to what the *kahuna* had to say—and there hasn't been a particle of trouble with dry docks at Pearl Harbor since.

Do you know why so many Hawaiian words sound and look alike to the uninitiated? There are only twelve letters in the Hawaiian alphabet. The vowels *A, E, I, O,* and *U,* and the consonants *H, K, L, M, N, P,* and *W.*

Although the luxury liner *Lurline* sails from Hawaii every fortnight, its skipper, Commodore Gillespie, still gets a kick out of the band blaring native airs and the hula maidens swaying in the breeze. He even shows passengers how to scale their flowered leis into the sea as the ship rounds Diamond Head, in a scene reminiscent of the finale of *From Here to Eternity.*

Tradition, quotes the commodore gravely, dictates that if the lei floats ashore, the tourist is destined to return to Hawaii another day. And since, because of the tide, the lei invariably does, everybody is happy. Aloha!

The Amazon

With its thousand tributaries, ten larger than the Rhine, author Willard Price points out, the Amazon contains a tenth of the world's running water and drains an area equal to 85 per cent of the United States. The main body of the river, of course, is in Brazil, but it sends feelers into Bolivia, Peru, Ecuador, and Venezuela. It is navigable for over 2,400 miles, at which point it is still 120 feet deep.

Nearing the Atlantic, the Amazon is more than 150 miles wide. Aboard Price's plane, a hostess told him, "We are beginning to cross the Amazon"; a half hour later she added, "We have finished crossing it." (A man I know calls his wife Amazon—because she has such a big mouth.)

At the end of the rainy season, the Amazon's waters roar down to the sea in a mighty torrent that upends trees and sends them hurtling into the air. Not a single bridge spans the river, because nothing made by man could resist its unleashed fury.

Heaven help any human caught in the Amazon's swirling waters! If he is not speedily drowned, he falls prey to the alligators or the piranhas, relentless little fish with razor-edge teeth and a taste for blood. Thirty-eight-foot anacondas slither along the river's banks to mop up what's left.

No place for a punster.

Ezio Pinza had an enchanted evening of his own in the Amazon country a few years ago when a Brazilian rubber magnate flew him a thousand miles and back, to give a single concert at a place outside Manáos.

Pinza was led in complete darkness down a narrow path, into a darkened building, and onto a dimly lighted stage. He felt that there was a large audience, but could see nothing beyond the footlights. He sang his heart out, but there was no applause. "They hated me," he remarked ruefully as he was driven back to Manáos.

"On the contrary, they adored you," said the impresario.

"Now that you have completed your performance, I can tell you that you have just rendered a great service. You have brought a little beauty to one of the largest leper colonies in the world."

The first known descent of the Amazon by a white man was made in 1541 by Francisco de Orellana, whose bug-eyed reports of the beautiful, seven-foot female warriors he encountered gave the river its name. Pinza confirms the fact that these ladies, alas, exist there no more. The theory is that the last of them long since were snapped up by model agencies, musical shows and soft-ball teams.

South of the Border

Life for public officials in the smaller South and Central American republics continues hazardous. News flashes always recall the late Willie Howard's summary of a south-of-the-border politico's career: "He run for mayor; he make it. He run for governor: he make it. He run for president: by golly, he make that too. But then he run for border: poor Manuelo, he no make *that!*"

The difference between tamales in the States and in Mexico, explains Pepe Montiguez, is that in the States they're merely hot; in Mexico, they're still sizzling ten minutes after you've eaten them. There's one place in Mexico City, swears Pepe, where, if three people are eating hot tamales at the same time, the automatic sprinkler system goes on.

A veteran cattleman from the Southwest was taken to his first bullfight in Mexico City, and was obviously fascinated by the various tricks of the picadors and matadors. Finally the big star of the show strode into the arena. A savage bull made straight for him, but the bespangled hero, armed only with a gorgeous cape, twirled it about in the air and avoided the animal's lunges by a fraction of an inch.

The crowd roared its approval, but the old cattleman did not join in. Obviously disgusted, he finally hollered, "Mister, if you don't hold that sack still, how in heck do you expect the critter to run into it?"

It was in Mexico City, too, just outside the magnificent new university that a señora said to her luscious friend, "Pepita, you must be mighty proud of your husband Juan. He is so big and strong."

"Pah," sneered Pepita. "You should have seen the Juan who got away!"

CHAPTER TWENTY-THREE

UNACCUSTOMED AS I AM . . .

After delivering an interminable speech to a vanishing audience, an English author, beginning a cross-country tour, asked a Town Hall chairman, "How do you think it went?" "Smooth as silk," was the tactful answer. "For the first two hours you had them glued to their seats."

A speaker at a Detroit function, confides Harvey Campbell, couldn't get his audience to settle down in silence for his address. Finally he thundered over the loud-speaker system, "Mr. Chairman and Gentlemen-so-called: Your committee assured me I would be greeted here by a vast audience. As I look out into this great auditorium and see every other seat empty, I realize that what I have instead is a half-vast audience!"

This story was told in Kansas City by a prominent Democrat once stationed in Washington (you guess!). A garden specialist, in the course of a lecture at a women's literary club, mentioned blandly that one of the best fertilizers is old cow manure. At the conclusion of his talk, one of the richest ladies in the community told him that she had enjoyed his talk and meant to heed his suggestions. "But tell me," she pleaded, "where can I find an old cow?"

Suggested opening for a lecture by a gossip columnist: "Accustomed as I am to public peeking . . ."

A prominent speaker recently was engaged to address a women's club in Chicago. An ardent cigar smoker, the speaker lit one rich Havana cigar after another before he rose to make his address. A friend wrote him the next day, "I suggest that you smoke fewer stogies hereafter, when you are completely surrounded by ladies."

The speaker wrote back: "Where there are angels, clouds are nearby." They've hired him to talk again next season—at double the fee.

In Cleveland, David Dietz, famous science editor, received an invitation to deliver the annual address at a very exclusive club. He accepted and added that the subject on which he meant to discourse was "Adventuring through the Universe." When the club's dignified president arose to introduce Mr. Dietz, he began to read to the members a list of the speakers at fifteen previous annual meetings, along with the topics they had chosen. The fifth name on the list stopped him cold. "In 1943," he announced, "our speaker was David Dietz, and his subject—dear me!—was 'Adventuring through the Universe'!"

"I'm afraid it's the same old speech," began Dietz, "but by the same token, it's the same old universe."

In a class by itself as a road attraction on the lecture circuit at the turn of the century was the joint appearance of Mark Twain and James Whitcomb Riley. Nothing comparable to it, in fact, came along until fifty years later, when Charles Laughton and his troupe triumphed in *Don Juan in Hell* and *John Brown's Body*. Twain would read from his own works. Riley would tell folksy anecdotes and recite his poems ("When the Frost Is on the Punkin" and "Little Orphan Annie" wowed them in particular), and the goose generally hung high—except on such occasions when Mr. Riley got higher than the goose. Horace Gregory, in *Poet of the People*, tells of some of the subterfuges to which Twain resorted in his efforts to keep Riley on the straight and narrow. One day he even locked the Hoosier poet in his room and kept both keys in his own pocket. Riley proved equal to the occasion however. When Twain finally released him for their walk to the local athenaeum, he was, if possible, more intoxicated than at any previous moment of the tour. He had imbibed a whole bottle of whisky through a keyhole with a straw, the bottle reverently held by a bellboy on the other side of the door.

To watch one of the nation's leading statesmen spellbind an audience with the greatest of ease, one would never suspect that just a few short years ago he was terrified at the mere prospect of opening his mouth in public.

Yet I happen to know that when nomination for his first important governmental post was offered to him, he almost refused because he knew acceptance entailed an endless series of after-dinner speeches to crowds of total strangers.

One story saved him and made possible his subsequently brilliant career, and because it may bail out timorous readers of *The Life of the Party*, too, if ever they are called upon to deliver a few impromptu remarks, I think it is worth repeating.

"If ever you sit trembling while the chairman is delivering the usual flowery introduction," the teller of the tale counseled his candidate (and how I wish I could tell you the candidate's name!), "just close your eyes for a few seconds and imagine that every blessed member of the audience is sitting there *in his un-*

derwear. Suddenly what you have imagined to be a sea of angry hostile faces will lose all its frightening aspect; they'll simply look ridiculous. Addressing them after that will be a breeze."

One man who heard the statesman recall the incident remarked, "Of course, if the underwear fantasy had failed to work, you might have gone one step further!"

Undoubtedly the most famous and adroit after-dinner speaker of our time is Georgie Jessel, who has been dubbed, with good reason, America's Toastmaster General. Georgie speaks because he loves to—at the drop of a hat, or even the wiggle of an ear. George Burns said of him, "Spring is the season when the birds and the bees follow Jessel—taking notes." And the immortal Will Rogers added, "George has only to see half a grapefruit and he's on his feet saying, 'Ladies and Gentlemen, we have with us tonight . . .'"

He confesses that one day he made four public appearances —at the christening of an infant, the launching of a destroyer, a funeral, and a screen writers' dinner.

"What's more," he adds, "I made the same speech at all four occasions!"

Spyros Skouras, of Twentieth Century-Fox, is an outstanding American today and a great philanthropist, but he never has lost his rich Greek accent. Introducing Mr. Skouras at a big convention, George Jessel observed, "Spyros sailed here from Athens over forty years ago, but judging by the way he speaks English, he doesn't land till next Tuesday."

At a dinner honoring New York's Governor Harriman, Jessel remarked, "Life's been good to Ave from the very beginning. He was born with the Union Pacific in his mouth."

I point with pride to one record I have compiled in the past three months. Invitations received to testimonial dinners and fund-raising banquets: thirty-one. Invitations declined: thirty-one. Batting average: one thousand. As far as I am concerned, banquets are an abomination.

I am convinced that most people would cheerfully double their donation to the worthy charity involved if they were permitted to stay home with their slippers, easy chairs, a good book —or even a fixed wrestling match on television.

Consider the average public dinner. The food is cold, badly served, and indigestible. Table companions usually are total strangers, even less interested in you than you are in them. The one fate worse than being planted at a table in the far corner next to the kitchen, is to be seated on or near the dais, where strategic retreat is completely cut off.

An internationally famous scientist became so irked by the series of bumbling long-winded speakers who preceded him at one banquet that, when he finally was called upon, he declared, "It seems I finally have been asked to give my address. Gentlemen, it's the Belvedere Hotel, and that's where I'm headed this very moment, since it's two hours past my usual bedtime. I thank you!" And with this, he strode out of the hall.

When Calvin Coolidge was Vice-President of the United States, Washington chairmen soon discovered that he promptly accepted all banquet invitations. Once present, however, it was well-nigh impossible to pry a word out of him.

The effervescent Alice Roosevelt Longworth volunteered to draw him out one evening, but she never had a chance. Finally she snapped, "I wonder why you come to all these affairs, Mr. Coolidge, when obviously they bore you so."

"Well," observed the frugal Cal, "a man's got to eat."

Because everybody appreciates words of sound advice, especially when you have to look up many of them in the dictionary, I pass on to you the admonition of a Florida jurist, memorized faithfully by A. B. Clark, of Jacksonville:

"Beware of platitudinous ponderosity. Let your communication possess coalescent consistency and concatenated cogency. Eschew all flatulent garrulity and asinine affectations. Use intelligibility and veracious vivacity without rodomontade or thrasonical bombasity. Sedulously avoid all prolixity and psittaceous vacuity."

In other words, "Be intelligible, think for yourself, and be brief."

An English magazine recently listed six rules for a good talker that are worth remembering:

1. Never tell funny stories about your own children unless you are certain you would be amused if Mrs. Whoop-te-do told them to you about hers.

2. Never try to start a long conversation with someone who obviously is busy, with his mind on something else.

3. Never talk to yourself in the middle of talking to others. (Let's see: was it really the last week in August? Maybe it was the first week in September. I know it was after Aunt Minnie left. Yes—it was August.)

4. Never describe the plot of a film your victims haven't seen, or a book they have not yet read.

5. Never apologize for something you're really proud of (I don't know anything about art, music, or poetry—*but . . .*).

6. Above all, *never* forget that other people also prefer *talking* to *listening*. Allow others to get in the last word—or the last laugh—occasionally. You'll be better liked for it—and may learn something besides. Incessant talkers learn *nothing!*

CHAPTER TWENTY-FOUR

WHERE THERE'S AN ILL

In virtually every office there is one deluded soul who takes fanatical pride in slaving twelve hours a day, and hasn't had a vacation worth mentioning in years. For good measure, he usually bolts down a sandwich at his desk at lunch time and takes home a portfolio full of documents and reports to foul up his weekend too.

If you'd like to help one of these benighted souls, hell-bent for a breakdown, you might tell him you've nominated him for A. S. Kettunen's mythical "Coronary Club." Mr. Kettunen, himself the victim of a heart attack, compiled this list of eligibility rules for candidates:

1. Your job comes first. Forget everything else.
2. Saturdays, Sundays, and holidays are fine times to be working at the office. There'll be nobody else there to bother you.
3. Always have your brief case with you when not at your desk.

This provides an opportunity to review completely all the troubles and worries of the day.

4. Never say "no" to a request. Always say "yes."

5. Accept all invitations to meetings, banquets, committees, etc.

6. All forms of recreation are a waste of time.

7. Never delegate responsibility to others; carry the entire load yourself.

8. If your work calls for traveling—work all day and drive all night to keep that appointment you made for eight the next morning.

9. No matter how many jobs you already are doing, remember you always can take on one more.

——And the next stop, of course, is the hospital!

The patient in Room 726 was apopleptic with rage when the doctor stopped in on his morning rounds. "That idiot nurse that came on at 8 P.M.," he roared, "plugged my electric blanket by mistake into the automatic toaster on my night table—and every four minutes I kept popping out of bed!"

A very rich lady loved to read a very successful magazine because every month it gave the details of a rare new disease, which the rich lady immediately imagined she was suffering from herself. Several doctors made a handsome living out of this. Up in Maine for the summer, however, she suddenly ran into one old country doctor who wasn't having any of her nonsense.

"You couldn't possibly have this disease you say is destroying you," he told her gruffly. "In the first place, if you did have it, you'd never know it. It causes absolutely no pain or suffering whatever."

"Just as I suspected," crowed the rich lady triumphantly. "Those are my symptoms precisely!"

A doctor in a Milwaukee maternity ward was making his morning rounds. "Nurse," he inquired, "on what day does this little lady expect her bundle from heaven?" "May fourth," was the answer. "And the next lovely patient?" "May fourth." "And this one?" "May fourth also, Doctor." The doctor appeared mildly surprised. "What a coincidence," he mused. "Don't tell me this other charming soul is also expected to be a mother on May fourth." "I wouldn't know, Doctor," admitted the nurse. "She wasn't at the picnic."

Mr. Haydn admitted to his wife that he was feeling much better since his operation, but couldn't account for the enormous bump on the back of his head. "Oh, that," chuckled Mrs. Haydn. "In the middle of your operation they suddenly ran out of ether."

The Mayo Clinic, in Rochester, Minnesota, is not only one of the biggest and best equipped in the world, but it cures minds as well as bodies. A friend of mine went out there to lose his arthritis, and managed to get rid of an inferiority complex and habitually harassed expression at the same time. One of the young doctors on the staff gave him a bit of philosophy from the Deep South which he claims has changed his whole life: "When you works, work easy; when you rests, rest loose; when you worries, roll over and go to sleep!"

Groucho Marx was so impressed with the daily routine at

Mayo's that he went around himself for weeks feeling people's pulses. He frightened the wits out of one poor lady by dropping her wrist like a hot potato and solemnly assuring her, "Madam, you have mice!" Her reaction, in fact, was so satisfying, the line was inserted in his next picture.

The biggest shot seen in Rochester in many a day, they say, was a coot who had made a couple of quick millions in the Williston Oil Basin, and arrived at the clinic in a big limousine with solid-gold trimmings and platinum ash trays. He was about as near-sighted as it's possible for a man to be, so a fellow townsman was astonished to see him driving through heavy traffic without glasses. "Don't tell me," cried the townsman, "that they cure acute myopia at Mayo's too!" "Not so's I know about it," admitted the big shot, "but you don't have to worry about my driving, son. I've got my prescription built into the windshield."

The whole Mayo Clinic owes its inception to a tornado that swept over Minnesota some sixty-six years ago. The two Mayo brothers, William and Charles, had just graduated from medical school, and in their own words, were "greener than grass," yet they pitched in with their father, who was one of the pioneer surgeons of the Northwest and, through three sleepless days and nights, and with inadequate equipment, saved the lives of scores of victims of the big blow. Impressed both with their skill and their dedication, Sister Albert, Mother Superior of the Convent of St. Francis, offered to finance a new clinic if the Mayos would undertake its direction. It opened its doors in 1889, with a policy still in effect: no set fees. A patient is billed according to his ability to pay. At first the clinic specialized in surgery, but long before both Mayo brothers died in 1939, it had spread all over the medical map. One enthusiastic patient insisted, "They've got drugs out there so new they haven't even discovered diseases for them yet."

A delectable Virgil Partch drawing shows a surgeon performing a delicate operation before a gallery of enthralled spectators. But one important thing is missing: there's no patient on the operating table, just a long piece of cord! The explanation is whispered into the ear of one spectator by the nurse: "Poor Dr. Goldbrick is operating on a shoestring!"

The phone rang at Polyclinic Hospital the other morning, and a voice demanded a connection with the nurse in charge of the seventh floor of the private ward. "I'm calling to find out about Julius Schwartz," this nurse was told when she picked up her receiver. "How's he progressing?" "Just fine," said the nurse. "And when will he be allowed to go home?" the voice continued. "Saturday morning," said the nurse, "and may I ask who this is calling?" "You may," said the voice, with a chuckle. "I'm Julius Schwartz. Nobody would tell me a damn thing around here!"

A doctor's most important patient demanded his presence at her bedside just when he was whooping it up at a class reunion. He endeavored to sober himself sufficiently to take her pulse, but gave it up, muttering disconsolately, "Blotto! Boiled to the ears!"

The following morning he received a fat check, with a note reading, "Thank you for your prompt and expert diagnosis. It will be appreciated if you keep it strictly to yourself."

Mr. Jones had been tossing nervously in his hospital bed for an hour when he had his first visitor. There was a knock on his door. He called, "Come in," and in walked the prettiest nurse he ever had seen. "We'll just give you a little preliminary check-up," she announced cheerfully. "Remove your pajamas, please." Mr. Jones complied a bit sheepishly, and the nurse then examined him carefully. "That's it," she said finally. "Hop back under the covers. Any questions?" "Just one," said Mr. Jones ruefully. "Why did you knock?"

Never in my life have I actually seen a beautiful night nurse, but I know they must exist because they keep bobbing up all the time in funny stories.

Authors, too—to hear them tell it—have always been singularly fortunate in drawing pulchritudinous hospital attendants, and it's probably just my bad luck they're never on duty when I happen to be around.

It was Heywood Broun's proud boast, for instance, that he was the only paying guest ever asked to leave a certain expensive rest home favored by overtired writers. "My trouble was I couldn't sleep," he explained. "So I took a turn for the nurse."

Irvin Cobb also had tales to tell of frolics in hospital corridors. One smart nurse soon put a stop to his marauding, however. She took the tires off his wheel chair.

In Rochester, Nelson Winter's nurse confessed to him that she had kissed every doctor in the hospital. "Intern?" queried Winters. "No," she giggled, "alphabetically."

There's a story about an Arab lady who didn't return to her husband's bed and board until the gray of the dawn. Her explanation: "I was sitting up with a sheik friend."

Offhand, I can recall the names of only four nurses who achieved world fame in modern times, though I am sure readers of this book will come up with many more nominations. My four: Florence Nightingale, Edith Cavell, Clara Barton, and Sister Kenny.

And I guess everybody's ideal of what a nurse should be was Ensign Nellie Forbush of *South Pacific*—especially when she was portrayed by Mary Martin!

There is no end to the situations in which a nurse is continually embroiled. There was the case of a much-publicized railroad official, for instance, who was rushed to the hospital following an exceptionally gay celebration, moaning with anguish.

Don't ask me how he did it, but he had swallowed a big gold watch his father had given him for his twenty-first birthday.

When his nurse showed him the X-ray, the railroad man leaped from his bed of pain, crying, "Let me out of here! I'm three minutes late!"

When I addressed an audience of doctors in San Diego, one

of them assured me he was the hero of the story, widely circulated, about an operation on a bad-tempered old lady of eighty. She came through with flying colors despite all her dire prognostications, but set up a new clamor when the doctor told her that, in accordance with the rules of the hospital, she'd have to walk ten minutes the very first day after her surgery and would have to get out entirely in a week, since beds there were at a premium.

Well, she had her ten-minute walk the first day, tottering but under her own steam, lengthened it to twenty minutes the second day, and by the time she went home was stomping all over the hospital—including rooms where she had no right to be.

Later, her family tried to pay the doctor a premium for his "wonderful job." "Nonsense," he laughed. "It was just a routine operation." "It's not the operation we're marveling over," said a grandson. "It's her walking. The old girl hadn't taken a step in six years!"

The patient shook his head gingerly and slowly regained consciousness. "Well, Doc," he said weakly to the face bending over him, "was the operation a success?" "Sorry, son," was the gentle answer, "but I'm St. Peter."

In London, a new reviewer has appeared who will bear watching. She signs herself "Jersey Lily," and her first efforts were devoted to appraising the merits of a book, published by the National Association for Mental Health, called *Do Cows Have Neuroses?* Miss Lily's review, in its entirety, read, "As a cow, I did not find this book very helpful."

A worried, twitching little man signed up for the full treatment with a prominent psychoanalyst. On his first visit he lay on the couch for thirty minutes without opening his mouth. The second visit was a replica of the first. Halfway through the third session he finally spoke. "Say, Doctor," he inquired, "am I allowed to ask you a question?" "Ah, ha," thought the doctor, "the floodgates are about to open!" To the patient, he said encouragingly, "I hope you'll tell me absolutely anything that enters your mind." The patient admitted, "I'm curious to know what you charge me for every visit here." "Fifty dollars," answered the doctor. The patient was silent again for ten minutes. Then he asked meekly, "Say, Doctor, wouldn't you like a partner?"

Even kiddie stories have a different twist when psychiatrists tell them. What do you think, for instance, of this one, included in the after-dinner speech of a famous analyst recently: A mother was entertaining three other ladies at tea when her nine-year-old son burst into the room, decked out in a shimmering white evening dress, a flowered hat, rouge on both cheeks, and his mouth smeared with lipstick. "Wilfred!" cried his horrified mother, "you nasty boy! Go upstairs and take off your father's clothes this very minute!"

Two roommates in a compassionately run nuthouse were comparing ailments. "I'd be all right," mourned one, "if I didn't have a hole in my head." "You're lucky," disputed the other. "I have *two* holes in my head." "Ba-a-h," grunted Number One. "You and your holier-than-thou attitude!"

A famous psychiatrist grimly informed one of his most difficult patients, "No, it is *not* all right for you to marry an octopus." "Drat it," grumbled the mortified patient, "then here I am stuck with eight engagement rings."

Dave Antman would have you believe that a banana sought out a psychoanalyst and wailed, "Doc, you've got to help me. A soda jerk has been trying to tell me I have a split personality."

Professor Harold Rome has come up with the proper distinction between a psychotic and a neurotic. A psychotic, avers the good professor, says, "Two and two are five and I'll fight any man who says me nay." A neurotic says, "Two and two are four, and I simply can't stand it."

The analyst stroked his chin and admitted to the tortured-looking character across the desk, "You're one of the most difficult cases that ever came here seeking my help. Is there any insanity in your family?" "There must be," maintained the character. "They keep writing me for money!"

A prominent Chicago psychiatrist told a patient, "Ridiculous that you should still be frightened of thunder at your age. Thunder is a mere natural phenomenon. Now the next time it storms, and you hear a couple of claps of thunder, just you do like I do—put your head under a pillow and stuff your ears until the thunder goes away."

Two old friends, lunching together for the first time in months, suddenly discovered that they were being analyzed by the same doctor. "Let's give him a problem that really will floor him," proposed one. "We'll make up an elaborate dream with all kinds of ramifications that I'll describe at my morning session tomorrow. Then you'll tell him you had precisely the same dream when you hit the couch in the afternoon."

With fiendish glee, the conspirators perfected their plot, and in accordance therewith, patient Number One reeled off the gory details the following morning while the analyst filled his pad with notes. At four-thirty patient Number Two gave an identical report. The analyst said not one word until the recital was completed. Then, however, he slapped down his pencil, jumped from his chair in great agitation, and exclaimed, "This is the most remarkable coincidence in my professional career." "What has disturbed you, Doctor?" inquired his tormentor innocently. "You won't believe this possible," answered the analyst, "but you're the *third* patient who has had that exact dream in the past twenty-four hours!"

Are you one of those timid souls who shudder at mere mention of a dentist's chair and regard his exploratory apparatus as far too bitter a drill to swallow? Drink a toast then to Max Grogle and Arnold Roe, of Barranquilla, Colombia, whose device— patent Number 2,648,043—enables any unfortunate in the chair to holler at will the electrical equivalent of "Ouch," though his jaws be jimmied wide apart and his mouth be cluttered with cotton, machinery, and the dentist's left arm. By merely pressing a switch in his hand he automatically shuts off the power that operates the drill—there's nought the dentists can do about it.

Dentistry, of course, has made vast strides in the past twenty years, and most of the pain inflicted is now anticipatory rather than actual. False teeth fit so well and look so natural that one of Hollywood's most glamorous stars has been fooling the public with a set through ten features and more.

In Revolutionary days, however, false teeth were so painful and cumbersome that George Washington refused to wear his set while posing for his celebrated portraits by Gilbert Stuart. It was only when the foremost dentist in the colonies, John Greenwood, took him in charge that he achieved some degree of comfort.

(Another gentleman who practiced dentistry as a sideline in those days was Paul Revere.)

A set of choppers Greenwood made for General Washington, incidentally, is still on display in the museum of the Baltimore

College of Dental Surgery and is said to have inspired one practitioner to drop his implements, seize a set of golf bags, and call over his shoulder as he headed for the exit: "That reminds me! I've got eighteen cavities of my own to fill this afternoon!"

How much time do *you* spend cleaning your teeth? Devote just five minutes to that task immediately after every meal and the chances are you'll seldom need a dentist at all.

The catch is that most of us are dreaming about something else while we go through the motions—and what we think is five minutes of polishing the molars is probably closer to thirty seconds.

"Put it this way," Dr. Ed Pullman once told me. "The blood circulating in your gums is like trains coming into Grand Central Terminal. The old trains must be shunted back to the yards so that new trains can come in. And the old blood has to be massaged out of the gums so that fresh blood can circulate there. Isn't that clear?"

"You ought to write a book," I told him.

"I have," he announced cheerfully as he drilled off the tip of my tongue. "My assistant will give you the manuscript on the way out. I call it: *The Yanks Are Coming*."

CHAPTER TWENTY-FIVE

WORDS AND MUSIC

Perfection is a rare and wonderful thing, separated from mere competence by an unbridgeable gulf. It takes no trained eye to thrill instinctively when a Fred Astaire or Gene Kelly executes a dance routine, or a Joe DiMaggio drifts back to haul in a towering fly, or a Sonja Henie does a hula on ice skates, or a Judy Garland or Mary Martin bangs out a popular tune.

322

They represent the nearest to perfection any human can approximate. All of them will tell you, however, that perfection is only nine parts God-given talent. The tenth—and absolutely essential—part is painstaking practice and dedication.

When Lynn Fontanne, Alfred Lunt, and Noel Coward, perfectionists all, were co-starring in the latter's *Design for Living,* Miss Fontanne never succeeded in mastering one unimportant piece of business to her own satisfaction.

In the course of the very last matinee, however, she rushed off stage and hurled herself into Coward's arms. "That letter bit!" she exclaimed triumphantly. "I've just learned exactly how to play it."

"Rather on the late side, aren't you, my pet?" laughed Coward. "Have you forgotten this is our last day?"

Lynn Fontanne glared at him. "We still have a performance this evening, have we not?" she inquired coldly.

That's my idea of perfection.

Do you think the team of Alfred Lunt and Lynn Fontanne are a sure-fire draw in every big city in the U.S.A.? Not so, says Lunt. For some reason he cannot fathom, they've never fared well in Pittsburgh, Pennsylvania. The last time they were penciled in for a week there, Lunt decided to do something about it. "I'll take over in Pittsburgh next week," he informed the company manager. "Somebody has not been doing his job here properly in the past."

When the week was over, Lunt sought out the company manager. "I told you I'd fix everything," he announced triumphantly. "Look at these figures, man! Thirty-five hundred dollars net profit!"

"Uh-huh," agreed the manager coldly, "but there's one thing I must point out. You forgot to pay the Lunts!"

Graphic commentary on the present state of show business by Mike Connolly: Two actors passed each other on Route 66, one going from New York to Hollywood, the other from Hollywood to New York. As recognition dawned in both their faces, they jumped to their feet and hollered frantically to each other, "*Go back!*"

It is comic Bert Wheeler's boast that he never has told a joke he wouldn't tell in front of his own mother. "Where is your mother?" Fred Allen asked him one time. Confessed Wheeler, "She's with a burlesque show."

Robert Harris, known to millions for his TV characterization in "The Goldbergs," once played a season in support of the Yiddish star, Maurice Schwartz. Harris played the part of Schwartz's attorney. One scene called for him to sit down at a table and breathe a heavy sigh. Opening night he sighed so heavily he blew out eight candles on the table. As the curtain dropped, Schwartz whispered angrily, "Stop padding your part!"

Feel a bit depressed once in a while? Next time the blues overtake you, think how much better off you are than the actress who, in the space of a few hours, lost a wonderful part she had been gunning for, had her new convertible stolen, and learned that her daughter had run away with a married man. Just then the janitor yelled up through the dumb-waiter, "Any garbage today?" The actress answered wearily, "Okay. Send it up."

The old Shakespearean actor cupped a hand over his ear and apologized, "You'll have to speak a bit louder, my good man. I've become a wee bit deafened. All that applause, you know . . ."

In many a notable London stage production, Sir Ralph Richardson has co-starred with that dazzling pair, Sir Laurence Olivier and Vivien Leigh. The three are firm friends, bound together by the memories of shared theatrical adventures and misadventures. And yet the Oliviers, like other hosts in England, hesitate to invite Sir Ralph for a weekend—or even for dinner.

Not, heaven knows, because he's dull. It's just that when Sir Ralph puts in an appearance, things begin to happen. Thereby hangs a tale, imported and partially vouched for by publicist Irving Hoffman.

It seems that the Oliviers had just finished furnishing a new home in the London suburbs, complete with expensive decorations and invaluable mementos of their careers. The housewarming party was the event of the season—but Sir Ralph found something missing. "Where are the Roman candles, old boy?" he protested. "No housewarming is complete without one!" To prove his point, Sir Ralph produced a Roman candle forthwith. It popped up a single fireball and then sputtered out.

"Bad show," grumbled Sir Ralph, and angrily picked up the Roman candle. That's when fireball Number Two went off. It zoomed past the spectators through an open window of the new house and promptly ignited the drapes. It then plowed a furrow through the rug, ricocheted off an old master, and sizzled upstairs to the master bedroom.

In less time than it takes to tell, the Oliviers and their guests were warmer than ever—but there was no house left. "To think," ruminated Sir Laurence, "that the insurance policy would have gone into effect at nine tomorrow."

Miss Leigh's comment was more to the point. "Sir Ralph," she decreed, "get off these premises and see that you never come back."

In due course the Oliviers once more were ready to resume light housekeeping—this time in a fifteenth-century castle they had restored with the profits from three years of slaving in the theater and Hollywood. Sir Ralph remained in banishment, but he looked so wistful that Miss Leigh, against her better judgment, relented. "Come for the day," she conceded, "but it must be distinctly understood that you don't set foot outside the library."

Sir Ralph stuck to his bargain straight through dinner, and it was Olivier himself who precipitated the next disaster. He led Sir Ralph on tiptoe to explore the treasures in the attic. Both men carried candles and Sir Ralph was so afraid of causing another conflagration that he proceeded as though he were walking on eggshells.

Of course he lost his balance. It was while he was negotiating a stretch on an open rafter. He crashed headfirst through the ceiling of the room beneath (it happened to be Miss Leigh's silk-lined boudoir) and on through *that* floor, bringing up, bloody but unbowed, at the very feet of Miss Vivien.

"Ah ha," he observed to that properly outraged lady, "here we are, right back in the library!"

The Oliviers refuse to be panicked by stories of Russia's growing war potential.

"If worse comes to worst," they reason to friends, "we can always send Sir Ralph for a fortnight of repertoire in Moscow."

The leading man in a touring Feuer and Martin musical show recently behaved so shabbily to a young lady in the chorus that he was dismissed summarily by telegram. That night he phoned the producers long distance and wailed, "How could you do this to me? Wasn't I giving a satisfactory performance?" "Your performance on stage couldn't have been better," they told him, "but we fired you because in private life you are the most unmitigated scoundrel we have ever encountered." "Thank heaven," exclaimed the actor. "You've made me feel like a new man again!"

George S. Kaufman recently characterized a familiar stage personality as "the most painsgiving director in the New York theater."

Variety recalls the time in World War I when a ham actor was attempting to sell Liberty Bonds from the steps of the Sub-Treasury in Wall Street. Not a soul had bought a bond and the actor was getting desperate. Finally one man came to the rescue and subscribed for a five-hundred-dollar bond.

"What town are you from, mister?" asked the actor.

"Topeka," said the man.

The actor turned to the crowd and declaimed, "Think of that! A man from a lousy little town like Topeka takes a five-hundred-dollar bond and you Wall Street pikers won't put up a dime!"

One of the most frustrating telephone conversations in history is recorded by *Theatre Arts* magazine.

A subscriber dialed "Information" for the magazine's number. "Sorree," drawled the lady, "but there is nobody listed by the name of Theodore Arts." "It's not a person; it's a publication," insisted the subscriber. "I want *Theatre Arts.*" The operator's voice rose a few decibels. "I told you," she repeated, "we have no listing for Theodore Arts." "Confound it," hollered the subscriber, "the word is 'Theatre': T-H-E-A-T-R-E." "That," said the operator with crushing finality, "is not the way to spell Theodore!"

Three typical debonair New Yorkers—director Josh Logan (born in Texarkana), author Sam Behrman (born in Worcester), and composer Harold Rome (born in Hartford)—were on their way to a rehearsal of their new musical play, *Fanny*, when Logan suddenly opined, "There's a spot in Act I that's made to order for a good, red-hot, talk-provoking belly dancer."

While Behrman and Rome were looking up yellowing press clippings, detailing the triumphs of a former torso gyrator who called herself "Little Egypt" at the Chicago World's Fair way back in 1893, Josh phoned Istanbul to sign up a Turkish delight named Nejla Ates for his new production.

Nejla (pronounced "Nella") Ates had as much to do with the plot of *Fanny* as my aunt Ruby, but there is no question that she stopped the show cold—or rather, hot. When this harem-scarem lassie goes into her act, all of her four-feet-eleven is moving—and what's more, it's moving in several different directions at the same time. Maybe it's something she Ates. Nor did her costume materially hinder her plan of campaign. Josh Logan certainly did right by his little Nejla.

With *Fanny* ensconced at the Majestic Theatre for what obviously was to be a long and well-deserved run, I felt that I owed it to my readers to seek an interview with Miss Ates. My arrival backstage prompted Walter Slezak, one of the big attractions of *Fanny*, to comment bitterly, "This wraps up the woes of the Broadway stage show in a nutshell. Here we have a great new musical, starring people like Ezio Pinza and Walter Slezak—and everybody comes to write a story about the belly dancer!"

Miss Ates, however, refers to her specialty as a *danse orientale*. Even off stage, she's an active miss. She speaks nine languages, she says, though I'd hardly call English one of them. In a few short weeks in America she acquired a mink coat and a diamond ring, both contributed by a love-smitten Texas gallant. When his ardor cooled, he made an effort to retrieve the loot.

"This fellow," reported Nejla dreamily, "is American, so okay he Indian giver. But Nejla Turk, not Indian. No give back!"

Nejla takes her new fame in stride, likes to stand in front of a flamboyant twelve-foot mural of herself that is plastered on the wall of the theater, and assure bedazzled passers-by, "Is me. Crazy, no?"

The first time that producer David Merrick, Logan, Behrman, and Rome actually saw Miss Ates do her number in costume, they remained rooted to their front-row seats for a full minute after her exit.

Author Behrman broke the silence: "Gentlemen, that's the best dialogue I have ever written!"

A couple of beaten-up old acrobats had been closing bills at vaudeville houses so long with the same act, they could go through their routines in their sleep. One week they finally made the Palace and, at the opening Monday matinee, stood in the wings while the late John Barrymore gave his magnificent rendition of the soliloquy from *Hamlet*. The audience went into raptures. One acrobat turned to his partner and muttered angrily, "If that's the kind of junk they want today, I guess we better work out a new act for next season!"

Charles Frohman, the famous theatrical producer and "star maker," was the man who discovered Billie Burke and developed her into one of Broadway's all-time box-office champs. When it became evident that she was falling for the charms of his bitter rival, Florenz Ziegfeld, however, he flew into a rage. Invading her dressing room one day, he declared, "I am off for London and, to remind you not to get married, I'm going to leave my hat here. Don't do anything idiotic while I'm gone." He had not yet reached London when Miss Burke and Ziegfeld slipped across the Hudson and were married in Hoboken. Frohman cabled her, "Send me my hat." She never saw or heard from him again.

When David Belasco produced Eugene Walter's *The Easiest Way*, he chose for his leading lady the relatively unknown Frances Starr. In rehearsal she did everything that was expected of her except in one scene, where her hysterical scream was several pitches below the result desired by the "Master." In the dress rehearsal Belasco tiptoed behind her, and Miss Starr gave a shriek that stood everybody's hair on end.

"That's what I want," exulted David Belasco, throwing the

safety pin he had used into the wings. "It's the effect I've been working for these last three weeks!"

One of the few failures produced by John Golden was a gambling story by Winchell Smith called *The Wheel*. The second-act climax was a dramatic scene in which the hero lost his last cent playing roulette on a crooked wheel. On the morning of the premiere, Golden realized that the balcony audience would be able to see the numbers into which the ball finally plopped. He called his friend, the police commissioner, and wailed, "Where can I get a rigged roulette setup before sundown?" "Leave it to me," said the commissioner. He raided a well-known gambling joint, and Golden had his crooked wheel three hours before curtain time.

P. G. Wodehouse, creator of the famous English comedy butler, Jeeves, recalls a theater manager who discovered one day that his box-office treasurer had been shortchanging him for years. He sent for the culprit and asked, "What's your salary here?" "Sixty a week," was the answer. "It's raised to a hundred. No, by George, make it two hundred," said the manager. "Thank you," burbled the treasurer. "I'm overcome." "There's just one thing more," added the manager cheerfully. "You're fired!"

"You see," he explained to Wodehouse later, "I wanted to fire the crooked so-and-so from a really *good* job."

One of the funniest backstage mishaps in theatrical history occurred during rehearsals of an old Bolton and Wodehouse musical at the Century Theatre. The Century, like the show's producers, Messrs. Ziegfeld and Dillingham, is, alas, gone forever, but in its day it was a beautiful structure with the biggest revolving stage in the country.

The plot called for an Italian tenor, and a gent who called himself "The Neapolitan Nightingale" showed up for an audition. He barely had launched into "Ridi Pagliaccio" when the revolving stage suddenly started off at Number Three speed and swept him into the wings.

"Why he didn't jump off, or at least stop singing," laughs Bolton, "we'll never know. Maybe he sang with his eyes closed. Maybe he thought the spinning turntable was part of his big test. At any rate, he suddenly popped into view at the other end of the stage, singing lustily, and after being seen briefly, whirled off on his second journey. By this time everybody in the theater was in convulsions. He ended the song out of sight, back of two tons of scenery, and everybody cheered. Unfortunately the part was cut out of the show and 'The Neapolitan Nightingale' got nothing for his pains but a magnificent run-around."

On the Bowery in New York there still exists the dilapidated restaurant in which, many years ago, a penniless lad named Irving Berlin waited on tables and picked out tunes on the piano for a living. Every guide includes the spot in his itinerary. The night I made the trip, our informant even declared that it was on that very battered piano that Berlin had composed "White Christmas."

One evening Irving Berlin himself decided to visit this haunt of his early days. In a nostalgic glow, he seated himself at the old piano and began to hum "Oh, How I Hate to Get Up in the Morning." In the middle of the rendition, a bus load of sightseers shuffled in, and their gravel-voiced guide began his spiel.

"Yes, sir, folks," he declared, "this is the very place the great Oiving Boilin began his career—singing songs on that same pianner you see standing in the corner. As a matter of fact, the song that Bowery bum is playin' this minute happens to be one of Boilin's own songs!"

The guide then walked over to the piano and dropped a heavy hand on Berlin's shoulder.

"Fella," he announced, "if Oiving Boilin could hear the way you're moiderin' one of his greatest songs, he'd toin over in his grave!"

Today plutocrat Berlin is one of those fellows who's firmly convinced he never sleeps a wink. One night he was a member of a big houseparty at cinema-magnate Joe Schenck's house when the family Saint Bernard created a tremendous uproar by falling into the swimming pool about 4 A.M. By the time he had been rescued, not only the entire household but neighbors for half a mile around had been aroused—that is, everybody but Berlin, who slept like a babe throughout the hullabaloo. Next morning somebody asked him innocently, "How did you sleep last night, Irving?" "Same old story," mourned Berlin. "I took four sleeping pills and still didn't catch a wink."

Another time he was forced to admit he had slept a few hours. "But," he added triumphantly, "I dreamed I didn't!"

In *Fun with Musical Games and Quizzes,* David Ewen and Nicolas Slonimsky quote two excerpts from contemporary reviews of musical compositions that later became famous. You wouldn't guess what pieces were on the griddle in a thousand tries! Number One: "It has no more real pretension to be called music than the jangling and clashing of gongs and other un-euphonious instruments with which the Chinaman, on the brow of the hill, fondly thought to scare away our English bluejackets." (From the London *Musical World,* June 30, 1855.) Number Two: "This music is only half alive. How trite and feeble and conventional the tunes are, how sentimental and vapid the harmonic treatment, under its disguise of fussy and futile counterpoint! Weep over the lifelessness of its melody and harmony, so derivative, so stale, so inexpressive." (Lawrence Gilman in the New York *Tribune,* February 23, 1924.) Well, the London *Musical World* was reviewing Wagner's *Lohengrin;* Mr. Gilman was polishing off George Gershwin's *Rhapsody in Blue.*

There was a composer in Munich one time, continues Slonimsky, named Max Raeger, who felt that a derogatory critic had overstepped all bounds. Raeger wrote him as follows: "Sir: I am sitting in the smallest room of my house. I have your review before me. In a moment it will be behind me."

Can you name the fourteen biggest popular-song hits of the past sixty years? The list, as compiled by historian Richard B. Morris, contained some surprises for me, and it will, I think, do the same for you. Here it is:

"The Sidewalks of New York" (1894), "The Stars and Stripes Forever" (1897), "Sweet Adeline" (1903), "Take Me Out to the Ball Game" (1908), "Ah! Sweet Mystery of Life" (1910), "End of a Perfect Day" (1910), "When Irish Eyes Are Smiling" (1912), "St. Louis Blues" (1914), "Dinah" (1925), "Ol' Man River" (1927), "Star Dust" (1929), "Easter Parade" (1933), "God Bless America" (1939), and "White Christmas" (1942).

The great Maestro Arturo Toscanini is noted for his temperamental outbursts, but his good friend Sam Chotzinoff has learned that he can dispel the wildest of Toscanini's rages by producing some childish practical joke. Wine glasses with a hole in the bottom, trick knives that collapse, fake "butlers" who spill things on purpose send him into gales of laughter. He concentrated for an hour on playing with a seven-year-old boy's toy magnet.

Another sure-fire way to restore his radiant good humor is to question him on his encyclopedic knowledge of music, or the countless other greats of the musical world he has known through the years.

"I will tell you all about Richard Strauss," he announced on one visit with the Chotzinoffs. "In 1906 I wrote to him for permission to give the first performance of *Salome* in Italy at La Scala. He replied yes. Very good. Then one day I read in the newspaper that Strauss *himself* would give *Salome* in Turin one week *before* my performance in Milan. I was crazy. I could not eat. That night I took the train for Vienna and confronted him in his own house. 'Strauss,' I told him, 'as a *musician* I take off my hat to you. But as a *man,* I put *on* ten hats.'"

As the maestro finished his story, Chotzinoff recalls that "his face shone with scorn and he feverishly put on ten imaginary hats."

333

The classic Toscanini story concerns the day he passed a hurdy-gurdy man, half asleep, who was lazily droning through the Toreador song from *Carmen*. Toscanini shook the startled player violently and commanded, "Faster, you fool! You play that as if it was a funeral dirge."

The next day the hurdy-gurdy man had a new sign on his battered instrument. It read, "Pupil of Toscanini."

Joan Carr attended a concert at Carnegie Hall that ended in a spontaneous ovation for the conductor. Applauding more madly than anybody else were a couple of uniformed ushers. Miss Carr had just whispered to her partner, "Those boys appreciate music more than all the frauds who pay seven dollars a ticket," when she heard one usher say happily, "If we can keep this applause going five minutes more, we'll collect overtime!"

A famous orchestra concluded the season with its usual deficit some years ago and the management went to Andrew Carnegie for help. "I'm getting a bit weary of being the patsy every season," grumbled Mr. Carnegie. "Somebody else will have to carry part of the load. You get him to make good half the deficit, and I'll give you my check for the rest."

The management called the very next day to report success. Mr. Carnegie made out his check and asked, "Mind telling me who coughed up the other half?"

"Not at all," he was assured. "It was Mrs. Carnegie."

An old and broken-down orchestra conductor made an ill-starred farewell tour in America. After the debacle at Carnegie Hall, the first violinist was asked, "What did he conduct tonight?" The violinist answered, "Lord knows what he conducted —but we played Tschaikowsky's Fifth."

Rumor is that a pedestrian on Fifty-seventh Street, Manhattan, stopped Jascha Heifetz and inquired, "Could you tell me how to get to Carnegie Hall?" "Yes," said Heifetz. "Practice!"

An amateur musician was making horrendous sounds on his saxophone in the middle of the night when the outraged landlord burst into his apartment, yanked the instrument out of his hands, and roared, "Do you know there's a little old lady sick upstairs?" "I don't think I do," admitted the amateur. "Would you mind humming the first few bars of it?"

Ad in a Providence newspaper: "For sale cheap: my son's collection of be-bop and rock-and-roll records. If a fourteen-year-old's voice answers the phone, hang up and call later."

Titian-haired Lucy Monroe has sung "The Star Spangled Banner" so often that several legislators have discussed admitting her as the forty-ninth state. From the Supreme Court to Milwaukee —home of the plea to the land of the Braves—she's warbled our national anthem in fair weather and foul, and become so identified therewith that every time she appears with a new male escort, wits immediately presume his name is Francis Scott Key.

When Lucy gives with the high notes the lyrics come across as clear as a bell. Obviously there was nobody like her around when columnist Franklin P. Adams was a lad. He confesses that, until he reached the age of twelve, he was convinced that the first line of our anthem was, "Osage, Kansas City."

When Mama made up her mind that little Nathan was destined to become a great violinist, Papa's complaints about the racket and the expense fell on deaf ears. Finally on the music teacher's recommendation he bought Nathan one of those "half violins" specially designed for the kiddies.

To the surprise of everybody but Mama, Nathan turned out to be a born fiddler. First thing you know, the teacher demanded that he have a full-sized violin.

Complaining at every step, Papa hied himself to the music store, where his eye fell on a big violoncello. "There's the one I'll take," he announced happily. "Let the little so-and-so learn to outgrow that!"

CHAPTER TWENTY-SIX

THE GRAB BAG

Pet Peeves

There are certain minor irritations in workaday life in the city that make everybody fume. It takes no terrible-tempered Mr. Bangs, for instance, to start spluttering at impatient motorists forever tooting their horns in a hopeless traffic snarl, or fat ladies who block aisles in theaters, resolutely refusing to pull in their feet or their middles an eighth of an inch, or ill-mannered oafs who shamelessly try to barge into the front of a line that's been queuing for an hour.

337

In addition to universal annoyances of this sort, however, every one of us has a special list of private peeves that make our gorge rise. Often they are inconsequential and irrational, but we cannot laugh ourselves out of them.

Less than a year after he retired from the presidency, Calvin Coolidge flew into a tizzy when a hat-check girl wouldn't put his fedora and his friend's on a single check. Columnist Franklin P. Adams conducted a personal war for years against house owners who didn't display their numbers plainly on the outsides of their doors. As mild-mannered a matron as ever I've known works herself into a tantrum when her husband tears the Sunday newspaper apart and leaves sections all over the floor.

Walter McConkle of Detroit is aroused because national syndicates are buying up famous old hotels and renaming them without regard for local tradition or sentiment. "Farewell, the Book-Cadillac," he mourns. "Good-by, the Copley Plaza and other landmarks we knew so well. The Hiltons and the Sheratons have got you 'cause you didn't watch out!"

Mrs. Porter Lucas of Crane, Missouri, sees red when she enters an American restaurant and they hand her a menu printed in French. "And what French!" she continues. "Even the headwaiter is often unable to translate it. They charge American dollars; let them print American menus!"

Compton Brooks of Paoli, Pennsylvania, waxes indignant at the mere thought of commuters who hog double seats for bridge games on crowded trains.

"Although no seats are reserved and they have no justification whatever, these buzzards take it for granted that that cardboard which they have bribed the conductor to throw across the seat is enough to hold four places for them, while other passengers are already standing in the aisle, and not one player has put in an appearance.

"The other evening I said to myself, 'Tradition be blowed.' I threw the board aside, sat down, and opened my newspaper. Believe it or not, I not only had to take abuse from the four bridge players when they finally showed up just before train time, but the other passengers took their side!"

Here are a few of my own pet peeves: Elevator starters who engage in long social conversations with the operators while I'm itching to keep an appointment on the twenty-ninth floor . . . TV-conscious baseball managers who interrupt a game five times to whisper advice to pitchers or batters, or dispute every close decision with umpires . . . Wives who won't let you put the top of a convertible down on a perfect summer day because they "don't want my hair to blow" . . . Advertisements—usually for autos—showing fascinating stretches of scenery without identifying them . . . Water taps in bathrooms that must be held on to keep them running . . . Proverbial and incurable no-check-grabbers . . .

There must be a special space in Hades reserved for people who solicit funds from strangers over the phone for unknown charities, using names of well-known figures to assure attention. Author-actor-producer Howard Lindsay has a wonderful way to stop such miscreants dead in their tracks. The moment he hears, "Judge Goofenswoggle was sure you'd be interested in the bazaar he's whipping up for——" he interrupts in a deceptively silken tone: "I'm sorry, but haven't you heard? I've just been elected president of the Anti-Solicitation-by-Telephone Association!" Then he hangs up.

A definite menace to society are the goons who persist in confronting comparative strangers with a simpering "Guess who this is," or "I'll bet you don't remember who I am." A few can be squelched with an emphatic "I most certainly do not." Most hang on, however, until it finally develops they sat next to you at a football game nine years ago, or had some equally intimate relationship with your cousin at prep school in 1928.

Habitual "Guess-who-I-ammers" ought to be marked with a

warning red light or a tolling bell buoy. They obstruct navigation.

It's a different kettle of fish, however, when you fail to identify or recall the name of somebody you've known perfectly well for years. We can't all be like the late Wendell Willkie, who never forgot even the first name of a person he had met in an elevator or at a crowded cocktail party. Jim Farley and Groucho Marx are blessed with similar total recall, though Groucho was moved to inform a pest, "I never forget a face, but I'm willing to make an exception in your case."

At the opposite end of the picture was the mighty Babe Ruth, who never remembered *anybody's* name. Five years after he joined the New York Yankees, he was still referring to everybody on the bench, including his roommate, Lou Gehrig, as "Kid" and "Whatchamacallit."

I'm not always so good at remembering names myself. In theater lobbies, I attempt to cover up with a hasty, "You know my good wife, Phyllis, of course," which suffices unless the little woman, in a perverse mood, counters demurely with, "What did you say the gentleman's name was, Bennett?" This leads to some interesting conversation after we get home.

One day a passer-by grabbed me and demanded, "Why haven't you answered all my phone calls?" Not knowing him from Adam, I replied heartily, "I've tried a dozen times, but you're never in. How much longer will you be in town?" This proved to be the wrong gambit. "What are you talking about?" he demanded. "I'm your dentist!" All I could manage was a weak "Why aren't you wearing your white coat?"

Sign Language

"Silly standardized country—America," grumbled a distinguished English author recently as he completed a U.S. lecture tour, his pockets bulging with silly standardized American dollars. "Your cities look so much alike, I had to consult my itinerary to see whether I was in Milwaukee or Memphis, Sioux City or Spokane. Same hotels, same stores, same signs . . ."

Same signs, my eye! This land of ours abounds with individualistic merchants who would rather be caught dead than hang a conventional sign outside their place of business. They'll stew for weeks thinking of a new twist—and one in a hundred is worth the effort! For instance:

Outside a Phoenix auto-repair shop: "May we have the next dents?" and "Second-hand cars in first-crash condition." A Dallas dealer has a more subtle approach: "Be a wealthy pedestrian. Sell us your car!" The shop next door displays clothes for debutantes, featuring "Convertible sun dresses. Very sporty with the tops down."

Offered by a dry-goods emporium in Allentown, Pennsylvania: "Bath towels for the whole damp family"; by a chicken incubator in Vermont: "Cheepers by the dozen."

A furrier in Kalamazoo begs, "Be our miss in lynx," and an alert fortuneteller in Asbury Park promises, "Your problem solved, or your mania cheerfully refunded."

Owners of restaurants and grogshops are in the forefront when the whims blow. A tavern keeper in Lexington advises, "If you drive your husband to drink, drive him here." A sign on the wall of a diner along Route 101: "What foods these morsels be!"; on the gas pump outside: "Four gals., one buck. May we suggest Ethyl?" In Hollywood, one proprietor cautions, "Not responsible for ladies left over thirty seconds."

And a Broadway delicatessen advertises: "Today only! Home-made imported caviar." Another sign inside the store warns, "If you don't smell it, we ain't got it."

Designed for motorists: In New Jersey: "Crossroad 200 yards ahead. Better humor it." In Connecticut: "Give our children a brake." At the bottom of a precipitous hill in West Virginia: "Resume breathing." On the back of a massive furniture van: "Watch my rear, not hers." On the water tank of a small college north of St. Louis: "This university was founded by our beloved president, William Johnson. Born 1855. Died 1911. Capacity, 150,000 gallons."

Humorists commandeered a paintbrush at the San Diego air base and indulged in some gay signing off. Outside a phone booth, they hung a placard reading: "Please limit calls to six girls"; on the bulletin board: "For sale cheap: one slightly defective ten-inch TV set. For details, see Lt. Squinty." And near a runway: "Absolutely no flying permitted over nudist camp 8.3 miles SSW on a true course of 177 degrees."

Atop California's seven-million-ton Shasta Dam some wag planted the sign, "U. S. Government property. Do not remove!" At Wellesley, a bright miss hung over a dormitory bathtub the reminder, "Don't forget your ring." And for several weeks (an unimaginative cop removed it) a sign above the entrance to the New York morgue advertised, "Remains to be seen."

A haberdasher in New York ran a chain of stores whose windows always were plastered with big signs proclaiming, "Going out of business," "Must vacate," and "Positively last twenty-four hours." One day he told his lawyer, "My son graduates from college tomorrow. Should I take him into business with me?" The lawyer suggested, "Open a new store for him and let him go out of business for himself."

Tall Tales

I've heard a lot of very tall tales in my day (my office is located smack in the middle of the highest-powered advertising agencies on Madison Avenue), but the yarn told with a perfectly straight face by David Vikomerson certainly takes the cake.

David insists that he and some convivials were prowling for sailfish in the Gulf Stream off Miami when suddenly one of them felt a tremendous strike. "It's a whale," he gasped, while his reel began to whip around like an airplane propeller. By turning on this cruiser's full power, they managed to tow the monster to shore and anchored him momentarily near the naval station at the edge of the causeway.

Then several fourteen-story hotels nearby, finished that Tuesday, began to sway ominously, and an admiral, experimenting with an electric razor, was hurtled clear across the base. "It's the Soviet Navy attacking," he hollered wildly. "Don't shoot, boys, till you see the eyes of their Reds!"

"So we cut the line pronto," concludes David. "If we hadn't, the whole of Miami Beach undoubtedly would have been towed to somewhere near the Azores.

"We did manage to get a snapshot of the monster before he headed for the open sea—and, believe it or not, the snapshot alone weighs thirty-one pounds."

That fish story reminded British author Eric Partridge of another whopper wherein a carpenter made and painted three wooden decoy ducks so lifelike that a deluded cat promptly bit the heads off two of them. The third one? He flew away!

"It was on my last safari in the jungle," recalled another tall taler at the Explorer's Club, "that a man-eating tiger sauntered into our camp at sundown. One of my trusty beaters just threw a glass of water in his face, and he slunk away with his tail between his legs.

"You doubt my veracity? Strolling later in the moonlight, I encountered this very tiger and playfully stroked its whiskers. Gentlemen, those whiskers were still wet!"

Mr. Bee McIntyre prevaricated his way to a hard-won championship of the Burlington, Wisconsin, Liars Club with his account of a wind so powerful that it picked up his brass wash kettle (which weighed two hundred pounds) and blew it clear out of the county.

"Furthermore," was his clincher, "that wind blew the kettle

so fast that, while it was sailing across our front yard, lightning struck at it five times—and missed!"

And yet that wind of Bee McIntyre's was but a gentle zephyr compared to the one that smote a blooming liar named Honest Dick McCardle, of Athens, Georgia. "It blew so hard," avers Honest Dick, "that our local creek ran backward, threw the mill wheel into reverse, and unground a thousand sacks of flour so fast that when the bags were opened the wheat wasn't even ripe enough to harvest."

There was a bit of a breeze out Lew Owens' way in Independence, Missouri, too. It picked up all the telephone poles and set them down in the same order—along with the operators —clear out in California. A subscriber, unaware that she, too, had been wafted over a thousand miles off base, asked for Kansas

City 0080. "Have to change the exchange, dearie," the operator told her. "We're just three miles out of Beverly Hills now."

The son of one of Minnesota's hardy Swedish pioneers was visiting a friend out West. The Westerner began to brag about the wonderful echo in his valley. "If you stand and call 'John Smith,'" he declared, "you will hear no less than thirteen echoes of it." "That's nothing at all," belittled the man from Minnesota. "Just outside of Minneapolis there's a high hill. If you climb to the summit and call 'Ole Oleson,' you'll immediately hear the echo saying, 'Which one?'"

The late Wilson Mizner was a wonderful storyteller, with no particular regard for the truth. Coming back from the Yukon gold rush—owning, alas, precious little of the gold himself—Mizner read in a Chicago paper that turkeys were in short supply that year and were bound to bring fifty cents a pound by Thanksgiving Day.

So, avowed Mizner, he bought five hundred baby turkeys from an Oregon farmer for a dime apiece, invested twenty dollars more in feed, and started driving them across country on foot. He figured he'd reach the Windy City in ten weeks flat—just in time for the holiday market and fortune.

"I got the turkeys clear through to Chicago too," he mourned, "but with the stockyards in sight, and a flock of five hundred nicely fattened fowl bound to net me five bucks apiece, cruel Fate stepped in.

"The turkeys developed sore feet and flew away."

In a mammoth and extensively publicized liars' contest in Milwaukee, a man named Butler was unanimously declared in a class by himself. The chairman noted, however, a certain reservation when the winner walked up to claim his prize.

"What's the matter?" demanded the chairman. "Gold cup not big enough to suit you?"

"It isn't that," confessed Mr. Butler. "I'm deeply honored.

But it's taken so long to get this meeting over with. *What will I tell my wife when I get home?"*

Tongue Twisters

Probably the two best-known tongue twisters in the English language are, "She sells sea shells by the seashore," and "Peter Piper picked a peck of pickled peppers." But there are hundreds more, as Duncan Emrich, chief of the folklore section at the Library of Congress, discovered when he appealed to listeners on an NBC radio program to send in any they happened to remember.

At last reports, Chief Emrich still was trying to dig out from under the bags full of mail that descended upon him, but he managed to list some of the twisters that popped up most frequently for an article in the historical bimonthly, *American Heritage.*

Take a deep breath, suggested Dr. Emrich, and see how quickly you can say "Sarah saw a shot-silk sash shop full of showy, shiny shot-silk sashes." Or: "She sawed six slick, sleek, slim, slender saplings." Or:

> *Bitty Batter bought some butter*
> *"But," said she, "this butter's bitter."*
> *So she bought some better butter,*
> *And she put the better butter in the bitter butter.*
> *And made the bitter butter better.*

When Duncan Emrich got himself straightened out, he added that several informants wrote about a tongue-twisting game they had played in their youth—a game that consisted of concocting long sentences whose every word began with the same letter.

Examples were "Six sick soldiers sighted seven slowly sinking ships," and "Frivolous fat Fannie fried fresh fish furiously Friday forenoon for four famished Frenchmen."

During World War I, Al Jolson popularized a song in similar

347

vein that called for a deal of rehearsing. It was called "Sister Susie's Sewing Shirts for Soldiers."

Tongue twisters work particular hardships on stutterers. In the speech department at the State University of Iowa, writes Gilbert Barnhill, it was decided that one way to help stutterers overcome their reticence in speaking to strangers was to send them to an Iowa City establishment in quest of an item obviously not carried in stock. They then were instructed to ask where it might be found and how to get there.

This season, every stutterer was sent to a campus bookstore to ask for ping-pong balls. The first dozen were turned away empty-handed, of course, but the thirteenth, to his amazement, found enough ping-pong balls on the premises to outfit the whole country. "I don't know why a bookstore should be expected to carry anything like this," admitted the clerk, "but we've never disappointed our customers before and we're not going to start now.

"What gets me, though, is this," he added. "Why does everybody who plays ping-pong *stutter?*"

Shaggy Doggerel

Today's wave of prosperity has swept the animal world, too, if the headlines in leading zoospapers can be trusted, but as is so often the case, the wealth has not been evenly distributed. Complains one disgruntled orangutan, "Bull markets may be great for bulls, but what the heck good are they for orangutans?"

Another disturbed soul is a leopard of my acquaintance. He sought the advice of a neurologist. "You've got to help me, Doc," he pleaded. "Every time I look at my wife, I see spots before my eyes." "Of course, dear boy," soothed the neurologist. "You're a leopard, aren't you?" "Sure, I'm a leopard," was the answer, "but my wife is a zebra."

A calf-é society columnist reports that a curvaceous piggy from Paree is sporting the season's most dazzling wardrobe, just for saying "oui, oui, oui" all the way home.

Night-club favorite, Joe E. Lewis, in an improbable foray into the animal world, tried crossing one rooster with another rooster. All this netted him was two very cross roosters.

A confrere of Joe's, meanwhile, wangled a date with a musical-comedy producer to exhibit his trained dog—a creature who could add, subtract, mambo, and recite "Casey at the Bat." The performance concluded, the dog's owner said, "Amazing, what?" "Not bad," conceded the producer. "Let's see her legs."

A couple of pigeons flew over the Bowl at New Haven just before the annual Yale-Harvard football game. "Who do you like?" asked one pigeon. "Well," replied the other with a knowing wink, "I've just put everything I have on Yale."

A cowboy once rode into town on his favorite pinto mare and reined up to watch a poker game in progress on the porch of Ray "Two Gun" Washburne's book, liquor, and grocery emporium. One of the players looked up and asked, "Like a little stud?" The mare answered, "Sure! Where is he?"

Walter Carroll tells about a prisoner sentenced to ten years in solitary confinement. The first year, he found an ant in his cell and determined, "I'll keep myself occupied teaching this ant some tricks, so that when I get out I can make a fortune with it."

By the time the prisoner was released, he had taught that ant, by exercise of infinite patience, how to do somersaults, speak fluent Greek and Latin, and explain the Einstein theory. He put it in a little box and headed for his first drink in ten years.

Here was his chance to show off his miraculous ant! He placed it carefully on the bar and called the barkeeper. "Hey," he cried. "Have a look at this!"

The bartender nodded grimly. He brought the flat of his hand down with a squash and complained, "That's the third darn ant I've killed on this bar today."

A cocker spaniel from the country was trotting down a busy street with a companion from the city and paused at what he thought was a mere hitching post. Too late he discovered it was a parking meter. He barked disgustedly and asked, "Do you mean to say you've got to pay now?"

There was the devil to pay when Pat Knopf's singing canary fell into the meat grinder. All week the family ate nothing but shredded tweet.

A thirsty gentleman entered a saloon with the peaceful intention of buying himself a beer, when he noticed that the bar was being tended by a horse. "Whassa matter?" snarled—or neighed —the animal, as he deftly flicked the collar off the beer. "Ain't you never seen a horse before?" "It's not that," the man assured him hastily. "I just never thought the cow that used to own this gold mine would sell."

Stanley Jr. and Livingston Jr. were having a hot toddy in their tent while shooting an African adventure film for M-G-M. "I think I'll go out and shoot a lion before dinner," boasted Stanley Jr. "I've got five says you can't do it," scoffed Livingston Jr. Stanley seized his rifle and exited. About an hour later a lion poked his head in Livingston's tent and asked, "Do you happen to know a screwball named Stanley?" "I do," said Livingston. "Well," said the lion, "he owes you five dollars."

An octopus became entangled in the propeller of an ocean liner, causing a sympathetic observer to murmur, "Crazy, mixed-up squid!"

A pig in California had to be taken to a mountain cleanery. He splattered himself with purple oink.

A cat presented the family tennis racket to a psychiatrist, who quickly diagnosed, "Your brother is too high-strung." This probably was the same analyst who made such a name for himself in the laboratory, pulling habits out of rats.

And in a garden, two caterpillars were lazing in the sun when a lovely butterfly fluttered by overhead. Declared one caterpillar firmly, "You'll never catch *me* going up in one of those things!"

Farmer Klopfer bought a perky young rooster in Flemington, with the thought that it would add vigor to his flock. The new rooster started out being courteous indeed to the old one on the job, but the old one wasn't having any of his soft ways. "Divide the harem 50-50?" he snorted, when the new rooster mildly suggested this solution, "I should say not!" He even turned down an 85-15 split.

Finally, the old rooster put forward a suggestion of his own. "See that tree across the field?" he asked. "I'll race you to it, and the winner takes the entire flock. I ask only that in view of my rheumatic condition you stake me to a modest ten-yard handicap."

"Done and done," agreed the newcomer, confident that youth would have to be served.

The race started. For a few seconds the young rooster let his rival maintain his lead. Then he lit after him in earnest—but just as he was about to catch him, Farmer Klopfer upped with his shotgun and decapitated him.

"Dunno why," mused Farmer Klopfer as he hung the gun back on its pegs, "but that's the third queer rooster to show up in my flock this month!"

A Scotch terrier took his wife and puppy to see a dog show and promptly was pulled out of the audience to receive first prize in his class. Startled and gratified, the Scottie stopped off at a tavern on the way home to celebrate his good fortune and inadvertently left his prize on the bar. He discovered his loss the moment he got home and sent the puppy to retrieve it.

The puppy ran briskly to the tavern and nudged his way through the swinging doors. The bartender noted his entrance and, pointing a long finger at him, demanded, "What'll *you* have?" The pup, of course, answered, "Pap's blue ribbon."

And for an appropriate tailpiece to this volume, there's the story of young Jonathan, who had been promised a new puppy for his tenth birthday, but had a tough time choosing between a dozen likely candidates at the neighborhood pet shop.

Finally he decided upon one nondescript shaggy pup who was wagging his tail furiously.

Explained Jonathan, "I want the one with the happy ending."